IN LINCOLN'S SHADOW

In Lincoln's Shadow

The 1908 Race Riot in Springfield, Illinois

Roberta Senechal de la Roche

SOUTHERN ILLINOIS UNIVERSITY PRESS
Carbondale

11 10 09 08   4 3 2 1

Library of Congress Cataloging-in-Publication Data
Senechal de la Roche, Roberta, 1950–
In Lincoln's shadow : the 1908 race riot in Springfield, Illinois /
Roberta Senechal de la Roche.
p. cm.
Rev. ed. of: The sociogenesis of a race riot. c1990.
Includes bibliographical references and index.
ISBN-13: 978-0-8093-2909-0 (pbk. : alk. paper)
ISBN-10: 0-8093-2909-3 (pbk. : alk. paper)
1. Race riots—Illinois—Springfield—History—20th century. 2. Springfield (Ill.)
—Race relations—History—20th century. 3. African Americans—Illinois—
Springfield—Social conditions—20th century. I. Senechal de la Roche, Roberta,
1950– Sociogenesis of a race riot. II. Title.
F549.S7S46 2008
305.896'073077356—dc22   2008027334

The paper used in this publication meets the minimum requirements of American
National Standard for Information Sciences—Permanence of Paper for Printed
Library Materials, ANSI Z39.48-1992. ⊗

For Marion and Robert Senechal

Contents

List of Maps and Tables   ix
Preface to the Centennial Paperback Edition   xi
Acknowledgments   xvii
Abbreviations   xix

Introduction   1

Chapter 1: "Riot, Ruin and Rebellion . . ."   15
Prelude / The Black Image / 14 August / 15 August
The Riot Redefined

Chapter 2: The Community   55
Springfield's Economy / The Black Community
Residential Patterns / Riot as the Wages of Urban Sin
Race and Politics / Riot as Reform

Chapter 3: The Rioters   93
Identifying Riot Participants / Age and Sex
Birthplace and Ethnicity / Class and Occupation
Homeownership and Residence

Chapter 4: The Victims   124
The Limits of White Consensus / Black Victims
The Levee and Badlands / Hit-and-Run Attacks
The Social Location of White Vengeance
Black Progress as Deviant Behavior

Chapter 5: The Aftermath   158
The Trial of Joe James / White Rioters, White Justice
Reading Race out of Riot / Black Law and Order Leagues
Local Impact of the Riot

Conclusion   190

Appendix   201
Bibliography   212
Index   226

Maps and Tables

Maps

Map 1.1. Springfield Wards and Black Neighborhoods, 1908   17
Map 1.2. Location of Black Businesses Attacked in Riot   36
Map 2.1. Black Residences: Badlands and Vicinity, 1892   69
Map 2.2. Black Residences: Badlands and Vicinity, 1907   70

Tables

Table 2.1. Population of Springfield, Illinois, 1840–1920   56
Table 2.2. Black Population of Springfield, Illinois, 1850–1920   60
Table 2.3. Black Population by Ward, Springfield, Illinois, 1910   66
Table 2.4. Males of Voting Age by Ward, Springfield, Illinois, 1910   79
Table 3.1. Occupational Distribution of Springfield Rioters
            ($N = 133$)   110

Appendix Tables

Table 2.1. Major Springfield Industries and Their Workforces,
            1912 and 1914   201
Table 2.2. Leading Occupational Categories, Springfield,
            Illinois, 1910   202
Table 2.3. Sangamon County Coal-Mining Statistics, 1906–10   203
Table 2.4. Blacks in Illinois Cities, 1890–1910   203
Table 2.5. Leading Occupations of Black Males, Springfield,
            Illinois, 1907   204
Table 2.6. White Foreign-Born Residents in Three Wards,
            Springfield, Illinois, 1910   204

Table 3.1.   Comparison of the Age Characteristics of Three
             Categories of Rioters   205
Table 3.2.   Comparison of Age of Rioters and White Springfield
             Males over Ten Years Old   205
Table 3.3.   Comparison of Ethnicity of Rioters and Springfield's
             White Population, 1910   206
Table 3.4.   Comparison of Ethnic Background of American-Born
             Rioters and Springfield's White Population, 1910   206
Table 3.5.   Occupations of Springfield Rioters, 1908   207
Table 3.6.   Occupations of Indictees, Arrestees, and Injured
             Rioters, 1908   208
Table 3.7.   Homeownership among Indictees, Arrestees, and
             Injured Rioters, 1910   208
Table 3.8.   Residential Location of Rioters by Ward, 1908   209
Table 3.9.   Marital Status of Springfield Rioters   209
Table 4.1.   Occupations of Black Riot Victims   201
Table 4.2.   Block-Length Street Sections with One Black
             Household, by Ward, 1907   211

Illustrations following page 54

Preface to the Centennial
Paperback Edition

THIS reprinting marks the centennial of a race riot that exploded in Springfield, Illinois, in August 1908. The volume's title, *In Lincoln's Shadow*, refers to a powerful and enduring symbolic connection between the riot and the city's most famous former resident: Abraham Lincoln. After the Civil War, northern whites generally assumed that violence against African Americans was a southern problem—and part of the South's moral inferiority. The Springfield riot shattered this assumption.

The irony surrounding the riot shocked the nation. It seemed unthinkable that African Americans might be attacked and violently driven from the Great Emancipator's hometown and final resting place, and it was front-page news—North and South—for weeks. For example, a *Washington Post* headline proclaimed, "Lincoln's City Scene of the Bitterest Race War Seen in Years," and the story continued in the same vein: "The city, which is richest in memories of the Great Emancipator, is tonight an armed camp because its citizens yesterday gave vent to the hatred of the race which Abraham Lincoln declared free and equal with all other people in this country." A Texas newspaper similarly spoke of Springfield's "war between the negroes and the white man" and reported, "As the blood red prairie sun sank tonight into the fields of waving corn that hedge about the city, where lie the bones of him who said: 'With charity for all and malice toward none,' the people trembled with terror and alarm." And a Mississippi newspaper stated, "The whites have decreed that Springfield, the home of Abraham Lincoln, who emancipated the black race from slavery, shall not be the abiding place of the negroes. The order is 'Move on,' and the negro is moving."[1]

The riot's details shocked the nation as well. The violence first erupted just a few blocks from the venerated Lincoln family homestead. Newsmen even reported hearing the rioters shout, "Curse the day Lincoln freed the slaves!" and "Lincoln freed you, we'll show you where you belong!"[2] The symbolism also extended to one of the riot's casualties, William Donnegan, an elderly black cobbler killed by a white crowd who cut his throat and hanged him from a tree outside his home. The press said that he had been a friend of Abraham Lincoln, and black ministers in New York lamented his killing "in the shadow of Lincoln's old homestead." One minister asked, "What would the emancipator of our race have thought had he witnessed the crimes of that horrible mob? Would he not have regarded his life as given in vain to see the people he freed subjected to such treatment?"[3]

At the time of the riot in Springfield, the city was even busy preparing to host a massive celebration, on 12 February 1909, of the centennial of Lincoln's birth that would feature speeches by numerous foreign as well as American dignitaries. The central event was a lavish banquet at Springfield's large State Arsenal building—which six months earlier had sheltered up to 300 black refugees, including the widow of Lincoln's friend William Donnegan. At least 700 distinguished guests and prominent speakers attended the dinner: judges and politicians from Illinois and other states; ambassadors from France and Great Britain; former presidential candidate William Jennings Bryan; and Robert Lincoln, son of Abraham Lincoln. Thirty aged Civil War veterans also "came in a body and marched gayly, with heads erect, to the strains of 'The Girl I Left Behind Me,' to the tables which had been reserved." Finally, some 3,000 female "society leaders" adorned the galleries overlooking the dining and speech making in the Arsenal's hall.[4]

But the Arsenal banquet excluded African Americans, and the press was quick to react. The *Chicago Daily Tribune* featured the issue in its headlines: "Black at Lincoln Banquet? Only Whites Are Welcome." The *Tribune* noted, for example, that a black attorney from Chicago, Edward H. Morris, had earlier purchased the necessary $25-per-plate ticket to attend the banquet, only to be stricken from the guest list when the Centennial organizers discovered his race. Springfield's black churches likewise tried to raise money to buy banquet tickets for their ministers, but the organizers apparently refused to have them as well. The *Tribune* observed sarcastically, "The colored population hereabouts will be represented only by the gents who slip the soup [to the white guests]." It added that Springfield's black citizens "are thoroughly aroused over the fact that they are deprived of participation in the big doings."[5]

The city's blacks responded by holding their own separate centennial celebration, at which Reverend L. H. Magee delivered a tribute to Lincoln that included a barbed reference to the all-white Arsenal dinner downtown: "I would rather be one of the number of the black devotees of Lincoln than toastmaster at a so-called Lincoln banquet at $25 a plate. O consistency, thou art a jewel! How can you play Hamlet without the melancholy Dane?" Meanwhile, at the all-white Arsenal banquet, speakers praised Lincoln as the savior of the Union, a great orator, and a man whose life exemplified America's abundant opportunities for the hardworking and virtuous to rise from humble origins. Originally the Arsenal banquet organizers did invite one African American—the popular Booker T. Washington, who was widely known, like Lincoln, as an exemplar of the self-made man. Although Washington declined the invitation because of previous speaking engagements in New York City on Lincoln's birthday, he sent a letter (to be read aloud at the Springfield celebration) in which he invoked the shade of another Lincoln—that of the Great Emancipator. And he was probably mindful of the recent riot when he wrote, "No white man who hallows the name of Lincoln will inflict injustice upon the negro because he is a negro or because he is weak."[6]

During the riot in August, reformer William English Walling had rushed to Springfield, arriving by train late on the second day of the violence to interview as many people as he could—from the authorities to the common folk on the streets. He published the results of his investigation two weeks later in a scathing article called "The Race War in the North" in a popular magazine, the *Independent*, where he reported finding widespread support for the riot among Springfield's white citizens. Springfield, he wrote, "stood for the action of the mob. She hoped the rest of the negroes might flee."[7] And he noted the historical irony of the riot by featuring on his article's first page a photograph of Lincoln's home with the following caption: "He [Lincoln] is very unpopular in Springfield just now, and the house was attacked." The rioters' message, he wrote, was that blacks "could not obtain shelter under the favorable traditions of Lincoln's home town," and he concluded that "the whole awful and menacing truth" was "that a large part of the white population of Lincoln's home . . . have initiated a permanent warfare with the negro race."[8] He invoked "the spirit of the abolitionists, of Lincoln, of Lovejoy [an abolitionist printer killed by proslavery partisans]" and finally challenged his readers with the question "Yet who realizes the seriousness of the situation, and what large and powerful body of citizens is ready to come to [the blacks'] aid?"[9]

Walling's article galvanized many northern progressives, including several New York reformers who successfully recruited the support of Oswald Garrison Villard, a wealthy and influential grandson of well-known Boston abolitionist William Lloyd Garrison. On 12 February 1909, Villard issued "The Lincoln's Birthday Call"—at once a protest against antiblack violence and a call to action—signed by more than fifty prominent individuals. In his "Call," Villard condemned the "lawless attacks upon the Negro . . . even in the Springfield made famous by Lincoln." Such violence, he added, "could but shock the author of the sentiment that a 'government of the people, by the people, for the people, should not perish from the earth.'"[10] Moreover, the northern reformist outrage stirred by the Springfield riot led directly to the formation of the National Association for the Advancement of Colored People. At the time of its creation and for many years afterward, the NAACP's major mission was to combat racial violence—in the North as well as the South. In still another irony, then, the riot "in Lincoln's shadow" was responsible for what became the most illustrious and powerful advocate of African American civil rights in American history.

I finally want to acknowledge my debts to several individuals who in various ways contributed to this new edition. I am especially grateful to Rick Beard, the executive director of the Abraham Lincoln Presidential Library and Museum for his enthusiastic and generous support. He and the Library graciously made available to me many previously unpublished photographs of Springfield's race riot, a number of which are included in the present volume. I also thank James Loewen for his advice and encouragement. Last but far from least, I thank my editor, Karl Kageff—and others at the Southern Illinois University Press—for their swift and skillful preparation of this edition in time for the centennial observances of the riot in Springfield.

R.S.

Free Union, Virginia
June 2008

NOTES

1. *Washington Post*, 16 August 1908; *Fort Worth Star-Telegram*, 16 August 1908; *Biloxi Daily Herald*, 17 August 1908.

2. William English Walling, "The Race War in the North," *Independent* 65 (3 September 1908), 529.

3. *Chicago Daily Tribune*, 16 August 1908; *New York Times*, 24 August 1908.

4. *Chicago Daily Tribune*, 13 February 1909.

5. *Chicago Daily Tribune*, 11, 13 February 1909.

6. *New York Times*, 13 February 1909.

7. Walling, "Race War," 531.

8. Ibid., 529–30.

9. Ibid.

10. Quoted in Robert L. Zangrando, *The NAACP Crusade against Lynching, 1909–1950* (Philadelphia: Temple University Press, 1980), 22–23.

Acknowledgments

THIS study of Springfield's race riot had as its initial inspiration a work far removed from the early twentieth-century Midwest: Paul Boyer and Stephen Nissenbaum's *Salem Possessed: The Social Origins of Witchcraft* (Cambridge, Mass.: Harvard University Press, 1974). Episodes of acute crisis in communities—whether hysteria over witchcraft or race riots—provide exceptional opportunities to trace the interaction of, as Boyer and Nissenbaum put it, "the 'ordinary' history and the extraordinary moment . . . to understand the epoch which produced them both." Their approach of identifying both witchcraft accusers and those accused suggested that detailed investigation of the identity of rioters in Springfield and those whom they targeted for attack might expose sources of interracial antagonism invisible under "ordinary" conditions in the city.

Writing history is at once a profoundly isolated and an intensely social endeavor. Persons too numerous to mention here helped at various stages of this project by reading drafts, uncovering new sources, providing support, and by offering advice (all of which was valued, but not always followed).

Funds for travel and research were provided in the initial stages of this work by the Carter G. Woodson Institute for Afro-American and African Studies and the Graduate School of Arts and Sciences, both of the University of Virginia. I am also grateful for the support of Washington and Lee University in helping me bring the manuscript to completion.

My debts to those whom I met in Springfield are many. In particular I wish to thank Nancy Hunt of the Sangamon State University

Archives and Karen Graff of the Sangamon Valley Collection, Lincoln Library, along with the rest of the staff at both institutions. Sangamon State's Oral History Office proved an invaluable source of material on the Springfield community at the turn of the century. Conversations and correspondence with Cullom Davis, James Krohe, Jr., Mike Townsend, Larry Golden, and William Craven helped me to understand more recent Springfield history and politics and its current state of race relations. Finally, I wish to thank Laverne and Daryll Thomas for their generous hospitality and their special insights into the Springfield community.

I would like to express my deepest appreciation to those who read the manuscript as it evolved, helping weed out infelicities of style and contributing many valuable suggestions. Special thanks must go to Cindy Aron, Edward Ayers, Donald Black, Paul Gaston, Kenneth Kusmer, Waldo Martin, and James Skalnik. I would also like to thank Beth Bower of the University of Illinois Press for her assistance in editing the manuscript in its final stages. Olivier Zunz, whose early faith in the project, steady encouragement, valuable criticisms, and moral support helped make the inevitable frustrations more bearable, deserves special thanks for his patience and many insights. Finally, I would like to thank my editor, August Meier, whose detailed and trenchant criticisms and suggestions helped make the final product far richer than might otherwise have been the case.

Abbreviations

CD   R. L. Polk & Co., *Springfield City Directory* (Springfield, Ill.: R. L. Polk & Co.). For years 1902–12.

CCF   Sangamon County Circuit Court Files

ISJ   *Illinois State Journal* (Springfield)

ISR   *Illinois State Register* (Springfield)

SN   *Springfield News*

SR   *Springfield Record*

SSU   Sangamon State University Archives

SSUO   Oral History Project, Sangamon State University

SVC   Sangamon Valley Collection, Lincoln Library, Springfield, Illinois

Introduction

IN the late afternoon heat of Friday, 14 August 1908, an angry white crowd gathered outside the county jail in downtown Springfield, Illinois. The police had just brought in a black man accused of raping a local white woman. Also lodged in the jail was another black man, awaiting trial for the murder of a white engineer in July. By early evening, leaders in the now menacing crowd demanded that the authorities hand over the two black prisoners. But the prisoners were gone—the police had secretly spirited them out of town. Its desire to inflict summary justice frustrated, the white mob turned its fury on Springfield's black community. What had begun as a lynching party quickly metamorphosed into a full-fledged race war. During two days of violence, white rioters gutted the capital's black business district, left blocks of black homes in smoldering ruins, and lynched two innocent black men. Four whites died and scores more were injured before several thousand state militia finally imposed an uneasy peace on the city. For weeks northern newspapers and magazines leveled scathing criticism at the Illinois capital and its inhabitants, making Springfield a byword for intolerance, corruption, and disorder. The southern press, meanwhile, made the most of the riot: finally, here was dramatic proof that the North, too, had a "Negro problem." The South had been criticized for its brutal record of lynchings and for a savage anti-black riot in Atlanta two years earlier. Now, with ill-concealed jubilation, southern writers and politicians pointed an accusing finger north of the Mason-Dixon line.

Race riots, however, were not new to northern cities. Numerous anti-black riots occurred in the first half of the nineteenth century, and between 1900 and 1908 they disrupted such cities as New York City (1900), Evansville, Indiana (1903), Springfield, Ohio (1904 and 1906), and Greensburg, Indiana (1906). But Springfield's violence came as a particular shock. Not since New York's draft riot of 1863 had the white public been so forcibly reminded of the vehemence of anti-black hostility in the North. The historical irony was too great to overlook: Springfield was Abraham Lincoln's hometown. Its riot presented the northern public with the startling spectacle of whites lynching blacks and burning their houses within a half mile of the Great Emancipator's homestead. The riot's potential import was not lost on Springfield's white mob, either. Local reporters who witnessed the violence overheard rioters yelling, "Lincoln freed you, now we'll show you where you belong!" Even the timing of the riot seemed outrageous: in several months the nation would observe the centennial of Lincoln's birth, and Springfield planned an extravagant celebration in honor of the martyred president. The unsettling symbolism surrounding the riot helped make it the best-known interracial clash of the century's early years.

The reformer William English Walling underscored the dismal irony surrounding Springfield's violence in a widely read article he wrote for the popular magazine, *The Independent.* "If these outrages had happened thirty years ago, when the memories of Lincoln, Garrison and Wendell Phillips were still fresh," he said, the North would have responded with utter indignation. Invoking Lincoln's memory, Walling warned reform-minded blacks and whites that if they did not revive "the spirit of the abolitionists," race war would soon be a permanent feature of northern life. He ended his article with a stirring challenge to northern reformers to organize to fight discrimination and anti-black violence. The publicity Walling and others gave the riot prompted northern activists to meet in 1909. Out of this meeting emerged the first effective national organization to further Afro-American rights: the National Association for the Advancement of Colored People. It was the Springfield riot's role as catalyst in the formation of the NAACP that would attract what little attention it would receive from historians.[1]

Influenced by sociological and psychological theories, historians of racial conflict emphasize what may be loosely termed a "social strain" explanation of anti-black violence. Some of the strains cited as contributing to racial violence are national or regional in scope and have little or no direct bearing on race relations. For example, one writer recently stated that "in the majority of the [race riots], some extraordinary social condition prevailed at the time of the outbreak: prewar changes, wartime mobility, postwar adjustment, or economic depression."[2] Psychologist Gordon W. Allport, in his classic work, *The Nature of Prejudice,* also captured the essence of strain theory, asserting that "most riots occur where there has been some rapid change in the prevailing social situation." Such unsettling changes might include black residential "invasion," a sudden rise in immigrant population, or strikebreaking during periods of industrial labor conflict.[3] Race riots, therefore, have been associated with rapid social and economic change and with periodic extraordinary conditions. Presumably the northern race riots were an outlet for the tensions or frustrations these strains generated.

Early social strain theory was further refined by sociologist Allen Grimshaw. The sources of interracial tension, conflict, and violence, he argues, can be found in "the structural arrangements of society itself," in certain "forms" of social interaction. In American race relations, that form historically has been a "classic accommodative pattern of superordination-subordination," in which whites, the dominant group, have expected "deference, obedience and compliance" from their black "inferiors."[4] As long as blacks "stayed in their place" and the boundaries defining white supremacy remained inviolate, there would be little trouble. Urban anti-black violence might result, though, "from reactions of the dominant group to real or perceived assaults upon the accommodative structure." Grimshaw adds that, "the most intense conflict has resulted when the subordinate group has attempted to disrupt the *status quo* or when the superordinate group has defined the situation as one in which such an attempt is being made."[5] Concentrating on anti-black violence from World War I to World War II, Grimshaw goes on to describe major areas in which blacks disrupted established patterns of race relations: housing, employment, politics, schools, and the use of recreational and transportation facilities. Blacks' rising militancy and determination to press for improved status added to whites' sense that blacks were becoming "uppity" or insubordinate in this period. Of course, most northern cities where blacks challenged the interracial status quo did not experience race riots. As Grimshaw notes, "There is no direct relation between the level of social tension and the eruption of social violence"; the effectiveness of "agencies of external control" (the police, the military, and the judicial system) is a key factor in determining whether a riot occurs or not in a particular city.[6]

Here, then, was a flexible theoretical model that historians could apply in case studies of anti-black collective violence in America— and they have. Most of the major histories of northern anti-black riots examine outbreaks from 1917 to the World War II era.[7] All attribute white fear and frustration to "real" challenges by blacks to the interracial status quo. All pay careful attention to the role of the police and the military in handling the violence. Two historians' works in particular—Elliott Rudwick's pioneering study of the 1917 East St. Louis riot and William Tuttle's examination of Chicago's 1919 outbreak—are influential examples of the application of Grimshaw's theories. Both point to the massive influx of blacks during the Great Migration as the major factor behind rising racial conflict in each city. Tuttle also argues that more general, national social strains helped make this an extraordinarily violent period. The wave of race riots in 1919, he says, was part of a national "climate of violence" created by postwar unemployment, labor disputes, anti-radicalism, and xenophobia.[8] Both studies argue that blacks were making real assaults upon the interracial status quo. Surveying three of the most serious racial clashes of the first half of the century (East St. Louis, Chicago, and the Detroit riot of 1943), Rudwick concludes, "In the three cities the racial violence resulted from: threats to the security of whites brought on by the Negro's gains in economic, political and social status; Negro resentment of the attempts to 'kick him back into his place'; and the weakness of the 'external forces of constraint'—the city government, especially the police department."[9]

The identification of periods of extraordinary social tension and the explanation of anti-black hostility in terms of assaults on the interracial status quo on the local level have significantly advanced our understanding of race riots. Social strain theory has forced serious exploration of the historical context and the urban structural changes that helped generate anti-black tension and violence. Even so, this approach has limitations. For one thing, it is difficult to identify a period from the 1830s on when tension was not present in northern urban areas. True, race rioting increased in the Jacksonian period and during the Civil War, World War I, and World War II eras, and each period witnessed a variety of unsettling social and economic changes, tensions, and strains. But the years between these peak times of interracial violence were not stable, either. After the 1860s, for example, the maturation of industrial capitalism, increasing immigration, economic depressions, labor strife, and advancing urbanization all were major sources of social tension. Thus, it cannot be said that fewer race riots in these years indicates a lack of social strain or rapid change.

Another problem with traditional interpretations of interracial collective violence—one that will likely continue to plague researchers—is the failure to explain why, given similar conditions, race riots occur in some cities and not others. Assuming some threshold of social strain beyond which whites become prone to anti-black violence, which variables—which specific strains—contribute most to aggression? It is difficult to be precise.[10] Allen Grimshaw suggests that the effectiveness of the police or the military may help explain why riots break out only in certain cities. Disorder can escalate rapidly in a city whose mayor hesitates to muster the force necessary to prevent rioting. Likewise, a riot can be prolonged or become more deadly where police either refuse to control crowds or actually join in the rioting themselves.[11]

It is possible—though no one knows for certain—that city police have occasionally prevented small-scale interracial clashes from escalating into full-blown race riots. Before World War II, however, the issue of urban police effectiveness in suppressing riots is largely irrelevant: regardless of their level of training and commitment to halting interracial violence, city police departments simply did not have enough officers to quell massive rioting. Springfield's police force, for example, at full strength could field only about forty patrolmen. Faced with crowds that numbered at times in the thousands, and which were spread over a wide area of the capital, the police could not impose control. Since restoring law and order in such cases typically meant separating the two races and protecting black neighborhoods from further attack, local authorities often had to call in state or federal troops. Moreover, the police lacked the technology that later would enable more efficient mobilization and coordination of riot suppression. Radio communication and automobiles were not factors in crowd control until well after World War I. Springfield's policemen patrolled either in horse-drawn vehicles or, more often, on foot, and they were out of touch with headquarters for long periods. Finally, not only were police departments highly decentralized before World War II, but they lacked policies for dealing with race riots, and, as one sociologist has noted, "the historical record indicates that they did not anticipate such happenings."[12]

The use of social strain theory—Grimshaw's theories in particular—has left us with an incomplete and oversimplified picture of the nature of northern urban race relations and the sources of anti-black hostility. As Grimshaw notes, white violence was the product of "real or perceived" black threats to the interracial status quo. For the most part, though, historians of twentieth-century racial conflict have not only focused upon blacks' "real" threats, but have primarily centered upon the largest and most visible of them: conflicts over jobs, housing, politics, and so forth, resulting from major increases in black population. But, as Richard Maxwell Brown emphasizes, from the 1820s to the 1960s white violence was often triggered by "white *perception* of black aggressiveness, not merely the act of black aggressiveness."[13] Attacks upon blacks did not always depend on overt or deliberate black challenges to their subordinate status. Neither did deference, passivity, and accommodation necessarily guarantee blacks' safety. To take the true measure of the extent and depth of northern white racism and anti-black hostility, we must carefully weigh the importance of white reactions to perceived black violations of place (or to smaller, less measurable, less perceptible "real" violations) before the extraordinary conditions created by World War I and the Great Migration.

Previous riot studies—especially of anti-black collective violence in the first half of this century—have also neglected another promising approach: the analysis of riot participants. We know very little about who actually took part in twentieth-century anti-black riots. Those who apply social strain theory identify many important structural changes in cities that heightened tensions, but they do not explain the connections between specific social strains and the people who actually comprised violent crowds. Case studies of race riots leave the impression that all whites were potential rioters and that all reacted with alarm and outrage to real black challenges to the interracial status quo. We are left to assume that all northern whites were committed to keeping blacks in their "place," and by violent means if necessary. Except for a few instances where single individuals or small groups of rioters are mentioned, the northern anti-black urban mob remains an unidentified, faceless abstraction. This lack of connection between riot theory and actual riot participation prompts a number of troubling questions. Were most whites in fact potential rioters? If interracial job or housing competition preceded a race riot, should we assume that the whites who rioted were mostly those whose interests were directly threatened by blacks? If labor conflict over the use of blacks as strikebreakers preceded a riot, should we assume that the rioters were drawn heavily from the industry in question? In other words, did directly aggrieved whites lead these riots? If not, why? The question of the actual influence of social strain and what motivated the rioters remains unclear when the identity and social position of riot participants are unknown.

The few scholars who have written about Springfield's 1908 race riot have relied heavily on social strain theory. Springfield, they argue, experienced much the same structural changes and social strains in 1908 as other cities did in the World War I era: large-scale black migration, job and housing competition, and labor strife.[14] Thus, for example, the *Encyclopedia of Black America* categorizes Springfield's violence as an "economic riot," generated by the fact that it "had recently received a sizable influx of black migrants." Increased numbers of blacks meant that "tension [over] the use of black miners as strikebreakers combined with general resentment against black competition for wages created a widespread feeling that the town's Negroes needed a lesson in the racial facts of life."[15] Another writer influenced by social strain theory concludes that a "huge Negro influx" into Springfield fueled interracial conflict. A burgeoning black population, this argument runs, "threatened the jobs of the whites as well as their superiority at the ballot box." In particular, "foreign-born Americans did feel a real competition from unskilled Negro workers in the Springfield area, and there is good indication that many of the rioters were of immigrant stock." This competition was said to be especially acute in Springfield's coal mines, which employed both blacks and immigrants. Too, white miners were said to harbor lingering hostility over black strikebreaking during the violent labor disputes of the late 1890s in nearby mining communities like Virden. In addition to foreigners, some scholars suggest, a southern white element in Springfield—presumably quicker to resent any black threats to the interracial status quo—was a major factor in the riot.[16]

However much black migration and consequent black threats to white dominance are pertinent to the analysis of race riots from 1917 on, they do not adequately explain earlier outbreaks. Springfield's 1908 riot is one case in point. First of all, in fact no sudden or massive influx of blacks into Springfield disrupted the interracial status quo or sparked heated competition in the late nineteenth or early twentieth century. Second, Springfield's patterns of black housing, politics, and employment remained much the same over that period. Hence, any black threats to whites' dominance in Springfield must have been present long before the riot. Third, many of the structural changes and social strains of the later war era were absent in Springfield. After the riot, Springfield's whites did speak of black "insubordination," but one is hard-pressed to trace such statements to any substantial or measurable black threats to the local interracial status quo. Finally, it should be noted that this was not a period of pervasive national tension. There was no extraordinary, general climate of violence in the North of the magnitude, say, of that of the "Red Summer" of 1919 or that of the turbulent 1830s. Taken together, these factors help explain the absence of a clear pattern of escalating interracial tensions before the 1908 riot.

The following examination of Springfield's race riot, therefore, begins where the earlier case studies end. Critical assessment of the origins and meaning of the outbreak must start with identification of the "faces in the crowd," as George Rudé put it in his important study, *The Crowd in History*. The technique of studying collective violence through an analysis of participants is not new, yet it has rarely been applied to outbreaks of urban American racial violence prior to the 1960s. Before we can generalize about the possible effects of social strain or, in Springfield's case, construct a modified explanation, we must know who the participants were—both rioters and victims. What was their social position? What possible connections, contacts, or relationships between the blacks and whites involved might have generated hostility? Explanation must be built from the ground up.

Though it is impossible to identify all of Springfield's white rioters, a surprisingly large number of names of active participants are available in the city's newspapers and court records. One can trace participants' residence, occupation, birthplace, and age in the federal census and city directories. The typical white rioter emerges from these sources, enabling us to identify the kinds of whites most willing to translate their grievances against blacks into street violence. Most observers at the time described Springfield's rioters as riffraff, criminals—the scum of the community. Later writers claimed that a foreign or southern element was to blame for the violence. Data on riot participants make it possible to test such generalizations and to clarify the relationship of class, ethnicity, occupation, and other social variables to violent behavior.

A second important question pertains to the position of Springfield's white nonparticipants. What social strata did they come from? Is it true, as is often said, that the city's leaders and its middle and upper classes were not involved in these early twentieth-century riots? Those studying riots typically focus on the response of city authorities and the police, especially that of the latter, to interracial violence. Although their actions are important to our understanding of urban riots, they shed little light on the part other whites played in such outbreaks. Springfield's middle- and upper-class whites, for example, asserted that they had nothing to do with the violence—that they were merely shocked spectators to a drama created, sustained, and applauded solely by dangerous criminal rabble. Were they in fact as far removed from the origins, progress, and aftermath of the riot as they claimed? And what of less affluent white nonparticipants? Did they differ in any significant or systematic fashion from more riot-prone whites? Analysis of individuals who refused to riot is another important key to understanding those who did.

A third analytical approach involves a systematic examination of the social characteristics and position of the victims of Springfield's white rioters. This method—which may be termed historical victimology—is rarely applied to the study of collective violence in America's past. Put simply, knowledge of relevant social strains, of who the rioters were, and of what role white nonparticipants played does not tell us all we need to know about the origins and nature of race riots. Attacks on blacks (and some whites) during Springfield's riot were not entirely random. Neither were all blacks equally at risk during the outbreak. The riot's shifting course and ecology, viewed together with the riot victims' socioeconomic characteristics, reveal a distinct and deliberate pattern of targeting. Were the individuals who were targeted for attack early in the outbreak socially similar to those victimized in its later stages? If not, why? The intent of this victimological approach is not simply to cast all of Springfield's blacks as passive or helpless victims of white aggression, but to infer from their identity what previous interracial contacts and interactions may have contributed to their being singled out for attack. In other words, examining the identity of riot victims, black as well as white, allows us to probe deeper into the origins of anti-black hostility in Springfield. It helps us identify what black activities and behaviors whites perceived as intolerable violations—real or imagined—of the boundaries of white supremacy.

During social crises such as riots, fundamental divisions in communities—ideological and behavioral—often stand out in bold relief. For a brief time the violence in Springfield exposed white disunity over the role and destiny of blacks there. One major finding of this study, besides the fact that whites were not equally likely to riot, was that whites also sharply disagreed on the causes, goals, and significance of the violence. As the Springfield riot unfolded, it became increasingly clear that it represented more than a conflict between blacks and whites: whites were pitted against other whites as well.

The implications of this white disunity are important. Previous work on northern interracial conflict often implies that most whites shared similar opinions about blacks' proper place in society. Actually, in some critical areas they disagreed over what the boundaries of white supremacy were or what constituted black challenges to the interracial status quo. White racism was not monolithic. It was unevenly distributed across the community.[18] When two of the most critical pieces of the puzzle are combined—the identity of rioters and their victims—we see more clearly that whites' racist beliefs and their behavior toward blacks varied significantly with their social position. Although structural conditions were not entirely irrelevant, whatever sense of grievance some whites harbored against blacks, it involved factors less visible and less tangible than a measurable shortage of jobs, black residential expansion, or labor strife. The following chapters explore the elusive yet vital factors behind Springfield's riot, and the nature and significance of white disagreement on racial issues for patterns of discrimination and anti-black violence.

This study, then, is more than an anatomy of a particular race riot. Springfield's outbreak provides us with a special opportunity to explore anew the broader dynamics of race relations in the urban North. Knowledge of the riot's participants provides crucial insights into the previously neglected, but vital and complex, interaction between class, racism, and anti-black violence. I have attempted, wherever possible, to account for the part played by all levels and segments of the Springfield community. Although there is much here about black life in Springfield early in the century, my intention was not to produce a detailed black community study. Discussion is largely limited to those black institutions, behaviors, and individuals directly connected to or affected by the 1908 riot. Admittedly, aspects of this and other riots stubbornly resist analysis, and inference must often serve where data are lacking. Difficult questions regarding timing, motivation, and causation underscore the complexity of riots. Nonetheless, it is possible to refine our understanding of this type of collective violence. A close analysis of the actors in Springfield's riot enables us to assess and improve the fit between theories of social conflict and actual racial violence on the local level.

NOTES

1. William English Walling, "The Race War in the North," *The Independent* 65 (3 September 1908): 530, 534; James Crouthemal, "The Springfield Race Riot of 1908," *Journal of Negro History* 45 (July 1960): 164–81.

2. Joseph Boskin, ed., *Urban Racial Violence in the Twentieth Century*, 2d ed. (Beverly Hills, Calif.: Glencoe Press, 1976), 14. For examples of this kind of interpretation as applied by historians, see Leonard L. Richards, *"Gentlemen of Property and Standing": Anti-Abolition Mobs in Jacksonian America* (New York: Oxford University Press, 1970), 47–81; William M. Tuttle, Jr., *Race Riot: Chicago in the Red Summer of 1919* (New York: Atheneum, 1970), 3–31; Michael Feldberg, *The Philadelphia Riots of 1844: A Study of Ethnic Conflict* (Westport, Conn.: Greenwood Press, 1975), 1–16.

3. Gordon W. Allport, *The Nature of Prejudice* (Reading, Mass.: Addison-Wesley Publishing Company, 1954), 59–60.

4. Allen D. Grimshaw, "Changing Patterns of Racial Violence in the United States," *Notre Dame Lawyer* 60 (Symposium, 1965): 539–40; idem, "Factors Contributing to Colour Violence in the United States and Britain," *Race* 3 (May 1962): 4. Grimshaw's major thesis first appeared in 1959 in his "A Study of Social Violence: Urban Race Riots in the United States," (Ph.D. diss., University of Pennsylvania, 1959), and "Lawlessness and Violence in America and Their Special Manifestations in Changing Negro-White Relationships," *Journal of Negro History* 44 (January 1959): 52–72. Restatements and elaborations on the theory may be found in these later works by him: "Urban Racial Violence in the United States: Changing Ecological Considerations," *American Journal of Sociology* 64 (September 1960): 109–19; "Negro-White Relations in the Urban North: Two Areas of High Conflict Potential," *Journal of Intergroup Relations* 3 (Spring 1962): 146–58; "Actions of the Police and the Military in American Race Riots," *Phylon* 24 (Fall 1963): 271–89; and "Three Views of Urban Violence: Civil Disturbance, Racial Revolt, Class Assault," *American Behavioral Scientist* 11 (March-April 1968): 2–7. These articles and several others by him are reprinted in Grimshaw, ed., *Racial Violence in the United States* (Chicago: Aldine Publishing Company, 1969). This volume is a valuable compendium of short pieces on racial conflict by historians, psychologists, and sociologists.

5. Grimshaw, "Factors Contributing to Colour Violence," 4.

6. Ibid., 5–7, 18.

7. Extensive treatments of early twentieth-century race riots include Tuttle, *Race Riot;* Elliott M. Rudwick, *Race Riot at East St. Louis, July 2, 1917* (Carbondale: Southern Illinois University Press, 1964); Scott Ellsworth, *Death in a Promised Land: The Tulsa Race Riot of 1921* (Baton Rouge: Louisiana State University Press, 1982); William Ivy Hair, *Carnival of Fury: Robert Charles and the New Orleans Race Riot of 1900* (Baton Rouge: Louisiana State University Press, 1976); and Robert V. Haynes, *A Night of Violence: The Houston Riot of 1917* (Baton Rouge: Louisiana State University Press, 1976).

8. Tuttle, *Race Riot*, 13–20.

9. Rudwick, *Race Riot at East St. Louis*, 217.

10. Sociological studies comparing riot cities with non-riot cities have had little success in detecting patterns distinguishing riot-prone communities. See, for example, Stanley Lieberson and Arnold R. Silverman,"The Precipitants and Underlying Conditions of Race Riots," *American Sociological Review* 30 (December 1965): 887–98. This study examined seventy-six riot cities and found that neither changes in the size of black population nor a high unemployment rate among whites accounts for riots. See also Milton Bloombaum, "The Conditions Underlying Race Riots as Portrayed by Multidimensional Scalogram Analysis: A Reanalysis of Lieberson and Silverman's Data," *American Sociological Review* 33 (February 1968): 76–91, and Albert Bergesen, "Official Violence during the Watts, Newark, and Detroit Race Riots of the 1960s," in Pat Lauderdale, ed., *A Political Analysis of Deviance* (Minneapolis: University of Minnesota Press, 1980), 155–57.

11. Grimshaw, "Actions of the Police and the Military," 271–89. See also Arthur I. Waskow, *From Race Riot to Sit-In, 1919 and the 1960s: A Study in the Connections between Conflict and Violence* (Garden City, N.Y.: Doubleday and Company, 1966); Morris Janowitz, "Patterns of Collective Racial Violence," in Hugh Graham Davis and Ted Robert Gurr, eds., *Violence in America: Historical and Comparative Perspectives* (New York: Bantam Books, 1969), 393–404, 409–11; Janowitz, *Social Control of Escalated Riots* (Chicago: University of Chicago Press, 1968), 7–28; and Michael Feldberg, *The Turbulent Era: Riot and Disorder in Jacksonian America* (New York: Oxford University Press, 1980), 7, 104–5, 108–19.

12. Janowitz, *Social Control of Escalated Riots*, 7–15.

13. Richard Maxwell Brown, *Strain of Violence: Historical Studies of American Violence and Vigilantism* (New York: Oxford University Press, 1975), 206.

14. For discussions of the relationship of black migration to interracial violence, see Tuttle, *Race Riot*, and Rudwick, *Race Riot at East St. Louis*.

15. Augustus W. Low, ed., *Encyclopedia of Black America* (New York: McGraw Hill Book Company, 1981), 232.

16. Crouthemal, "The Springfield Race Riot of 1908," 165, 177–78; James Krohe, Jr., *Summer of Rage: The Springfield Race Riot of 1908* (Springfield, Ill.: Sangamon County Historical Society, 1973), 3–4.

17. In part, the lack of study of crowd composition in riots of this period is due to the scarcity of sources that might yield the names of riot participants. In many cases, however, the question of who rioted was never addressed in the first place, except in a most general fashion. One likely reason for this is that participant analysis became more widely accepted after interest in race riot studies had waned. For examples of this method, see George Rudé, *The Crowd in History: A Study of Popular Disturbances in France and England, 1730–1848* (New York: Wiley, 1964); Natalie Zemon Davis, *Society and Culture in Early Modern France* (Stanford, Calif.: Stanford University Press, 1975), 152–87; *Report of the National Advisory Commission on Civil Disorders* (Washington, D.C.: Government Printing Office, 1968) (see especially Part 3 for a discussion of riot participants); Robert M. Fogelson and Robert

B. Hill, "Who Riots? A Study of Participation in the 1967 Riots," in Grimshaw, *Racial Violence*, 313–16; Boskin, "The Revolt of the Urban Ghettoes, 1964–1970," in *Urban Racial Violence*, 166–67; Richards, *"Gentlemen of Property and Standing"*; David Grimsted, "Rioting in its Jacksonian Setting," *American Historical Review* 77 (April 1972): 361–418; and Paul A. Gilje, *The Road to Mobocracy: Popular Disorder in New York City, 1763–1834* (Chapel Hill: University of North Carolina Press, 1987).

18. Barbara J. Fields, "Ideology and Race in American History," in J. Morgan Kousser and James M. McPherson, eds., *Region, Race and Reconstruction: Essays in Honor of C. Vann Woodward* (New York: Oxford University Press, 1982), 156–60.

CHAPTER 1

"Riot, Ruin and Rebellion . . . "

IT was midday on 1 June 1908 when the freight train bound northeast for Springfield left the Mississippi River town of Alton, Illinois. Concealed in one of the boxcars was Joe James, a young black drifter from Alabama. For three years he had been on the move, looking for work in the larger cities of Missouri and Illinois. Were it not for the events of the next two months, James's existence, like that of thousands of other southern blacks who were moving northward searching for a better life, would have remained shrouded in obscurity. Even so, very little is known about his background. He was born in Birmingham, Alabama, into a poor family. His father died when he was a small child, and from the age of seven he was raised by relatives. Before he left Alabama James had worked in a brush factory, in brickyards, as a moulder's helper, and at various odd jobs. Though he apparently had received no formal schooling, he had somehow acquired the rudiments of reading and writing. He also knew how to play the piano, a skill that enabled him to pick up small change in city saloons and dance halls. Joe James—perhaps nineteen or twenty years old by the time he headed for Springfield—was already well versed in the art of surviving in cities on very little money. Still, despite the poverty and transiency he had experienced, he apparently had never been in trouble with the law before he went to the Illinois capital. In flight from the bleakness of his Birmingham past, he seems the archetype of the "travelling man," living by his wits and by occasional labor. What drew him to Springfield, according to later accounts, was the hope of a steady job.[1]

Late in the afternoon of 1 June, Joe James got off the railroad boxcar in Springfield. The capital city, situated near the geographic center of Illinois, was a logical choice for a black migrant. It had a modest-sized black community—about 2,500 out of a total population of nearly 47,000—and the city's coal mines, brickyards, and small black-owned businesses held out hope of employment.[2] James walked downtown to a district of cheap boardinghouses and saloons Springfield residents called the Levee. It lay just east of the courthouse, roughly bounded by Seventh and Tenth Streets on the east and west, and East Jefferson and East Washington Streets on the north and south (see Map 1.1). The Levee consisted mostly of two- and three-story brick buildings, which housed saloons, small restaurants, pawnshops, and assorted small businesses on the ground level and cheap, squalid rental units on the upper floors. The East Washington Street blocks of the Levee contained most of the city's black businesses: barbershops, saloons, little restaurants, pool halls, and grocery stores. A few businesses—both black and white—concealed less legitimate enterprises behind their doors. Indeed, the Levee was the neighborhood where local "sports," tourists, and others could indulge their taste for liquor, gambling, and "ladies of the evening." Some of the activity in the Levee and surrounding vice district was technically illegal, but unofficially sanctioned as long as it remained within traditional and recognized geographic bounds—that is, away from the more respectable business and residential districts to the west and south. Springfield authorities paid less attention to the expansion of vice and crime to the north and east of the city's center. Northeast of the Levee (between Reynolds and Jefferson Streets on the north and south, and east of Ninth Street for several blocks) lay a large settlement of poor blacks known as the Badlands. This neighborhood, like others of its kind in American cities, was vulnerable to invasion by gambling dens, brothels, and other assorted "dives" (See Map 1.1).[3]

In 1909 a zealous anti-saloon crusader penned a vivid description of Springfield's Levee. It was, he said, "a mass of dive saloons, pawn shops, questionable hotels, fourth rate lodging houses and brothels from the lowest ramshackle hovels to the most richly and elaborately equipped which can be found anywhere in the State."[4] Walking east on Washington Street from the courthouse to Tenth Street four blocks away, the indignant prohibitionist counted twenty-five saloons, "most of them . . . vile and stenchful." Revealing not a little middle-class and nativist bias, the reformer went on to picture Levee saloons at their worst:

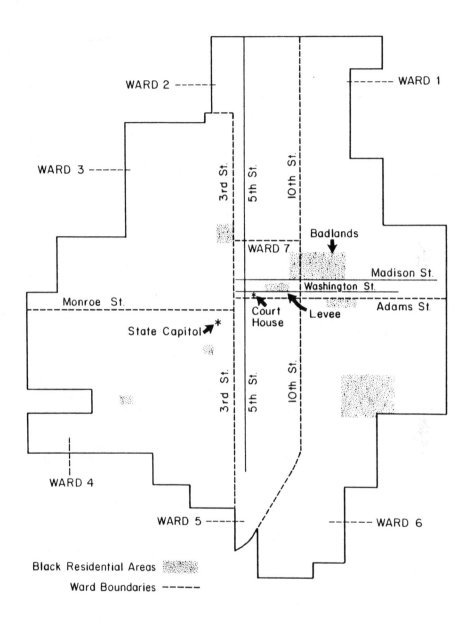

WARD 2

WARD 1

WARD 3

3rd St.

5th St.

10th St.

Badlands

WARD 7

Madison St.

Washington St.

Monroe St.

Court
House

Levee

Adams St.

State Capitol *

3rd St.

5th St.

10th St.

WARD 4

WARD 5

WARD 6

Black Residential Areas

Ward Boundaries ------

Map 1.1 Springfield Wards and Black Neighborhoods, 1908

Negro dive saloons, Bohemian saloons where the English language is never spoken. Blazing lighthouses of Hell and recruiting stations for the penitentiary. You enter one of these places and low-browed brutish red eyed animal men will stare at you. The air is foul and stifling. Faded, vulgar pictures look down at you from dirty, dust-covered walls. The mirrors behind the bar are so covered with fly specks and other accumulations of filth that you can scarcely see your reflection. Low-browed, pig-eyed, pug-nosed, pot-bellied products of the saloon with shirts unbuttoned in front and breeches bagging at the knees are lined up at the bar, drinking goblets of sheeny booze. . . . Over nearly every door hangs the unpronounceable name of a Roman Catholic foreigner, and in and around these places loaf the porch climber and yeggman, who would take your life for a dollar.[5]

Prelude

For Joe James, the Levee was a logical destination upon arriving in Springfield. Nearly all of Springfield's black-owned saloons were in this neighborhood, and he headed to one of these on his first day in town, seeking information about the city and soliciting work. He asked about odd jobs at several saloons and later claimed that one had hired him as a cleaning man. James passed that evening playing pool with several local blacks, apparently for money, and won most of his games. According to James, his troubles began the next day. The local men he had played with were angry at their losses. To get even, they pointed him out to the police as a suspicious stranger. Two black city detectives confronted James and arrested him for vagrancy. The authorities ordered him to leave town, giving him a couple of hours to clear out. When James insisted on staying, he was rearrested. Perhaps for the first time in his life, the Alabama migrant found himself in jail.[6]

During his stay at the city prison, Joe James proved a model prisoner, and by the end of June he became a "trusty." Early in the evening on 4 July, one of the guards at the jail sent him out to buy food. In the middle of his errand, James succumbed to temptation and decided to find some amusement in the Levee. He entered "Dandy Jim" Smith's saloon, a black establishment on East Washington Street, and began to play the piano in return for free drinks and small change. A little later he won money in a crap game at a second black saloon. He spent the better part of the evening drinking, gambling, and playing the piano. A black porter who saw him that night later recalled that James seemed to be "loading up" for a "big-jag." Some time after 11:00 in the evening, James, now thoroughly drunk, was thrown out of a saloon, and he stumbled off into the night.[7]

The same night that Joe James was having his spree in the Levee, Blanche Ballard, the sixteen-year-old daughter of Clergy Ballard, a white mining engineer, was attending Fourth of July festivities at the White City amusement park on the eastern edge of the city. She returned home to 1135 North Ninth Street around midnight, and she and the rest of her family went to bed. A little before 1:00, Blanche awoke suddenly and found someone sitting or lying at the foot of her bed. In the darkness she could not see who the person was, and when she questioned him she got no answer. Alarmed, the girl cried out for her parents, and the intruder fled the house. Exactly what happened next is unclear, but it seems that Clergy Ballard ran outside in pursuit. Unarmed, Ballard caught up with the intruder in the front yard. The two struggled; Ballard was stabbed several times and mortally wounded. His assailant fled, and the family helped the wounded man back to the porch where he collapsed from loss of blood. Before he lost consciousness, Clergy Ballard told his family that his attacker was black and that he had run northward on Ninth Street. He died the next day in the hospital.[8]

Early the next morning, four girls spotted a black man sleeping by the side of the road several blocks north of the Ballard home. They, like many other residents in the northern section of the city, had heard the news of Clergy Ballard's death. They telephoned both the police and the Ballard family to tell them they had seen a black man in the neighborhood. Clergy Ballard's sons and neighbors reached the spot first. They concluded that the sleeping man was the murderer and began beating him severely. The police arrived just in time to prevent what probably would have been a lynching and carried the man off. The next day, the front pages of the city's newspapers featured large photographs of Joe James, his face puffy and his eyes swollen shut from the beating he had received at the hands of Clergy Ballard's friends and relatives.[9]

Ballard's murder was front-page news in Springfield for several days, and residents of the predominantly white, working-class north end were heard to suggest kidnapping and hanging Joe James. Not long after the police had taken James back into custody, an angry crowd formed at the Ballard residence. "The cry of 'kill' emanated from the crowd which had gathered, and the sons of Ballard were

urged to do the deed"—to lynch Joe James—reported one newspaper. "Murmurs and whisperings coupled with threats of vengeance disturbed the Sabbath quiet of the whole north end of the
city." The excitement in the north part of the city stemmed partly
from Clergy Ballard's popularity. He was a long-time resident there
and, having worked on the railroads, in the mines, and at the large
Illinois Watch Company, had a wide network of friends and
acquaintances.[10]

What made the murder newsworthy was not just that it had involved a black, but that it had occurred in an unexpected part of
town: in a quiet, predominantly white residential neighborhood
some distance from the Levee and vice district downtown. For many
years the area bounded by East Washington, East Adams, and Seventh and Eighth Streets was known as Springfield's "Block of
Crime" for its high incidence of assault and murder. As much as
forty years earlier, East Washington from Sixth to Eighth Street had
earned the title "Bloody Row." The Levee had been the rough part
of town for a long time.[11] Of course, a certain amount of lawlessness and disorder was part of the price Springfield and many other
turn-of-the-century American cities had to pay for their toleration of segregated "sporting" neighborhoods with their high concentrations of saloons and vice. But Springfield's newspapers were
quick to point out that in the case of Clergy Ballard's murder,
crime—black crime in particular—had ventured beyond its recognized territory. While most articles in the press expressed hopes for
a quick trial and speedy execution to resolve the Ballard affair,
others called for, or hinted at, broader retribution. One newspaper,
for example, issued a thinly veiled demand for revenge: "If blood
ever did cry out for vengeance, that of Clergy Ballard's does. It cries
out not alone for punishment of the man who spilled it. It cries out
for an end of the dives on the levee. . . . It is time to clean out the
levee."[12]

In the end, the tensions generated by the Ballard murder dissipated without incident. The newspapers, after a few days of inflammatory coverage of the murder, shifted their attention back to the
upcoming elections in August. Joe James's trial was postponed for
six weeks, in part to wait until the white community was in a calmer
frame of mind. In jail once again, James resumed his role as a
model prisoner. Under intensive questioning by police, he insisted
that he knew nothing about the murder of Clergy Ballard—that,
indeed, he had been so drunk at the time, he scarcely remembered
the beating he had received the next morning.[13]

The Black Image

In covering the Ballard murder, the Springfield press emphasized the issues of black crime and miscegenation, reflecting white concerns about the social control of blacks in the North. Of course, concern over the maintenance of black subordination involved much more: a wide range of economic, social, and political anxieties fueled urban interracial conflicts and violence. Black crime and racial amalgamation, however, were among the most dramatic and emotionally charged symbols of failure to control black urban communities. The press both reflected and furthered a belief that blacks were somehow naturally criminally inclined and lascivious. The reiteration of these stereotypes also reinforced the notion that blacks were unfit for life in the North, and it revealed a thinly disguised wish that blacks might disappear from the region, or even the nation, altogether. In short, for some northern whites, the issue was one of social isolation, quarantine, or even expulsion of blacks. After the riot, one Springfield resident, for example, described most of the city's black residents as lazy, dishonest, and vicious. He did concede that "there is a saving element of the thrifty and law-abiding class" in the black community, but went on to assert that "the majority are worthless or genuinely bad." He concluded with the hope that "the city will be purified." Presumably he meant, in this context, that the majority should be induced to leave.[14]

Stereotypes of blacks as innately prone to criminal acts and deviant behavior were in no small part shaped by the conspicuous and often lurid coverage of black crime in the nation's white press. Indeed, the unsuspecting reader scanning northern urban newspapers in this period might easily have concluded that a major black crime wave was underway. In 1908, for example, scarcely a week passed in which a Springfield newspaper failed to display a headline highlighting black misbehavior. Articles entitled "Negroes in Gun Fight," "Loses $10 to Negress," "Negro Attacks Housewife," and "Negro Slashes Woman With Razor" were typical fare.[15] As historian David A. Gerber has concluded, such coverage "revealed a deep-seated belief that fighting, drinking, gambling and prostitution were the peculiar characteristics of an undisciplined, irresponsible people."[16]

Concern over black misbehavior was not limited to Springfield's white press. One of Springfield's two black newspapers fretted constantly over the bad impression made by those of the city's blacks who habitually visited saloons and gambling dens, fearing that a disorderly minority might bring trouble to the whole black community. Springfield's black *Forum* at times showed more venom in denouncing black conduct in the Levee than the most racist writers of the white press. Launching a "crusade against bad joints," the *Forum* railed against the black "loafers [and] loud obstreperous Negroes" who frequented them. Its editor complained of "colored girls roaming the street," and "a certain class of Negro men . . . who are bestially inclined and lay by the high-ways, winking and flirting at girls and men's wives." He concluded angrily: "It is a scandal, an abomination and an irreparable sin. . . . Such curs should not be lynched but legally and summarily dealt with. The time has arrived for young men to form clubs and cowhide such beasts. . . . They should be made to leave town."[17]

Jealous of the reputation of the majority of blacks in the city, the *Forum* reflected the middle-class values and sensibilities of the more successful and established black Springfield residents, and their desire for security and respectability in an age that saw increasing anti-black hostility and growing discrimination in the North. To be sure, the *Forum's* editor did not absolve whites from responsibility for the deterioration of race relations. But, observing the tendency of the white press to dwell upon black criminality, he turned his anger upon those he felt were the most visible but the least representative of the black community: black Levee habitués. The *Forum* scolded: "There seems here in Springfield . . . a set of indolent young men whose ambition never runs higher than a fine suit, excursions and hanging around saloons. Whenever they think the law will not be enforced they gather themselves together and form a crap game usually on Saturday evenings. . . . Sunday morning they are written up in the dailies."[18]

That blacks were conspicuous and disorderly in the Levee involved more than just embarrassment for the city's black elite—realistic fears lay behind the *Forum's* rebukes. Painfully aware of the grotesque stereotypes of blacks circulating in white American popular culture, the *Forum* editor was concerned that black impropriety, especially in public places, would contribute to increased discrimination locally and might even trigger white violence. Incensed over the "profanity and vulgarity" of black men who liked to "congregate about the front doors of saloons and curse," the black editor warned, "these young men seem to forget that they are a part of the nation and their deeds will build up or tear down; make history great or 'paint it red.' "[19]

Press accounts of Clergy Ballard's murder raised the issue of racial amalgamation along with that of black crime, and in doing so catered to many whites' view of the black man as a sexually depraved brute. Since theft did not seem to have been Joe James's motive for entering the Ballard residence (no property had been stolen), the city newspapers assumed that he had intended to rape Ballard's daughter.[20] Like crime, interracial sexual contacts were supposed to remain within the confines of the Levee and the downtown demimonde. The press usually treated incidents of miscegenation in the vice district and Levee with condescending humor, and it sometimes offered stories of interracial escapades there for public amusement.

In March 1908, for instance, the robbery of Polish immigrant Nicholas Ministinski was presented as a sort of local burlesque comedy. His experience stood in part as an example of how some recent immigrants were slow to assimilate American ideas of proper racial etiquette. Nicholas and a friend visited a black saloon in the Badlands that had a reputation as a rendezvous for prostitutes. There he had "fallen under the spell of a dusky maiden. The influence of her smiles, aided, perhaps, by the booze he had soaked up, caused the separation of a ten dollar bill from the man's pocket." The article's message was clear: Nicholas, the ignorant foreigner, got what was coming to him; he should have known better. When he went to the police, demanding that they "getta back da ten," his difficulty speaking English, combined with his drunkenness, meant that he could expect little aid from that quarter. Returning to the police station the next day, sober, and no doubt frustrated with the workings of American law enforcement, Nicholas reportedly "struck his breast with his clenched fist and in true dramatic fashion exclaimed, 'I finda da mon, I no come back!' " and left to conduct his own search for the black woman who had picked his pocket.[21]

Springfield's press also took an indifferent or neutral stance when those involved in interracial encounters were "lowlifes" or "Levee characters." Undoubtedly some persons regularly violated white racial norms in the saloon and brothel area downtown, but it is impossible to gauge how much interracial sexual behavior actually took place. Neither is it possible to determine the extent of interracial marriage or cohabitation in the city. A careful search of the manuscript censuses of 1900 and 1910 reveals no more than a half-dozen instances of persons of the opposite sex and of different race living under one roof. Given the tendency of census enumerators and city directory compilers to overlook residents in poorer urban neighbor hoods, the actual number of interracial couples was probably underreported. Moreover, some individuals "changed" their race over time; whites living with blacks were sometimes listed as "black" or "colored" in the city directories and censuses, and some light-skinned blacks occasionally appeared as "white."[22] Nonetheless, a close reading of Springfield's newspapers clearly indicates that many people of varied backgrounds and nationalities mixed freely in the shady district of the city. The press usually took this as a matter of course.

The experiences of Helen Bates, a white prostitute, suggest the kind of blurring of the color line that occurred in the vice district. In the spring of 1908 Bates and several others were arrested for smoking "hop" in an "opium den" on East Adams Street. Two of her fellow smokers were black men. During a short series of police cleanup raids in August, the authorities arrested Bates again at the same stand for possession of an opium "smoking outfit." The court ordered her and the rest of the "undesirables" netted in the raid to leave town. But just three weeks later the police caught her yet again, this time at a "hop joint" in a Chinese "chop suey parlor" on North Seventh Street. She had been sharing opium with four "yellow dope fiends."[23] As long as such interracial liaisons remained within the confines of the Levee and vice district, they were tolerated, even winked at, by the city's press.

Still, the white press in America often did treat racial mixing as an important national issue. White concern over miscegenation had a long history in the North, but by the late nineteenth and early twentieth centuries, debate over it had taken a decidedly nasty turn. By 1908 the stereotype of the black man as a wild beast unable to control his sexual passions had pervaded white American popular culture and received serious attention in intellectual circles as well. Along with this view of the black man as beast went the assumption that the preferred object of his passion was the white woman.[24]

One measure of the ubiquity of the notion of the black man as a savage, lustful brute was the popularity of the unabashedly racist novels of Thomas Dixon. Both of his novels, *The Leopard's Spots* and *The Clansman*, were best-sellers in the North as well as the South. Dixon reworked *The Clansman* into a play by the same name. Later it would provide the foundation for D. W. Griffith's popular film, *The Birth of a Nation*. In the fall of 1905 the play "The Clansman" began a long and successful tour of the country. One of its major messages was that the black man was "an animal . . . the sport of impulse, whim, and conceit . . . a being who, left to his will, roams at night and sleeps in the day, whose speech knows no word of love, whose passions, once aroused, are as the fury of the tiger."[25]

The appearance of Dixon's play in a northern community occasionally stimulated lively controversy and sometimes interracial violence in and around the theaters that offered it.[26] Dixon's stage creation appeared several times in Springfield during the year and a half before the race riot. When it came to town, the *Forum's* black editor denounced the play as "calculated to stir up race friction." The *Forum* reported that in December of 1907, shortly before a repeat performance, a committee of worried black citizens approached the mayor, asking him to ban the show from Springfield's theaters. When the mayor rejected their request, they asked him, "What would you do in the case of a riot?" The mayor retorted, "I should stop it soon enough." Calling a conference with the city council and the manager of the theater who wanted to stage the play, the mayor forged a compromise: the theater would sell tickets to whites only.[27] Eight months after Springfield's stage had hosted "The Clansman's" dramatization of a Ku Klux Klan lynching of a black rapist, it appeared that the city's press and a large part of its white population agreed with Dixon's assessment of blacks' future in America: "Can we assimilate the negro? The very question is pollution."[28]

14 August

On Friday, 14 August, Springfield's newspapers confirmed what many whites in the north end of the city probably had already heard by word of mouth: that on the previous evening, a black man had sexually assaulted a white woman, Mabel Hallam, the wife of William Earl Hallam, a city streetcar driver, at their home on North Fifth Street. Mrs. Hallam delivered a brief statement to the press two days later recounting her ordeal. She had been alone that Thursday evening, as her husband had been working a late shift. "It was just 11:20 o'clock," she continued,

> when that negro came into our home and came directly to my bed. He laid on the bed and grabbed hold of me. This, of course, awakened me. My husband does not possess such habits, and I asked him the question, "Why, Earl, what is wrong with you?" to which the negro replied, "I am drunk." Then he commenced gagging me, telling me all the time that if I made any outcry he would kill me. . . . The fellow dragged me into the back yard, carrying and pulling me through the kitchen of our home. He pulled and jerked and yanked at me until we

were in one of the outbuildings. All the time his fingers were buried
into my neck and the pain was intense. Finally he released me. . . . [29]

When she recovered her senses, Mrs. Hallam screamed for help and
her neighbors rushed to her aid and telephoned the police.

As the search for Mrs. Hallam's assailant intensified Friday morning, the city's newspapers printed the story on their front pages with
boldface headlines. Some, such as one that blared "Dragged From
Her Bed And Outraged By Negro," were clearly inflammatory.[30]
Throughout the day crowds of angry friends and neighbors milled
about the Hallam house. Some voiced the opinion that one of the
black workmen who had been remodeling a nearby building was responsible for the assault. Since these were the only blacks who had
visited the neighborhood recently, their proximity made them suspect. Following this lead, the police brought the workmen one by
one to the Hallam home in the hope that Mrs. Hallam might recognize one of them. She tentatively picked out George Richardson, a
hod carrier, as the man who had attacked her Thursday night. The
police then placed Richardson in a lineup with other black men, and
Mrs. Hallam picked him out again without hesitation. At 3:30 Friday afternoon, Richardson was taken to the county jail where inmate Joe James was awaiting his trial for the murder of Clergy
Ballard.[31]

All day Friday, as news of the Hallam assault and the police drag-
net spread, groups of men began to gather in front of the county
jail at the corner of Jefferson and North Seventh Streets. By noon
the crowd was getting large, but, as the editor of the *Forum* later
reported, "It only looked like similar occasions when a man accused
of some bad crime is brought in."[32] Other signs indicated that trouble was brewing. At 2:00 that afternoon a mob of whites in the
north end cornered a lone black man and beat him with bricks and
baseball bats. As the hot August afternoon wore on, a few in the
crowd at the jail began to talk loudly of lynching. Word-of-mouth
news must have traveled quickly in the city, for while the authorities
were serving George Richardson with his arrest warrant at the
courthouse two blocks away, a second crowd had gathered there—a
crowd menacing enough that County Sheriff Charles Werner ar-
ranged for an armed escort to get his prisoner to the jail safely. During the afternoon Sheriff Werner took the precaution of securing
extra rifles and swearing in additional deputies, and he stationed
armed guards outside to patrol the jail grounds. The crowd outside
grew, as did talk of seizing Richardson and Joe James. No one had

menaced the jail yet, but by 4:00 the sheriff began to fear that his force might be too small to hold the building, and that it was only a matter of time before some kind of leadership emerged to turn hostile spectators into active rioters.[33]

At about 4:30 in the afternoon, Colonel Richard J. Shand of the Third Infantry of the Illinois state militia, a Springfield resident, received news of the trouble at the county jail. Shand sped there in his carriage, hoping to persuade Sheriff Werner to ask the mayor to make the necessary formal request of the governor to call out the local militia. Werner proved reluctant to take this step, despite Shand's arguments. This was the first of a series of disagreements between the colonel and the sheriff that took place Friday evening over what measures were necessary for crowd control. (Shand later turned in a very unflattering report of the sheriff's conduct that evening.) After arguing at length, Colonel Shand persuaded the sheriff to make the request for local troops, who were to assemble at the State Arsenal and wait there in case they were needed.[34] Sheriff Werner had a plan to move Richardson and James from the jail, and no doubt he hoped that once they were safely out of reach, the angry crowd outside would break up and go home.

Werner had telephoned several wealthy Springfield residents who owned reliable fast cars; of these citizens, Harry Loper volunteered to aid in the escape plan. Loper had been in business in Springfield for nearly twenty years and began as the proprietor of a small lunchroom downtown. By 1908 he ran "the largest and most popular" restaurant in town outside of the hotel dining rooms, an elegant eating place near the corner of Fifth and Monroe Streets. Decidedly one of the city's elite, Loper held other valuable property besides his restaurant and had the distinction of being one of the first in town to own an automobile.[35] Loper recognized the risk involved in volunteering his services, but, as he later explained, he had felt it was his civic duty: "I was in Cincinnati in 1863 when the riots occurred there in which 100 people were killed and that the court house was burned. I didn't care whether the negroes [Richardson and James] were hanged if they were guilty, but I wanted to avoid the bloodshed that would be the result of an attack on the jail."[36]

City Police Chief Wilbur Morris and the fire department coordinated the escape strategy. As city patrolmen and deputies pushed the crowd back from the building, a prearranged fire alarm was turned in, sending fire trucks clanging down a nearby street, thereby diverting the crowd's attention. In an alley behind the jail, a cordon of armed deputies hurried Richardson and James into Loper's waiting automobile. Harry Loper, two deputies, and the frightened prisoners sped northward out of the city and met a Chicago and Alton train, which carried Joe James and George Richardson to more secure lodgings in a jail at Bloomington. As an added precaution, Sheriff Werner asked the city newspapers to report that the prisoners had been carried further, to Peoria, in order to prevent determined Springfield whites from attacking the jail at Bloomington. The press complied.[37]

It was growing dark by about 7:00 and the crowd, its numbers augmented by men just off from work and by weekend shoppers, began to threaten the jail. Sheriff Werner went out to the steps and announced that the two prisoners were no longer inside. The crowd thought he was bluffing and drowned out the sheriff's appeals with cries of "Lynch the nigger!" and "Break down the jail!" The thin line of bluecoats guarding the jail found themselves steadily pushed backward. With the throng now numbering in the thousands, and with the local companies of the state militia still unassembled, Sheriff Werner asked the mob to select a committee to search the jail to confirm that Joe James and George Richardson were in fact gone. Several streetcar employees, including William Hallam, the husband of the woman Richardson had allegedly raped, checked the building twice and finally convinced the crowd that their intended prey had indeed escaped.[38]

At 7:30 Colonel Shand returned to the county jail from the State Arsenal. He noted that even though the mob knew by then that the prisoners had been spirited away, they showed no signs of dispersing and "kept up a running fire of comments on negroes and ropes and lynchings." Shand raced his carriage back to the Arsenal to gather the twenty-six soldiers who had assembled thus far and marched them back to the county jail. There the troops formed a skirmish line and, under a barrage of bricks and insults, pushed the crowd away from the building and set up ropes to keep them back. It was then about 8:00 in the evening.[39]

Somehow those at the county jail got word that Harry Loper had helped the prisoners escape. When someone in the mob shouted "On to Loper's," the rioters made a great rush south and east to his restaurant three blocks away. There they regrouped, at first contenting themselves with shouting threats and obscenities. Hundreds of curious onlookers, including businessmen and women with children in tow, were attracted by the disorder and swelled the ranks of those already thronging the street in front of Loper's place. Harry Loper was inside his restaurant with a handful of employees, armed, but exceedingly reluctant to shoot anyone. At around 8:10, the Gatling gun platoon of the local militia, consisting of a lieutenant and eight men, was ordered to Loper's. The governor had asked that the platoon not take their Gatling guns to Loper's. In the confusion at the State Arsenal, the platoon rummaged for weapons, finding a box of new rifles, but no ammunition. Worse, the ammunition supply wagon that was supposed to meet them on their way to Loper's never materialized. When the tiny contingent arrived at Loper's, it was overwhelmed by volleys of bottles and brickbats. The mob quickly disabled four of the militiamen and stole their weapons.[40]

Rioters next overturned Loper's automobile and began to throw bricks and bottles at the restaurant's large plate glass windows. With each cascade of broken glass, the crowd applauded and cheered. "Curse the day that Lincoln freed the nigger!" shouted one attacker. "Abe Lincoln brought them to Springfield and we will run them out!" As the rioters busied themselves with demolishing the front of the restaurant, Loper and his employees took cover in the rear of the dining room. With so many outside and with so little help from the authorities, Loper felt it wiser not to fire into the crowd. The four patrolmen on the scene were helpless; according to one disgusted observer, they were even criminally indifferent. He and others commented upon one incident in particular, which probably had a great deal to do with the later indictment of the four officers for "failure to suppress riot." Murray Hanes, the young son of a prominent Springfield architect, was a spectator in the crowd at Loper's during the early stage of the attack. He witnessed the following scene:

> As we stood there in that milling crowd, there was a policeman immediately in front of us. He was well known to both of us [Hanes's grandfather was with him]. He was complacent. Immediately in front of the policeman a boy, I would say of eighteen years, had dug a brick out of the pavement and was attempting to throw it into the plate glass. The denseness of the crowd prevented the swing of his arm. His arm moved backward into the stomach of the policeman. The policeman pushed backward to give the boy room for the swing of his arm. . . . The policeman was quite amicable. And the boy threw the brick. The policeman did not remonstrate.[41]

Another witness also remembered the patrolman making space for the boy to throw his brick. He saw the boy "turn about as the mob cheered, look the policeman squarely in the face, and swagger back into the mob, the policeman seeming to say by his manner, 'That was well done.' "[42] Given the size of the mob, however, Springfield's beleaguered patrolmen could do little but look on helplessly. Had they attempted an arrest, the rioters surely would have quickly overwhelmed them.

Soon most of the windows from Loper's elegant restaurant lay in shards on the sidewalk. Now, having destroyed the exterior, the mob hesitated. Then Kate Howard, the heavy-set proprietor of a small downtown boardinghouse, taunted and challenged the crowd: "What the hell are you fellows afraid of? Women want protection and this seems to be the only way to get it." This hefty "Joan of Arc," as some city newspapers later dubbed her, then led a charge into the restaurant. Loper and his workers fled to the basement and barricaded themselves behind a door at the bottom of the stairs. Once inside the dining room, the rioters threw tables, chairs, drapes, chandeliers, and bar fixtures out the door, while others piled the furnishings in the street, making a bonfire out of them. In less than an hour the rioters reduced the restaurant to a shambles, even tearing out pieces of wall paneling to toss into the fire. Looters later completed the destruction, carrying off plates, silverware, liquor, and food.[43]

Part of the mob crowded down the stairs to the basement, hoping to get at Loper and to plunder the bar and supply room. Loper, fearing that the worst was at hand, fired two warning shots through the top of the door that stood between him and the rioters, hoping to drive them back upstairs. Among those on the stairway were two north-end teenagers, Roy Wilson (later arrested as a rioter) and Louis Johnson, an operative at a shoe factory. At an inquest one week after the riot, Wilson described the events in the stairwell: "The mob found that Loper was downstairs and they all made a rush for the cellar. Neither one of us could get out of the way and were pushed down the stairway. I fell all the way down backwards, and as I reached the bottom of the stair, somebody fired a shot just as I was raising up, and that is when I lost track of Louis."[44] Louis Johnson had fallen, mortally wounded with a bullet wound in the neck, the riot's first fatality. The police later found his body buried under furniture and debris at the bottom of the staircase.[45] Meanwhile, hearing the mob talk of burning the building, Loper and his employees had crawled out a basement window and hidden under a raised wooden sidewalk outside until the rioters had left the area and more police had arrived on the scene to secure the building.[46]

A little after 9:00, the rioters at Loper's put the finishing touches on their work of vengeance, slashing the tires on Loper's offending automobile and then setting it afire. The gasoline in the car ignited, sending flames nearly as high as the surrounding buildings. The mob prevented the city fire department from extinguishing the blaze, and reportedly "around this burning machine the crowd danced in frenzied delight and fiendish glee." At this point, Springfield's Mayor Roy R. Reece appeared in the midst of the crowd to appeal for law and order. As he spoke, some cheered him; others shouted obscenities and demands that Joe James and George Richardson be handed over. Then several rioters tried to seize the mayor; others began hurling bricks at him. A few friends surrounded the mayor and rushed him into a nearby cigar store and out a back door into an alley to safety.[47] The crowd had reached its greatest size—about five thousand, according to most newspapers and the military.[48]

Although the mob at Loper's was the largest remnant of the crowd that had menaced the county jail earlier in the evening, smaller groups had headed downtown to hunt for blacks. Word-of-mouth news spread as quickly in the black community as in the white, and by 8:00 most blacks had deserted the downtown area and the Levee. If they had not heard the news of their danger, the growing disorder and the shouted threats of passing groups of whites were probably sufficient warning that the neighborhood was becoming unsafe. Even so, a few isolated individuals ran afoul of armed bands of white men downtown early that night. On the east side of the courthouse square, E. W. Chafin, the Prohibitionist party candidate for president, was addressing a rally. In the middle of his speech, around 9:00, Chafin noticed a disturbance in the crowd and saw a lone black man, with about five hundred whites in hot pursuit, running toward the speaker's platform. "A negro tried to get upon the platform," Chafin reported, "when several leaders of the mob pulled him back into the crowd. I saw the determined faces before me, faces that meant no good for the colored man if they secured complete control of him. I went to the edge of the platform and lifted my left hand, and went to my hip pocket with my right hand as if to draw a pistol. I never carry a revolver, but the bluff worked and the crowd held back."[49]

While the rioters hesitated, those on the platform lifted the black man out of the crowd and handed him over to an officer, who hurried him into the courthouse. When Chafin withdrew his hand from his pocket, the rioters realized he had duped them. Several of the bolder rioters jumped upon the speaker's platform and threatened the candidate, but Chafin's friends managed to shove the attackers off the stage. Chafin resumed his speech, but rioters began hurling bricks and stones. One caught Chafin a staggering blow on the side of the head, forcing the prohibitionists to call off their rally.[50]

Other blacks were less fortunate than the man rescued at the rally. A few remained at their places of employment, either unaware of the extent of the disorder in the city or unwilling to leave their workplaces for the danger of the streets. Many white rioters knew where blacks were employed, however, and early in the evening visited several establishments in search of victims. While one group of rioters disrupted the prohibitionist rally, another, traveling along North Fourth Street, found Walter Reilly, a black porter at the Silas Hotel. Reilly escaped into the hotel and the rioters left, but not before they directed a barrage of bricks at the hotel's dining room windows, sending surprised patrons fleeing from their meals. The same group next marched over to North Third Street, where they burst into the Chicago and Alton railroad station. They found one black porter, Will Stewart, still at work, and beat him into insensibility before railway employees could remove the man to safer quarters. Another black porter, surprised at the Illinois Central terminal, received similar treatment at the hands of the mob. A few blacks who were still downtown early in the evening, finding the crowds of whites there becoming even more hostile and threatening, attempted to leave the area on city streetcars. But since the throngs of people on the downtown streets made it difficult for the streetcars to make headway, black passengers found themselves extremely vulnerable to attack, and several were pulled off cars and roughed up. The virtual absence of any effective law enforcement downtown meant that assaults upon isolated blacks would continue throughout Friday evening.[51]

By 9:00 it was obvious to the authorities that the combined forces of the sheriff, the city police, and the local militia could not restore peace to the city. At 9:15 the city authorities asked Governor Charles Deneen to call out more troops, but it would take hours to assemble and transport militia from other parts of the state. The first reinforcements, thirty men from a Decatur company, did not arrive until after 2:00 Saturday morning. The city authorities had underestimated the seriousness of the situation earlier in the evening. Now Springfield would pay dearly for the delay.[52]

With the sack of Loper's complete by about 10:00 Friday evening, the rioters at the restaurant showed no signs of dispersing. It only took one mob leader's suggestion—"Let's go down to Washington Street!"—to precipitate a rush for the Levee two blocks away. Their target was the small concentration of black businesses on East Washington Street between Seventh and Tenth Streets. No doubt they also hoped to surprise some of the black residents who lived on the second and third stories of some Levee buildings. The mob began ransacking and vandalizing businesses near Seventh and Washington and methodically worked their way eastward.[53] The destruction, as one newspaper put it, "was done with deliberation and without any attempt at concealment." Coming upon a black establishment, "leaders of the crowd would start a bombardment of missiles . . . and with hatchets or axes would begin the work of destruction on the interior. Others following would continue the work . . . leaving a small army of hangers on and looters to finish the job."[54]

The mob reportedly exercised care in attempting to destroy only black businesses. If rioters began to assault a white business by mistake, the others would shout, "That's a white man's place! Pass it up!"[55] In fact, a number of white businesses in the Levee sustained damage at the hands of the mob that night, much of it accidental. With so much rock-throwing and gunfire, and with many white businesses situated next door to black ones, not surprisingly, a number of white establishments suffered broken windows and shattered doors. However, it is possible that the rioters singled out Jewish businesses in the Levee for looting and vandalism. Many of the city's Jewish-owned businesses were interspersed with the black ones on East Washington Street. Although some only suffered broken windows, a small number sustained damage beyond what one might expect from a mob that attempted to spare "white men's places," and two Jewish businesses not on East Washington were also vandalized.[56] The first Jewish store attacked was Reuben Fishman's pawnshop at 719 East Washington Street. The press suggested that the rioters entered Fishman's and other pawnshops in search of weapons, but the nature and extent of damage done to these and other Jewish businesses casts some doubt on this interpretation.[57] Fishman fled at the approach of the mob, and the rioters stole most of his stock and did considerable damage to the interior of his shop. The next day Fishman tentatively estimated his losses at $3,000. Characteristically succumbing to the temptation to caricature an unpopular ethnic group, one newspaper quoted Fishman "in his broken English" as saying, "I vill now haf to go in der poorhouse!"[58] Led by a man who shouted, "He's a nigger lover!," the crowd also looted and vandalized a pawnshop belonging to John Oberman.[59] Other Jewish businesses—a shoe store and a clothing store, for example—had their windows broken, interiors damaged, and stock pilfered. Only one other white business—a saloon—suffered this kind of attack, but in this instance it was not possible to determine with certainty whether or not the owner was Jewish.[60]

The rioters visited every black business in the Levee. First, the rented rooms over the shops were riddled with bullets; then the shops were looted. The crowd's work was thorough: "The plate glass fronts were first smashed in. The mob would then enter, overturn and tear to pieces all the furniture. What liquor in the saloons they did not carry away they poured out. All sealed packages they stole. The contents of the groceries and barber shops were thrown into the street and either cut to pieces or torn apart."[61]

The rioters' progress met with little resistance from the authorities. Most of the handful of troops in the city were stationed at the county jail, and the rest were assigned to guard duty at the Arsenal. Colonel Shand, frustrated by the sheriff's insistence upon holding the militia at the jail, made a brief reconnaissance of the riot area in his carriage. He went first to Loper's, arriving just as the last of the crowd was leaving for East Washington Street. After following these stragglers to the Levee and seeing the attack underway there, he raced back to the county jail, where he persuaded Sheriff Werner to allow him to lead a small band of troops to break up the Levee rioting. Werner shortly retracted his permission, however, and once again decided, much to Shand's consternation, to keep the troops at the jail, even though the riot no longer posed any real threat to the building. Only on the fringes of the East Washington Street rioting was there token police activity, as a few city detectives and patrolmen picked up isolated rioters who were carrying away articles looted from shops and saloons.[62]

When the mob finished with the black businesses on the 700 block of East Washington, and as they came to Eighth street, they encountered unexpected opposition. Several black men, armed with a variety of guns, had taken up positions at second-floor windows over "Dandy Jim" Smith's saloon. The snipers let loose a volley of gunfire into the crowd gathering in the darkness outside. The rioters returned fire, creating, according to one newspaper, "a cannonading which rivaled the battle of Gettysburg." The battle was short. It must have been obvious to the men in the building that their numbers and weapons were too few to hold off the mob for long, and that it would be only a matter of time before the rioters surrounded and entered the building. The black defenders kept up their firing for a short while, then retreated out a back door into an alley, escaping unharmed, but not before wounding a number of rioters, some fatally. Three white men, all allegedly bystanders according to

the newspapers, suffered fatal gunshot wounds during the gun battle at Eighth Street. They and others with less serious wounds
walked or were carried to St. John's Hospital three blocks north of
the Levee.[63]

After the firing ceased, the mob entered "Dandy Jim's" and
wrecked the place thoroughly, until "every thing on the inside had
been smashed and splintered until unfit for further use." They then
subjected the rest of the black business district on the 800 block of
East Washington Street to the same treatment.[64] At least twenty-one
black business establishments fell victim to the mob, and all but five
of these were located in the Levee (see Map 1.2).[65]

By about 11:00 the rioters had reached the end of the black business district at the corner of North Ninth and East Washington
Streets. Mob leaders next suggested an attack on the Badlands to the
northeast. The first black-owned building the rioters came across
was Scott Burton's wood-frame barbershop, which they burned
down in short order.[66] Rioters then fanned out over the Badlands
and began to set fire systematically to black residences along Madison and Mason Streets, and along connecting north-south side
streets. As was the case in the Levee, the mob generally exercised
care and deliberation in their selection of targets. Since a few white
homes were interspersed with black on some blocks, the rioters ordered white Badlands residents to pin white cloths to the front of
their houses so that they would not be accidentally burned. Nathan
Cohn, a Jewish immigrant from Romania who lived with his parents
on North Thirteenth Street, witnessed some of the destruction in
the Badlands that Friday evening. "You know, the riot was right
around there [Cohn's neighborhood] and I think there was a Jewish
fellow—I can't think of his name—Jewish fellow, and he went out
and hollered, 'All white folks hang out a white sheet and put it on
their fence.' " Cohn also remembered vividly that the "Jewish fellow"
he had seen was one of the more visible of the leaders of the crowd
engaged in burning houses in the area: "There was a lot of white
folks following this fellow."[67]

Another resident described the mob's progress through the Badlands: "I saw the work of the mob at close hand. A few men would
enter a shack and after tipping over the bed and tearing open the
mattress would pour on a little oil and apply a match. That was all
there was to it. They [the rioters] left them, feeling sure that the fire
would not be interfered with, and it wasn't."[68] Firemen arrived at
the scene, but the rioters prevented them from dousing the fires.
The firemen would no sooner direct water at a burning building

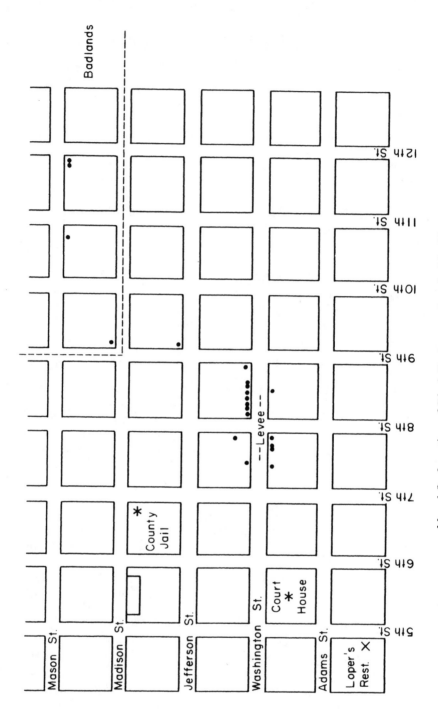

Map 1.2 Location of Black Businesses Attacked in Riot

than someone would cut the fire hoses. Finally, to prevent the complete destruction of their equipment, the firemen confined their efforts to extinguishing the embers of houses that had already been
reduced to ash heaps. As they worked their way eastward through
the Badlands, the mob tried to prevent the spread of the flames to
white property. On East Jefferson Street, rioters accidentally set fire
to a white woman's home, and though the fire quickly raged out of
control, many members of the crowd helped remove the woman's
furniture and belongings to the safety of the street. Such care did
not extend to all white homes, however. On the same street, rioters
deliberately burned another white woman's house to the ground
"because it was said that she was living with a negro."[69]

Colonel Shand, meanwhile, had returned to the streets in order to
track the rioters' movement and had followed their march up North
Ninth Street, arriving just in time to witness the burning of Scott
Burton's barbershop. Shand mingled briefly with those who stood
watching the flames and then reported back to Sheriff Werner. The
crowd, he told the sheriff, was made up mostly of cowardly "bums
and hoodlums," and he pleaded for a small force of troops and deputies to lead against the mob. Again the sheriff initially agreed with
Shand's suggestion, only to quickly change his mind a moment later.
Another excited argument ensued, but Werner remained determined to keep all available men at the county jail. The reasons for
the sheriff's hesitation to deplete the forces at the jail remain unclear. Probably he simply felt that, given the size of the mob, it was
unwise to divide the few men available. After the riot was over some
critics felt—as Shand evidently did—that a small, armed, and determined band of men could have put the rioters to flight. Perhaps so,
but—as had been the case with the Levee—the rioters were to have
free rein in their attack on the Badlands.[70]

Most black Badlands residents had abandoned the neighborhood
before the mob arrived. Some took refuge with friends and relatives
just outside Springfield or in neighboring towns and villages. Many
simply fled on foot into the surrounding countryside with no clear
idea of where to go or what to do. A few white employers sheltered
black refugees, hiding them in attics and storerooms. And a few
blacks secreted themselves in the city—in bushes, wells, and empty
railroad boxcars. However, several Badlands blacks who lived alone
and were too ill or old to escape fell prey to the mob. The rioters
surprised Harrison West, an elderly black man who lived by himself,
and beat him severely. In an old wood shack at the corner of Tenth
and Madison Streets, the mob discovered another black invalid,

William Smith, who suffered from paralysis. As one newspaper reported, "Smith is a helpless cripple and has been for a long time. The mob found him in the house and pulled him out into the weeds and began to beat him unmercifully. Some of the mob wanted to save him but they were overruled." Allegedly active in the assault on Smith was Kate Howard, the so-called "Joan of Arc" who helped lead the attack on Loper's restaurant earlier in the evening. A white bystander, disgusted by the spectacle, managed to get Smith away from the crowd and carried him to safety.[71]

In their progress through the Badlands, the rioters sometimes showed a certain perverse chivalry—black women they encountered were allowed to escape unharmed. When a crowd of whites arrived at the residence of Susan Crawford, an old black woman, for example, they told her to gather her belongings and leave the area before they burned her house down. No one attempted to injure her as she left. Even more fortunate was another elderly black woman, Mrs. A. J. Young, a "kindly looking old lady in glasses," whose home on Madison street was flanked on either side by white residences. When the rioters tried to burn her house, Young's white neighbors pleaded with the attackers to spare her home and to leave her and her children unmolested. The mob relented and told them to hang a white sheet on Mrs. Young's fence so that her house would be safe for the evening.[72]

After several hours of unimpeded looting and burning, at about 2:00 Saturday morning, the rioters reached the home of Scott Burton on Twelfth Street between Madison and Mason. The fifty-six year old black barber had sent his wife and children out of town to safety and had remained at home, armed with a shotgun, to protect their house.[73] As the rioters approached his front door, Burton fired at least two loads of buckshot into the crowd. Apparently the ubiquitous Kate Howard was again among those in the front ranks. After the riot she "exhibited . . . proudly the buckshot wounds in her fleshy arms" to a reporter as proof of her participation in the rioting.[74] Scott Burton tried to escape out a side door and through the backyard, but the crowd quickly overtook him and pummeled him unconscious. While some dragged Burton to the street, others went in search of a rope. They found a length of clothesline in a nearby yard and hung Burton from a dead tree in front of a saloon at the corner of Twelfth and Madison Streets. By the light of the flames from the burning buildings, the rioters mutilated the dangling corpse. The city newspapers chronicled the horror in detail. The crowd first riddled Burton's body with bullets. Then, "as the body hung from the tree all manner of fiendish cruelties were perpetrated upon it. Men gashed it with knives, others attempted to start a fire under the tree, and nearly all his clothing was torn from the remains."[75]

At about 2:30 in the morning, as the rioters were still busy disfiguring Burton's body, a skirmish line of troops quietly approached the crowd. The first militia reinforcements had finally reached the city. With Sheriff Werner and Colonel Shand in joint command, thirty men from a Decatur company, plus a handful of deputies and city patrolmen, had marched from downtown, driving rioters before them as they swept east through the Badlands. At Twelfth Street, the easternmost edge of the rioting, they encountered the large crowd of rioters and spectators at the Burton lynching. Werner commanded the troops to halt, then stepped forward and ordered the rioters to go home. He was greeted with a barrage of catcalls and obscenities. Colonel Shand, who had been chafing with impatience all evening, asked the sheriff for permission to fire a volley into the legs of the crowd, arguing that it was the only way to disperse them. Werner insisted on trying twice more to reason with the rioters, but they only became more abusive. Stepping back behind the line, the sheriff ordered the troops to fire a warning volley over the heads of the rioters. The gunfire had no effect whatsoever. Then, as Colonel Shand later reported,

> I immediately instructed Captain Walz to fire a volley low, but the sheriff protested and went along the left of the line, instructing the men to fire high [over the heads of the rioters]. Inasmuch as there was so much noise and confusion, it was impossible for the men to hear the commands of their commanding officer, he being on the right and the sheriff on the left, there were only seven or eight men on the right of the line who fired low, and as they fired into the crowd, there was enough multi-ball cartridges that took effect to convince the crowd that we meant business.[76]

Once again, the colonel and the sheriff worked at cross-purposes. Nonetheless, the troops' bullets abruptly put an end to large-scale rioting for the evening.

As the crowd dispersed and rioters left the Badlands in small groups, some of the white stragglers ran into trouble. William Bowe, the chief clerk of the county treasurer, and six white companions were walking east on Mason Street when they were surprised by a volley of gunshots and bricks from a group of about a dozen black men. Outnumbered, the whites fled, but Bowe, less fleet of foot than his companions, was captured, shot, and left for dead. Bowe survived the attack, and he and several of his friends later pressed charges of assault against twelve blacks. Calling the attack upon Bowe a "murderous assault," none of the city's four white newspapers raised the question of what Bowe and his friends were doing on the streets just outside the Badlands after 2:30 in the morning. Rather, the press assumed that an "angry mob," a "gang of maddened negroes," had committed an indefensible attack upon presumably innocent men. It is more likely that the blacks, all of whom lived nearby, had banded together to patrol the boundary of their immediate neighborhood, and had taken the approaching whites to be rioters fresh from the Badlands. There is no evidence to indicate that any blacks attacked or threatened whites who lived in the racially mixed neighborhood east of the Badlands. They were solely on the lookout for suspicious-looking bands of white strangers. In the eyes of the white press, however, active black self-defense was equated with hooliganism.[77]

15 August

Springfield remained quiet all day Saturday. By late afternoon at least 500 militiamen patrolled the city, and by 11:00 Saturday evening over 1,400 troops were on hand, with more on the way. The authorities placed companies of militia strategically in order to prevent further attacks on black neighborhoods. The Levee and Badlands each had large military patrols. A large working-class black enclave in the southeast section of the city, about two miles from downtown, also received its share of troops. It had not been attacked during Friday's rioting, but, given the rioters' threats against its residents and their apparent determination to drive all blacks from the city, the authorities thought it prudent to patrol the neighborhood. As a further precaution, Mayor Roy Reece ordered all saloons closed indefinitely and asked that businesses downtown shut down by 6:00 in the evening. A substantial number of troops also patrolled the city's north side, reportedly "one of the worst neighborhoods to handle." All day Saturday the city police kept busy rounding up suspected rioters and searching the homes of "suspicious characters" for items looted from Loper's restaurant and Levee shops.[78]

For those blacks who could not or would not leave Springfield, and for those who insisted on returning, Governor Charles Deneen designated the State Arsenal as a temporary refuge. A few other displaced blacks were accommodated at Camp Lincoln, the militia

grounds on the northern edge of town.[79] Riot refugees ventured
home during the day to salvage their belongings, but were careful to
return to the protection of the troops before nightfall. One of the
rare newspaper articles that expressed sympathy for the riot victims
described the scene at the Arsenal: "Innocent old men, who have
lived here for years, tottering old women in white hair . . . children
in their teens and babies are mixed up in this sorry spectacle, their
faces withered in anxiety. . . . When bedtime came all the older people placed chairs together and on comforts [quilts] rescued from
their homes during the day, made the children and the babies comfortable. The old women were sleeping on their chairs. The men
were making out on the hard floor."[80] The white press generally
showed little interest in the plight of the riot victims, preferring instead to dwell on the subject of how many blacks had fled the city.
One suspects that a certain amount of wishful thinking lay behind
such coverage—that the press expressed the hope of many whites
that the departure of black residents would be permanent.[81]

That Saturday Springfield's streets were filled with curious
crowds of white sightseers, lending the city an almost carnival air.
Special trains brought visitors eager to view riot sites in the Levee
and the Badlands. One major attraction was the tree where Scott
Burton, the black barber, was lynched. By midday the tree had van-
ished. Relic hunters had torn it apart, carrying off pieces as souvenirs. Also, some made money marketing riot mementos. Enterprising photographers bustled about making pictures of the damage
in the Levee and Badlands, and for days after the riot their souve-
nir photographs and postcards were in great demand. The *Springfield News* reported that "all sorts of views have been taken and
every negative is worth its weight in gold to the photographer. He is
selling prints as fast as he can turn them out. . . . The most photo-
graphed spots are the places where . . . the lynchings occurred. The
pictures have been going like hot cakes."[82] In one instance, the city
authorities felt that the picture vending had gone too far. The police
ordered off the streets a man hawking pictures of Mrs. Mabel Hallam, the woman whose alleged rape had precipitated Friday's riot,
for fear that her picture might somehow spark more trouble. The
press, however, continued to print her portrait for several more
days.[83]

Prevailing opinion in Springfield's white press on Saturday held
that the rioting had been inevitable, and that black, not white misconduct was to blame for the violence. Many claimed that the riot
was an effective and justifiable remedy for black misbehavior. "For

months, yes, years, past," stated one editorial, "it has been predicted that such an outburst of popular fury would sometime come in Springfield." The editor concluded: "The implication is clear that conditions, not the populace, were to blame and that many good citizens could find no other remedy than that applied by the mob. It was not the fact of the whites' hatred toward the negroes, but of the negroes' own misconduct, general inferiority or unfitness for free institutions that were at fault."[84]

In addition, a reporter for the *Illinois State Journal* claimed that Springfield's press had avoided criticizing the violence for fear of attack. The *Journal's* owner had called this reporter into his office during the weekend of the riot and told him, "Be awful careful what you run, because when this paper comes off the press this mob's still going to be in action, and if they don't like it, they'll tear down the plant."[85] Although fear of mob retaliation may have influenced the tone of the early news coverage of the riot, all four of the city's white newspapers were so consistently indulgent in their descriptions of Friday night's violence, that one suspects that caution or fear of reprisal played a small part. Even as the ruins of the Badlands still lay smoldering, some newspapers went beyond expressions of the inevitability of the "good citizens' " popular uprising against blacks' misconduct or inferiority, and printed inflammatory editorials that bordered on a call for more violence.

A Saturday editorial entitled "That Brutal Outrage," for example, reminded readers of the "hellish assault" on Mabel Hallam by "a negro fiend." The "devilish deed . . . must have been premeditated, and was in all its harrowing details so brutal as to arouse a feeling of righteous indignation among the people of the city. . . . What is there to prevent others from becoming victims of like outrages? Is there any way to relieve the community of this fear? That is the question in connection with this devilish crime for our people to consider."[86] In an ironic twist, the *Springfield News*, the newspaper that in July had called for the cleaning out of the Levee, accused its major competitor, the *Springfield Record*, of inciting whites to violence by printing "bloodthirsty riot dope" and by posting misleading riot bulletins in its office windows downtown. The *News* pointed out, for example, that its rival had printed the sensational headline "Negroes Arming in the Outskirts" on the top of the front page of one of its Saturday extra editions, but that "not a single word appeared in the paper elsewhere in substantiation of this terror-creating headline."[87] Some weeks after the riot, E. L. Rogers, the editor of the black newspaper, the *Forum*, expressed disgust over the white newspapers' coverage of the riot. As far as Springfield's blacks were concerned, Rogers wrote, "not one paper offered condolence nor cheer nor solace and comfort for the perturbed minds [of black residents]. . . . There are sins of omission as colossal as those of commission. 'As a man thinketh in his heart so is he.' "[88]

After about 7:00 Saturday evening, Major General Edward C. Young, now in command of the militia, began to receive alarming reports that crowds were again gathering downtown. Near the courthouse, one large group of whites was becoming especially loud and disorderly. Since the sheriff's department and the city police were supposed to be responsible for maintaining order in the downtown business district, Major General Young promptly telephoned Sheriff Werner to ask him why he had not prevented crowds from forming. The sheriff replied that he did not have enough men and that the militia would have to step in to deal with the problem. Young quickly ordered cavalry downtown to disperse the crowds, which they did in short order. It was to be a very busy night for the militia. Shortly after 7:30, Young got the news that two more mobs had formed just south of the downtown business district. Their target seemed to be the large black settlement in southeast Springfield. Again the cavalry dashed to the scene and routed the rioters. Major General Young began to realize that "conditions were such . . . that it was quite evident that small numbers would gather and attempt, under cover of darkness, to commit violence wherever opportunity presented itself." A call went out for more militia reinforcements.[89]

The authorities had already posted militia at likely trouble spots in the city: the Levee, the city and county jails, the Badlands, the larger black neighborhoods, and the north end. But smaller black settlements, particularly those in the predominantly white, middle-class southwest quarter of Springfield, had no protection. Major General Young later reported that Sheriff Werner told him that only whites lived in that part of town, and therefore it needed no troops. With only about a thousand troops available to police the city, the military and civil authorities decided to concentrate their manpower where they felt it was most needed. The rioters, however, noted the weak spots in the militia's defense.[90]

Rumors circulated Saturday that a mob was going to attack the residence of William Donnegan, an aged black man who lived with his family at the corner of Spring and Edwards Streets, about a block and a half south and west of the state capitol building. The Donnegans and a few other black families lived on one block of an otherwise all-white middle-class neighborhood—the one section of town where the authorities least expected trouble. William Donnegan was about eighty years old and had retired from his trade as a shoemaker because of his severe rheumatism. One black Springfield resident remembered that Donnegan was so infirm that "it would take him all day to walk downtown." Donnegan had lived in the city since 1845 and was well known in the black community. He was one of the city's wealthier blacks and owned his own home and other real estate in town. His wife, Sarah, was white, the daughter of German immigrants. The Donnegans had decided to stay home after Friday's outbreak, perhaps feeling relatively secure since their home was a good distance from the Levee and close to the State Arsenal and Governor's mansion.[91]

When the Donnegans heard of the threats circulating in the city, they tried to secure protection from the authorities. William Donnegan's sister recalled, "We had been warned that a mob was coming to kill us, but we knew of nothing to do but remain here and await their arrival. We telephoned the jail and the militia headquarters several times, asking for protection, and though we were promised each time that the soldiers would come, none came."[92] By Saturday evening it was becoming evident that the troops were spread too thin, and the persistence of disorder downtown absorbed most of the authorities' attention.

The crowds that the cavalry had dispersed downtown earlier Saturday evening regrouped once again near the courthouse. As one newspaper observed, "there was no lack of leaders" in the crowd. One of them shouted, "Forward, citizens! Let us complete the good work begun last night!" Following a rioter waving an American flag, the crowd marched in a deliberate and orderly fashion several blocks west and south to the State Arsenal. Their goal was to get at the black refugees who were under militia protection. Nearly a thousand rioters gathered at the Arsenal, but their resolve wavered at the sight of troops armed with rifles and fixed bayonets. The militia charged and quickly repulsed the mob, which scattered in several directions.[93]

Some of the rioters fleeing the Arsenal headed directly for the Donnegan residence several blocks to the south, passing around and over the state capitol grounds on the way. Blanche Hankins, the daughter of a white grocery merchant, and then a young girl, remembered that Saturday evening well. Her family lived near the Donnegan home. She reported that "after sunset, the mob of several hundred marched down Spring Street carrying all kinds of weapons—clubs of wood, and iron, and various kinds of firearms.

They were rendering a piercing yelling; cursing sounds in a wild manner. By the time they reached Spring and Edwards, they spread out over the block completely surrounding our home. By [that] time, the firearms were thundering shots in the air." Some of the rioters pounded on the Hankins' front door and demanded a rope from Mr. Hankins. The grocer told them to clear out, that he wanted no part in their activities. "Next morning," Blanche Hankins recalled, "our clothes line was missing."[94]

Sometime after 8:00 in the evening, the rioters reached the Donnegan home. Accounts of the attack differ in detail, but William Donnegan's sister later told reporters that her brother met the crowd at the front door and someone knocked the man to the floor. The old man was dragged outside to the front yard and beaten with bricks torn up from the sidewalk. One rioter produced a razor and cut Donnegan's throat. Dragging the dying man to the street, the rioters tied a small cotton clothesline around his neck and tried to hoist him to the limb of a small maple tree in front of the Edwards School across the street. Either their work was too hasty, or the rope proved too weak, for the rioters did not raise their victim's body off the ground. When the militia and police arrived, most of the crowd had already fled, and the authorities could do nothing but cut William Donnegan down and carry him off. By the time he received medical aid, he was beyond hope of recovery, and he died in St. John's Hospital the next day.[95]

Despite the large number of troops already in the city, and despite the arrival of trainloads of reinforcements throughout Saturday evening, Major General Young had his hands full trying to maintain order. As he had feared, rioters had decided to conduct hit-and-run attacks over much of the city. A continual stream of false alarms telephoned into headquarters by panicked black and white residents kept the exhausted troops busy dashing here and there checking out reports of violence. Occasionally they found small crowds and dispersed them. Angered by the attempt on the Arsenal and the Donnegan lynching, Major General Young told his troops to shoot if necessary.[96]

By Sunday morning, except for a few minor incidents, the riots were over. By Monday morning enough militia reinforcements had arrived in Springfield—nearly 3,700—to provide adequate patrols for the city. For a community of its size, it had been a major disaster. Two blacks and four whites had died in the two days of rioting, and over a hundred others, mostly white, had been injured. The riot had also caused indirect casualties. For example, one black couple's infant died of exposure when the family fled the city on foot. Rioters had damaged, destroyed, or stolen at least $120,000 worth of property, and over forty black families had lost their homes to fire. While the city's newspapers expressed virtually no sympathy for the black victims' losses, in the days after the violence they grimly calculated the riot's expense to the city and state. Providing militia had cost the state at least $125,000, and the city, which was legally responsible for compensating riot victims, was faced with a very large bill.[97]

Minor incidents of violence persisted after Saturday's rioting. No one expected a repetition of Friday or Saturday night's mass outbreaks, but many feared that sporadic anti-black guerrilla warfare would continue. Many believed that "the spirit of vengeance is only smoldering, ready to break out again at the first opportunity." Early Sunday morning after the Donnegan lynching, a group of rioters attacked a black residence at 1144 North Seventh Street. The militia arrived in time to prevent any injuries and escorted the family to the police station for protection. Sunday afternoon the militia was dispatched again to quell another outbreak at 417 North Fifth Street. The troops encountered a crowd of about 1,500 menacing the home of Samuel Willis, who, like the other blacks attacked earlier in the day, lived in an otherwise all-white neighborhood. The militia dispersed the crowd and then helped put out a small fire someone had started in one of Willis's outbuildings.[98] Attacks upon lone blacks walking through white neighborhoods, hangings of effigies, and occasional instances of arson persisted until early September.[99]

The Riot Redefined

William English Walling arrived in Springfield the morning after the rioters lynched William Donnegan. He spent hours walking the streets and talking to citizens about the riot and visited the city authorities and military commanders. Walling soon concluded that most of the city's whites approved of the mob's actions. The "masses of the people, the workingmen in the shops, the storekeepers in the stores, the drivers, the men on the street, the wounded in the hospitals," he reported, hoped that "the rest of the negroes might flee." Another out-of-town writer thought he detected a "passive sympathy with the mob" among many Springfield whites and reported that "there appears to be a feeling, even among the better classes, that good will finally result from the evil." After his extensive investigation, Walling concluded grimly, "Springfield had no shame. She stood for the action of the mob."[100]

When Sunday's newspapers hit the streets after the second night of rioting, however, it was evident that a definite shift in their interpretation of the violence had occurred. The press still showed no sympathy for the riot victims, but it did revise its assessment of the riot participants and their motivation. Now no one talked about the righteous indignation of "good citizens" who applied an illegal, but popular, remedy for black misbehavior; the rioters now appeared in a negative light. The *Springfield Record*, accused by a rival of eagerly printing "bloodthirsty riot dope," now editorialized: "The element that created such infernal havoc, Friday and Saturday, is no more representative of the real citizenry of Springfield than a rotten and foul smelling fruit is representative of true vegetation. The decent citizenry of Springfield have always been opposed to mob rule and always will be. . . . It was that undesirable class that did all the mischief."[101] The rioters, declared another paper, were persons without property or status, without a stake in the city: "law violators, burglars, thieves, prostitutes, keepers of disreputable resorts, the riff raff, the scum of the community." Only one of the four white city newspapers—the Democratic *Illinois State Register*—still seemed reluctant to blame deviant elements in the white community for the riot. Noting the growing claims elsewhere that the riot was the work of riffraff, the *Register* continued to assert that many "who are ordinarily well-disposed and law abiding citizens" had succumbed to "the hysterical mob spirit." But, like its competitors, the *Register* voiced increased concern that "mob rule" be suppressed.[102]

Several days after the riot, over three hundred prominent whites gathered for a joint meeting of Springfield's business and professional associations to denounce the rioters and to demand the return of law and order. The president of the Springfield Business Men's Club ventured his opinion of the mob in his introductory remarks to the meeting. "I believe that out of every ten men in this city nine are law-abiding, faithful citizens. Of the persons in that mob there was not one to which any of us would entrust a single dollar; not one has ever stood with any degree of responsibility in his community."[103] Like the press, the city's businessmen called for an end to "the rule of riot, ruin and rebellion," and similarly, they also expressed no sympathy for black victims of the violence. A bitter dispute broke out at the meeting when a committee tried to agree on the wording of a resolution calling for the protection of "life, liberty and property . . . without reference to nationality or

color." One committee member demanded that the words "nationality or color" be left out, arguing that otherwise many in the community would mistake the club members for "nigger lovers." The
resolution, he said, would "rouse a bitter race hatred." In the end it
passed in its original form, but clearly the businessmen felt more
comfortable calling for law and order than for justice.[104]

After the second day of rioting, then, whites in positions of influence and power in effect served notice that they would not counte-
nance further violence. It seems likely that the change in their view
of the riot and rioters was at least in part a face-saving operation.
After all, the nation's press was now filled with many critical and
unflattering observations about Springfield and its inhabitants. The
city's good name and reputation might be salvaged if the blame for
the violence could be pinned on a small element of irresponsible
lowlifes and hoodlums. Editors, businessmen, and religious leaders
who took this position could maintain that the majority of Springfield's citizens were law-abiding, rational, and peaceful. Later, in
covering the arrests and trials of rioters, Springfield's press would
devote most of its attention to a handful of suspects who fit the stereotype of rioter as lower-class deviant. One of them was the notorious and unsavory Kate Howard. Insofar as the press fixed blame
for the riot on such "undesirables," it did seem to be attempting to
repair the city's tarnished image.

The shift by the city's press and business community to condemnation of the rioters and the violence involved more than civic face-
saving, though. Better-off whites, by characterizing riot participants
as riffraff, were clearly distancing themselves from the event. They
were in effect denying that they had given any approval to the assault on the city's black community or that they had any responsibility for it. Of course, the sheer size of the downtown crowds on the
first night of rioting alone indicates that more than just riffraff were
involved. As Walling suggested, many from the ranks of the respectable were present as approving spectators, some of whom cheered
and applauded the mob at Loper's. Early press response echoed that
approval by portraying the violence as a regrettable but necessary
reaction to the city's "Negro problem": the mob seemed to be exe-
cuting the collective will of the entire white community. Even
wealthy white residents, Walling said, thought some good would
come out of the violence. But something went wrong, something
that turned that earlier approval to fear and outrage: the violence
continued. It ceased making sense to the city's better-off whites, who
began to realize that the rioters had far different social goals in

mind. At the same time, influential whites also realized that their authority and control in the community were being challenged. Thus they revised their descriptions of the violence—revealingly— to "mob rule," a "reign of terror," and "rebellion." This turnabout in attitude by the press and better-off whites represented far more than face-saving and far more than a guilty or hypocritical denial of their earlier approval of anti-black violence. Indeed, it was a major symptom of conflict and disagreement among whites over racial issues.

NOTES

1. Springfield's newspapers are the major source of information on Joe James's past and his activities while in Springfield. *ISJ*, 5–6 July 1908, 17–18 September 1908, 24 October 1908; *SR* 15–16 September 1908, 21 September 1908, 23 September 1908.

2. *ISJ*, 8 July 1908. A school census taken in 1908 indicated that the city's population was 47,587. U.S. Bureau of the Census, *Thirteenth Census of the United States Taken in the Year 1910: Population* (Washington, D.C.: Government Printing Office, 1913), 1:504. Springfield's black population in 1910 was 2,961.

3. Bruce Alexander Campbell, *200 Years: An Illustrated Bicentennial History of Sangamon County* (Springfield, Ill.: Phillips Brothers, Inc., 1976), 200; William Lloyd Clark, *Hell at Midnight in Springfield; Or a Burning History of the Sin and Shame of the Capital City of Illinois*, 4th ed. (Milan, Ill.: 1914), 9–10, 14–16. On vice in black neighborhoods see, for example, Roger Lane, *The Roots of Violence in Black Philadelphia, 1860–1900* (Cambridge, Mass.: Harvard University Press, 1986), 122, 139, 173.

4. Clark, *Hell at Midnight*, 9.

5. Ibid., 14–15.

6. *ISJ*, 6 July 1908, 16 September 1908; *SR*, 16 September 1908; *ISR*, 6 July 1908. Springfield's police checked with authorities in the cities James had lived in and could find no evidence of a criminal record for him.

7. *SR*, 16 September 1908; *ISJ*, 6 July 1908, 16 September 1908; The Chicago Commission on Race Relations, *The Negro in Chicago: A Study of Race Relations and a Race Riot* (Chicago: University of Chicago Press, 1922), 68.

8. *ISJ*, 5–6 July 1908; *SR*, 15 September 1908. One small piece of evidence suggests that James might not have been Ballard's assailant. A second assault occurred that evening, shortly after the attack on Ballard, involving a black man who stole another black man's coat. When the victim put up resistance, he was stabbed and seriously injured. The police took the victim to the hospital. This incident also occurred on North Ninth Street, about six blocks south of the Ballard home, between fifteen and thirty minutes after

Ballard fell. The assailant in this case—based on his black victim's description—clearly was not Joe James. At the time (before Joe James was arrested) the police believed this man "might be the same negro who cut Ballard." The incident was never mentioned again in the press, and apparently the police did not, or could not, pursue the lead further.

9. *ISJ*, 6 July 1908; *ISR*, 6–7 July 1908.

10. *ISJ*, 6 July 1908; CD, 1902, 1904–7; manuscript schedules of the population census for Springfield, Illinois, 1900.

11. *ISJ*, 16 August 1908.

12. *SN*, 6 July 1908.

13. *ISJ*, 6 July 1908, 18 September 1908; *ISR*, 6 July 1908, 8 July 1908; *SR*, 16 September 1908; William English Walling, "The Race War in the North," *The Independent* 65 (3 September 1908): 533. Walling indicated that the court had some doubt as to whether James was involved in Ballard's murder and that this was one reason the case was postponed.

14. "The So-called Race Riot at Springfield, Illinois," *Charities and the Commons* 50 (19 September 1908): 711; George M. Fredrickson, *The Black Image in the White Mind: The Debate on Afro-American Character and Destiny, 1817–1914* (New York: Harper & Row, 1971), 228–55.

15. *ISJ*, 8 March 1908, 17 March 1908, 30 August 1908, 24 September 1908. See also Donald F. Tingley, *The Structuring of a State: The History of Illinois, 1899–1918* (Urbana: University of Illinois Press, 1980), 283. After examining Illinois newspapers, Tingley discovered that "nearly half of the news articles about blacks had to do with crime." The criminal stereotype affected blacks even in small towns with tiny black communities. See James E. DeVries, *Race and Kinship in a Midwestern Town: The Black Experience in Monroe, Michigan, 1900–1915* (Urbana: University of Illinois, 1984), 81–106.

16. David A. Gerber, *Black Ohio and the Color Line, 1860–1915* (Urbana: University of Illinois Press, 1976), 107–8. White newspapers' heavy coverage of black crime persisted well into the century. See, for example, Gordon W. Allport, *The Nature of Prejudice* (Reading, Mass.: Addison-Wesley Publishing Company, 1954), 196–202.

17. *Forum*, 29 June 1907. As was the case in many other urban areas, Springfield's blacks accounted for a disproportionate number of police arrests. See "Report of the Chief of Police," in *Reports of the Officers of the City of Springfield, Illinois, for the Fiscal Year Ending February 28, 1891* (Springfield, Ill.: 1891), 66–67, SVC. Bureau of the Census, *Thirteenth Census, 1910* (Washington, D.C.: Government Printing Office, 1913), 2:504. The *Reports* were published annually until 1906. Only for the years 1886 to 1893 did the police department list the ethnic or racial background of offenders. In those years the number of black arrests was substantial, but there is no way to tell what kinds of crimes blacks were arrested for or how many black arrestees were repeat offenders. In 1890 blacks made up 7.2 percent of the city's population but accounted for 12.6 percent of all arrests.

Proportion of Blacks among Springfield Arrestees, 1886–92

Year	Total Arrestees	Black Arrestees	Percent Black
1886	3,002	361	12.0
1887	3,233	378	11.8
1888	2,539	290	11.4
1889	2,666	303	11.4
1890	2,890	365	12.6
1891	3,393	245	7.2
1892	3,732	382	10.2

Compiled from *Reports of the Officers of the City of Springfield, Illinois, 1887–1893*, SVC.

Investigators for the Russell Sage survey of Springfield noted that in 1913, 10.2 percent of all arrests involved black offenders, while blacks made up under 6 percent of the city's population. See Zenas L. Potter, *The Correctional System of Springfield, Illinois* (New York: Russell Sage Foundation, 1915), 1. For discussions of problems involved in using arrest records to assess the extent of criminal behavior, see Roger Lane, *Violent Death in the City: Suicide, Accident, and Murder in Nineteenth-Century Philadelphia* (Cambridge, Mass.: Harvard University Press, 1979), 6, 64; Lawrence M. Friedman and Robert V. Percival, *The Roots of Justice: Crime and Punishment in Alameda County, California, 1870–1910* (Chapel Hill: University of North Carolina Press, 1981), 26–28, 105–7; Eugene J. Watts, "Police Priorities in Twentieth-Century St. Louis," *Journal of Social History* 14 (Summer 1981): 649–73.

18. *Forum*, 27 April 1907.

19. Ibid., 5 January 1907, 7 September 1907.

20. *ISJ*, 6–8 July 1908; *ISR*, 6–8 July 1908.

21. *ISJ*, 8 March 1908.

22. Other researchers have encountered the problem of determining an individual's race in census and city directory records. See, for example, DeVries, *Race and Kinship in a Midwestern Town*, 11.

23. *ISJ*, 6 March 1908; CD, 1911; *ISJ*, 8 August 1908; *SR*, 26 September 1908.

24. Fredrickson, *The Black Image in the White Mind*, 262–82; I. A. Newby, *Jim Crow's Defense: Anti-Negro Thought in America, 1900–1930* (Baton Rouge: Louisiana State University Press, 1965), 135–40; Raymond W. Logan, *The Betrayal of the Negro: From Rutherford B. Hayes to Woodrow Wilson*, new enl. ed. (New York: Collier Books, 1965), 390; Joel Williamson, *The Crucible of Race: Black-White Relations in the American South since Emancipation* (New York: Oxford University Press, 1984), 111–24, 140–51, 339–40.

25. Thomas Dixon, Jr., *The Clansman: An Historical Romance of the Ku Klux Klan* (New York: Doubleday, Page, & Co., 1905), 290–93. The quote also appeared in Thomas Dixon, Jr., "Booker T. Washington and the Negro," *Saturday Evening Post* 178 (19 August 1905): 2. For an account of Dixon's life and works, see Raymond Allen Cook, *Fire from the Flint: The*

Amazing Careers of Thomas Dixon (Winston-Salem, N.C.: John F. Blair, 1968), 126–53. Cook's treatment is excessively flattering to Dixon and generally ignores his relationship to the decline of race relations early in the century. A briefer, but more critical, examination of Dixon's career may be found in Williamson, *The Crucible of Race*, 140–76.

26. Cook, *Fire from the Flint*, 149.

27. *Forum*, 9 February 1907, 28 December 1907.

28. Dixon, *The Clansman*, 291.

29. *ISR*, 15 August 1908.

30. Ibid., 14 August 1908.

31. *ISJ*, 15 August 1908; *ISR*, 15 August 1908.

32. E. L. Rogers, "A Review of the Springfield Riot: The Alleged Cause and the Effect," *The Colored American Magazine* 15 (February 1909): 75.

33. *ISJ*, 15 August 1908; *ISR*, 15 August 1908.

34. *Biennial Report of the Adjutant General of Illinois to the Governor and Commander-In-Chief, 1907–1908* (Springfield, Ill.: State Printers, 1909), 270–71. The *Biennial Report* is the only major source other than the newspapers that provides detailed information on the riot. Several of the officers present early in the rioting provided vivid accounts of the mob's actions. The *Report* also provides a means of testing the accuracy of newspaper accounts.

35. *Chicago Record-Herald*, 15 August 1908.

36. *ISR*, 15 August 1908.

37. *ISJ*, 15 August 1908; *ISR*, 15–16 August 1908.

38. *ISJ*, 15 August 1908; *Biennial Report of the Adjutant General*, 271.

39. *ISJ*, 15 August 1908; *Biennial Report of the Adjutant General*, 271.

40. *ISR*, 20 August 1908; *ISJ*, 15 August 1908; *Biennial Report*, 281.

41. Murray S. Hanes, "Samuel Jackson Hanes," typescript, n.d., G. Cullom Davis Papers, SSU.

42. "The So-called Race Riot at Springfield," 711.

43. *ISJ*, 15–16 August 1908, 21 August 1908.

44. *ISR*, 22 August 1908.

45. *ISJ*, 15 August 1908, 21–22 August 1908; *ISR*, 21–22 August 1908.

46. *ISR*, 21 August 1908.

47. *ISJ*, 15 August 1908; *ISR*, 15 August 1908.

48. *Biennial Report*, 271; *Chicago Record-Herald*, 17 August 1908; "The So-called Race Riot at Springfield," 709; *ISR*, 15 August 1908.

49. *Chicago Record-Herald*, 16 August 1908.

50. Ibid.; *ISR*, 15 August 1908.

51. *ISJ*, 15 August 1908.

52. *Biennial Report*, 272–74.

53. *Chicago Record-Herald*, 17 August 1908; *Biennial Report*, 272.

54. *ISJ*, 16 August 1908.

55. Ibid.

56. *ISJ*, 15–16 August 1908; *SN*, 15 August 1908; *ISR*, 15 August 1908; CD, 1907, 1908; manuscript schedules of the population census for Springfield, Illinois, 1900, 1910. In some instances newspapers mentioned that

shop owners were Jewish. The 1910 manuscript census also provided information on these proprietors. Most were Russian Jews. The census enumerators, for some reason, often filled in the space for place of birth with the entry "Russian-Yiddish."

57. *ISJ*, 16 August 1908; "The So-called Race Riot at Springfield," 710.

58. *ISJ*, 16 August 1908; "The So-called Race Riot at Springfield," 710.

59. *ISJ*, 15 August 1908.

60. Ibid., 15–16 August 1908; CCF, case number 23409.

61. *SN*, 15 August 1908.

62. *ISR*, 15 August 1908; *Biennial Report*, 272.

63. *ISR*, 16–18 August 1908; *ISJ*, 18 August 1908.

64. *ISR*, 16 August 1908.

65. Newspaper estimates of the number of black businesses destroyed ranged from 15 to 35. A count of those listed in the press indicates that 21 black businesses were attacked. *ISJ*, 16 August 1908, 2 September 1908; *SN*, 15 August 1908; CD, 1907, 1908. The number and type of black businesses attacked were as follows: barbershops, 7; saloons, 6; restaurants, 2; shoemaker's shops, 2; upholstery shop, 1; grocery, 1; bicycle shop, 1; undertaking establishment, 1.

66. The Chicago Commission on Race Relations, *The Negro in Chicago*, 69; *ISR*, 15 August 1908; *SN*, 15 August 1908; *ISJ*, 16 August 1908.

67. Nathan L. Cohn Memoir, SSUO; Walling, "Race War in the North," 531.

68. *Chicago Record-Herald*, 16 August 1908.

69. *ISJ*, 16 August 1908; *ISR*, 15 August 1908.

70. *Biennial Report*, 272; "The So-called Race Riot at Springfield," 709–11.

71. *SN*, 15 August 1908; *ISJ*, 16 August 1908.

72. *ISR*, 18 August 1908.

73. *ISJ*, 16 August 1908, 2 September 1908; *SN*, 15 August 1908; CD, 1907.

74. Walling, "The Race War in the North," 532.

75. The Chicago Commission on Race Relations, *The Negro in Chicago*, 69; *SN*, 15 August 1908; *ISJ*, 16 August 1908; *Chicago Record-Herald*, 16 August 1908.

76. *Biennial Report*, 272–73.

77. *SR*, 23 August 1908; *Chicago Record-Herald*, 23 August 1908; CD, 1907, 1908; *ISR*, 16 August 1908; *ISJ*, 16 August 1908.

78. *SN*, 15 August 1908; *ISJ*, 16 August 1908; *ISR*, 16 August 1908.

79. *SN*, 15 August 1908; "The So-called Race Riot at Springfield," 710.

80. *ISR*, 18 August 1908.

81. Walling, "The Race War in the North," 532–33; Rogers, "A Review of the Springfield Riot," 77; *ISR*, 17–18 August 1908; *ISJ*, 16–17 August 1908; *SR*, 16–17 August 1908.

82. *SN*, 15 August 1908, 21 August 1908; *Chicago Record-Herald*, 16 August 1908; *ISJ*, 16 August 1908.

83. *ISJ*, 15–16 August 1908; *SR*, 16 August 1908; *SN*, 15 August 1908.

84. *ISJ*, 15–16 August 1908; also cited in Walling, "The Race War in the North," 531.

85. Frank H. Madison Memoir, SSUO.

86. *ISR*, 15 August 1908.

87. *SN*, 22 August 1908.

88. *Forum*, 12 September 1908.

89. *Biennial Report*, 265–66.

90. Ibid.

91. *ISR*, 17 August 1908; *ISJ*, 16 August 1908; Clarence Liggins Memoir, SSUO.

92. *ISR*, 17 August 1908.

93. *SR*, 16 August 1908; *ISJ*, 16 August 1908; *Biennial Report*, 265.

94. Blanche Hankins Memoir, SSUO.

95. *Biennial Report*, 265; *ISR*, 16–17 August 1908; *ISJ*, 16 August 1908; *SN*, 16 August 1908, 22 August 1908.

96. *Biennial Report*, 266–70; *ISR*, 16 August 1908; *ISJ*, 16 August 1908.

97. *ISJ*, 2 September 1908, 5 September 1908.

98. *Biennial Report*, 270, 275; *ISR*, 17 August 1908; *ISJ*, 17 August 1908.

99. *ISJ*, 19–20 August 1908, 6 September 1908, 19 September 1908; *SR*, 1 September 1908, 18 September 1908; *SN*, 19 August 1908; *Chicago Record-Herald*, 17 August 1908; *Chicago Tribune*, 18 August 1908.

100. Walling, "The Race War in the North," 530–31; *Chicago Tribune*, 17 August 1908.

101. *SR*, 18 August 1908.

102. *ISR*, 16 August 1908, 19 August 1908.

103. Ibid., 19 August 1908; *ISJ*, 19 August 1908.

104. *ISR*, 19 August 1908.

The scene at Loper's restaurant, with the remains of Loper's automobile.
Courtesy of the Sangamon Valley Collection, Lincoln Library, Springfield.

Black firemen hosing ruins of a Badlands home after the riot.
Courtesy of the Abraham Lincoln Presidential Library.

Sightseers viewing burned Badlands buildings on East Madison Street.
Courtesy of the Abraham Lincoln Presidential Library.

"Scene on East Madison Street: In the Heart of the Black Belt."
Courtesy of the Abraham Lincoln Presidential Library.

Burned black residences on East Madison Street after the riot.
Courtesy of the Abraham Lincoln Presidential Library.

Illinois state militia encampment near downtown Springfield.
Courtesy of the Abraham Lincoln Presidential Library.

"Scene of Lynching." Crowds gathered at the tree where the black barber
Scott Burton was hanged during the first night of rioting. By the end of
the day, the tree was gone, torn apart by whites who wanted souvenirs.
Courtesy of the Abraham Lincoln Presidential Library.

Mabel Hallam. Her false allegation
of rape precipitated the riot.
Courtesy of the Abraham Lincoln
Presidential Library.

George Richardson, the man
whom Mabel Hallam accused of
rape. Courtesy of the Abraham Lincoln
Presidential Library.

Sightseers at Reuben Fishman's wrecked pawnshop on East Washington Street.
Courtesy of the Abraham Lincoln Presidential Library.

Troops guarding smoldering ruins of black homes on East Madison Street.
Courtesy of the Abraham Lincoln Presidential Library.

"Negro Residence 9th & Madison. Militia on duty."
Courtesy of the Abraham Lincoln Presidential Library.

"12th and Mason. Burnt Negro homes."
Courtesy of the Abraham Lincoln Presidential Library.

Springfield mayor Roy Reece.
Courtesy of the Abraham Lincoln
Presidential Library.

Sangamon County
sheriff Charles Werner.
Courtesy of the Abraham
Lincoln Presidential Library.

Alleged riot leaders, Ernest "Slim" Humphrey, left, and Abraham Raymer. Both were accused of taking part in the killing of William Donnegan.
Courtesy of the Abraham Lincoln Presidential Library.

Riot area on 700 block of East Washington Street. "Dandy Jim" Smith's wrecked saloon was in the building on the left. Blacks defending the building fired from its roof into the crowd of rioters. Courtesy of the Abraham Lincoln Presidential Library.

Black riot victims viewing the remains of their burned homes.
Courtesy of the Abraham Lincoln Presidential Library.

CHAPTER 2

The Community

E XCEPT for the presence of the state government, a relatively ample railroad service, and a large number of coal mines close at
hand, Springfield in 1908 was an average middle-size midwestern
city. The capital developed a diversified and vigorous economy, but
only a few diehard civic boosters expected it to become an industrial
and commercial giant like Chicago. First settled about ninety years
before the riot, until the late 1830s Springfield remained but one of
a number of small and undistinguished prairie villages in central
Illinois.[1] Many of its early settlers came from the South—especially
from Kentucky and Tennessee—but the 1820s also saw the arrival
of migrants from the North. Several distinct streams of American-
born settlers merged in central Illinois, and the region also attracted
a significant number of German and Irish immigrants before the
Civil War. By the 1860s Springfield was culturally diverse, though
the presence of southerners in terms of numbers and outlook was
more prominent than it would be later in the nineteenth century.[2]

Springfield's Economy

The acquisition of the state government lent Springfield political
importance and prestige, but it was the discovery and exploitation
of massive coal resources that, along with railroads, stimulated population growth after mid-century (see Table 2.1). Springfield is situated near the center of a massive coal bed that underlies nearly
three-quarters of Illinois.[3] Before the 1860s coal in Springfield and
elsewhere in the state was harvested in small quantities for local use

Table 2.1 Population of Springfield, Illinois, 1840–1920

Year	Number	Percent Increase
1840	2,579	
1850	4,533	75.8
1860	9,320	105.6
1870	17,364	86.3
1880	19,743	13.7
1890	24,963	26.4
1900	34,159	36.8
1910	51,678	51.3
1920	59,183	14.5

Compiled from U.S. Bureau of the Census, *Sixteenth Census of the United States: 1940, Population* (Washington, D.C.: Government Printing Office, 1942), 1:294.

from surface seams. Test holes drilled near the city in 1865 revealed wide coal seams a little over two hundred feet down, and the first shafts were operating within two years. Springfield's residents recognized the significance of the discovery of a seemingly inexhaustible supply of coal, and, when the first load was hauled in 1867, they marked the event with a day of celebration.[4] By the early twentieth century Illinois was second only to Pennsylvania in amount of coal mined, and the mines near the capital were prominent in this production. Sangamon County (including Springfield) enjoyed a six-year stretch, beginning in 1900, in which it mined more coal than any of the other fifty or so coal-mining counties in Illinois. From 1906 to 1908 it stood second only to Williamson County in productivity. In 1908, 37 Sangamon County mines provided employment for some 6,553 workers, most of whom were miners who extracted the coal with pick and shovel. Several years after the riot an intensive study of Springfield conducted by the Russell Sage Foundation mentioned that the 17 mines within four miles of downtown Springfield employed nearly 3,000 of the city's male workers. A few coal mines actually operated within city limits. "By the time the last shipping mine shut down in 1952," according to one account, "all but the central core of Springfield and much of the surrounding territory was undercut by abandoned coal mine tunnels."[5]

Railroad lines, in part attracted by the availability of coal, helped spur local development. The Northern Cross Railroad was the first to lay tracks into the capital in 1842, but this initial enterprise got off to a shaky start. Within a few years both tracks and rolling stock were in disrepair, and at one point mule teams temporarily took the place of locomotives. By the 1850s, however, effective and efficient rail service was in place. Three railroads served Springfield by the 1870s, and construction of three more was scheduled for the near future. In 1904 a local historian noted with pride that Springfield, served by a half dozen major railroad lines, had become one of the state's more important transportation hubs.[6]

The twin blessings of ample fuel and good transportation facilities would seem to have invited the development of industry in the city, but manufacturing never did dominate Springfield's economy. The capital ranked fourth among Illinois cities in population in 1910, for example, but stood eleventh in numbers of factory workers and fourteenth in the value of its products. At the turn of the century, factories loomed larger in the capital than they did earlier, or would later. Out of a total population of 24,693 in 1890, 3,269 workers (13.2%) were employed in factories; in 1940 there were only 5,111 factory workers (6.8%), even though the city's population had grown to 75,503.[7]

Springfield's major manufactures in the early twentieth century, in order of the value of their products, were as follows: flour and grist mill products, shoes, zinc products, watches, agricultural implements, electrical supplies, and malt liquors.[8] The largest factory, in terms of number of employees, was the Illinois Watch Company, located—as were many other factories—in northeast Springfield (see Appendix, Table 2.1). In the early 1880s the company counted 600 men and women in its workforce; in 1914 it had nearly 1,000 operatives engaged in assembling timepieces for railroad use.[9] Manufacturing, mining, and transportation were the chief employers in Springfield by the early twentieth century (see Appendix, Table 2.2).[10]

On the eve of the race riot, then, Springfield's economy had a broad and diverse base, yet it is tempting to attribute the timing of its riot to the brief national economic recession of 1907. One could speculate, for instance, that local high unemployment and economic distress generated the kinds of social strain that produce interracial tensions. But Springfield seemed to pass through the recession relatively unscathed. The local press mentioned no serious economic problems in the city in the year before the riot. Following the riot in August, the *Illinois State Journal* published an editorial entitled "Springfield is All Right," which provided an overview of the recession's local impact. It noted that "in the east the situation was more serious than here. In the west and particularly in this section the people have cause for thankfulness." Surveying the local scene, the editorial concluded:

Springfield has been peculiarly blessed in the fact that, even when the commercial depression was at its height there were few unemployed people in the city. Now that the industrial situation is steadily improving, there is work for all. A large number of paving, excavating and building contracts have recently been let which absorb the labor that is on the market and in every department of commercial and manufacturing activity the revival is noticed. The country is prosperous, the crop prospect good, prices of products high and labor generally employed.[11]

Did Springfield's press exaggerate the health of the local economy? Ideally one would analyze the production, employment, and profit records of Springfield's major industries and businesses to test the newspapers' claims, but these records generally no longer exist. Fortunately it is possible to examine the recession's impact on one major segment of the city's economy: coal mining. Beginning in the early 1880s, the Illinois Bureau of Labor Statistics published annual reports detailing the state of the industry in each county involved in coal mining. Its reports from 1906 to 1910, the years surrounding the recession, indicate that the economic downturn had no impact on mining in Sangamon County (see Appendix, Table 2.3).

After manufacturing, the coal mines employed the largest number of men in Springfield. In 1908 over two thousand miners worked in the pits in and near the city.[12] Severe unemployment in the mines would not have passed unnoticed, for it would have had economic repercussions beyond the mining community. The retail sector, for instance, would have been affected, since many small businesses—grocery stores, furniture stores, clothing stores, and the like—depended heavily on miners for their trade. One former miner recalled, with a bit of overstatement, perhaps, that Springfield resembled "a coal mining camp," with "about as many coal miners as there were any other type of people." He added that "practically the [whole] town depended on the miners' paychecks."[13] The stability of coal mining during the recession does support the claim by Springfield's press that the city was little troubled by the 1907 economic crisis.

The steady expansion of Sangamon County's coal mining before the riot is also important because it was precisely in mining, and not in industry or transportation, that potential for interracial competition over employment and wages existed. Of non-mining employment, one local newspaper noted that "there are not many positions held by blacks which are envied by whites to such an extent as to create disturbance."[14] Springfield had a relatively high proportion of black miners, though in terms of numbers their presence was small. In all of the 55 Illinois counties with mines in 1910, there were only 1,512 black coal miners—about 2.6 percent of the total mining workforce.[15] In Springfield nearly one out of every ten miners was black, and in 1907 there were 158 black miners living in the city.[16]

Some have claimed that the labor violence that flared in counties south of Sangamon in the late nineteenth century poisoned race relations among Illinois miners and later contributed to the riots in Springfield.[17] Interracial conflict at midwestern mines had been occurring at least since the 1870s. Nonetheless, race relations among Illinois miners—and among those in the United Mine Workers union in general—were complex, and blacks were not always found on the wrong side of the picket line.[18] Black UMW members often closed ranks with white members during labor unrest, and white miners were aware of their cooperation. During a bloody strike in Virden in 1898, for example, black union miners from Springfield joined the effort to fight the importation of black strikebreakers.[19] Just before the Springfield riot, violent strikes broke out in the Alabama coal fields. If white miners paid attention to the news regarding their union, the stories they would have read in the capital's press revealed that "negro and white miners are at present standing together side by side in a great struggle with the operators."[20]

Impressionistic evidence also suggests that relations among Springfield's black and white miners were, if not entirely cordial, at least peaceful. "The miners [in Sangamon County] are generally foreigners [who] fraternize during times of peace," said one newspaper. "The black and white miners have worked together in their unions without friction and mined together in the black recesses of the earth where color is not distinguishable."[21] Shortly after the riot the press expressed concern that violence might break out in the mines, as both black and white workers refused to enter the pits together, each side fearing that the other might be armed. A brief visit by United Mine Worker officials, however, was enough to reconcile the fearful miners and convince them to return to work. And even though the rest of the city remained tense, no further trouble between the races occurred in the mines.[22]

The Black Community

Springfield had a higher proportion of black residents than most Illinois cities in the early twentieth century, and some writers have suggested that this statistic somehow helps explain the 1908 riot.[23] It does seem commonsensical to suggest that cities with substantial numbers of blacks were more likely to have anti-black collective violence. After all, East St. Louis and Chicago had the largest black populations in the state, and both experienced major riots during the World War I era. On the other hand, it is clear that the outbreak of race rioting involves much more than numbers or percentages of blacks in a particular community. Springfield's whites probably did not keep close track of the proportion of blacks in their city, though at any given point they may have felt that there were "more" or "fewer" blacks in town. Except for the decade following the Civil War, the growth of Springfield's black population was gradual (see Table 2.2). From 1880 on, the city's white population grew at a faster rate than the black, and blacks' share of the total population slipped steadily after 1890, from a high of 7.2 percent to 5.7 percent in 1910. Springfield did have a higher percentage of blacks than most other larger Illinois cities from 1890 to 1910 (see Appendix, Table 2.4), but it certainly was not alone in having a large proportion of black citizens. Furthermore, cities like East St. Louis and Danville experienced a much more rapid increase in black residents from 1900 to 1910, and by 1910 Danville, Quincy, and Peoria each had acquired a large black community.

Table 2.2   Black Population of Springfield, Illinois, 1850–1920

Year	Blacks	Percent of Total Population	Percent Increase
1850	171	3.9	
1860	203	2.2	18.7
1870	808	4.7	298.0
1880	1,328	6.7	64.4
1890	1,798	7.2	35.4
1900	2,227	6.5	23.9
1910	2,961	5.7	33.0
1920	2,769	4.7	−6.5
1930	3,324	4.6	20.0

Compiled from the U.S. Bureau of the Census, *Sixteenth Census of the United States: 1940, Population* (Washington, D.C.: Government Printing Office, 1942), 1:294; *Thirteenth Census, Population, 1910* (Washington, D.C.: Government Printing Office, 1913), 2:504; Daniel J. Elazar, *Cities of the Prairie: The Metropolitan Frontier and American Politics* (New York: Basic Books, Inc., 1970), 182.

As for Springfield, its relatively high percentage of blacks does
not really explain why a race riot occurred there or why it took
place in 1908. Why, for example, was interracial unrest not greater
from 1890 to 1900, when the proportion of blacks in the city
reached its peak of over 7 percent during a time of significant labor
unrest and a major depression? Furthermore, incidents occurred
during this earlier period that, given the tensions evident in Springfield, ought to have evoked some expression of anti-black hostility, if
one accepts a social strain interpretation. For example, in October
1898, during the bitter coal mine strike at nearby Virden, an armed
battle broke out between mine guards and strikers who had been
trying to block the importation of black strikebreakers. Dismayed by
the violence, the strikebreakers asked to be taken home and were
given temporary shelter in Springfield. Several white Springfield
miners died of gunshot wounds during the clash, and their friends
carried their bodies back to the capital. White Springfield miners
organized a massive turnout for the funeral, which was attended by
members of other unions as well as many sympathetic Springfield
residents. Springfield's authorities feared an attack on the black
strikebreakers and saw to it that they were promptly removed from
the city. Nonetheless, despite the tense circumstances, the press
made absolutely no mention of any resentment or anger aimed at
the capital's own black community. No attacks on local blacks were
anticipated or reported, either before or after the bloody Virden
incident.[24]

In this instance the percentage of blacks in Springfield was not a
reliable indicator of the likelihood of anti-black violence. With respect to the size or proportion of black communities, there was no
predictable threshold that, once crossed, guaranteed heightened interracial conflict in this period. At any rate, when Springfield's
white press tried to explain the race riot, it never once mentioned
that whites were alarmed about the number of blacks in the city.
Rather, it described other local conditions in accounting for the riot,
including ones that had more to do with the character than the size
of the black community.

It is impossible to say exactly when blacks first settled in Springfield. As a local writer observed, "the history of the colored people
in Sangamon County, like the sources of the common law, is
shrouded in some mystery."[25] The first black settler seems to have
been William Florville, a West Indian who arrived in Sangamon
County in 1831. By chance Florville met Abraham Lincoln in nearby
Salem, who, when he discovered Florville was a barber, urged him to

set up shop in Springfield. Florville's business prospered in the capital, and he passed the management of his barbershop on to his son. By 1908 the Florvilles were among the wealthiest black families in the city. The black community the first Florville belonged to remained small until the decade from 1860 to 1870, when a sharp increase (298 percent) in the number of black migrants from the South occurred (see Table 2.2).[26]

Most black Springfielders at the turn of the century, as earlier, earned their living in unskilled and menial positions. One white newspaper remarked, "most of the work performed by blacks down town is work for which whites do not ordinarily make application."[27] The leading occupations for black men were laborer, miner, teamster, and waiter; most other occupations held by blacks were either dirty, dangerous, or regarded as beneath the dignity of whites, for example, bootblack, yardman, furnace stoker, or domestic servant (see Appendix, Table 2.5). Even within a less skilled trade like teamstering, blacks were often at a disadvantage. Margaret Ferguson, an elderly black Springfield resident interviewed in the 1970s, recalled that "Negroes drove all [the] brick wagons, because that was hard work. They had to load these bricks, and then they had to unload them where they went. Well, that didn't change, because whites weren't going to do that work anyway."[28]

Several areas of modest opportunity in the city were open to black workers, though; the expanding coal mining industry was one. Springfield's status as state capital also assured a large number of positions in personal service occupations catering to tourists and other transient visitors who needed to be housed, fed, and entertained. In addition, there were relatively few newly arrived immigrants (about 14 percent of Springfield's population was foreign-born in 1900 and 1910), who might compete for lower-status, personal service employment. Most of the city's twenty-five black barbers, for example, served a white clientele, and many blacks found work in Springfield's best hotels in the early twentieth century. Three large hotels—the St. Nicholas, the Illinois, and the Leland—employed blacks in positions ranging from headwaiter to dishwasher and busboy. Nearly one out of every twenty black men in 1907 worked in one of these three hotels. Others found employment as waiters in white-owned restaurants, including Harry Loper's elegant but ill-fated establishment on Fifth Street. The city's many saloons (nine of them run by black barkeeps in 1907) provided jobs for over 5 percent of black male workers, mostly as porters.

Blacks were almost entirely excluded from employment in two major sectors of Springfield's economy: transportation and manufacturing. The only industrial work open to blacks was backbreaking labor in the city's several brickyards. The 1914 Russell Sage Foundation survey of the capital said that in the brickyards "seasonal [un]-employment is at its worst." Irregular employment, combined with low pay meant "for many of their [brickworkers'] families nothing short of real penury."[29] Of the 1,064 black male workers listed in the 1907 city directory, only four held jobs in other industries: a machinist, an apprentice machinist, a polisher in a piano company, and an animal feed mixer (see Appendix, Table 2.5). The largest industrial employer in Springfield, the Illinois Watch Company, out of the hundreds of workers on its payroll, employed but one black, a janitor. In transportation the situation was little better: apart from drivers and teamsters, a few blacks served as railroad porters, and one man worked as a railroad boilerwasher; neither of the city's streetcar companies hired blacks in any capacity.

This extreme exclusion of blacks from jobs in transportation and industry in the North has been well documented for this period and has been attributed in part to the prevailing high level of anti-black sentiment and to demands by labor unions to exclude blacks from their trades.[30] What is striking about Springfield is that such thorough exclusion took place in a community in which only small numbers of foreign-born whites might have competed for manufacturing and transportation employment. The "color line" in the city's occupations was clearly the product of the prejudices of a predominantly native white population. Native whites had a virtual monopoly on industrial and transportation employment and were increasingly less attracted to the dirty and extremely dangerous work of mining coal, which, by the turn of the century was attracting growing numbers of recent immigrants as well as blacks.

Opportunity was limited for most Springfield blacks, but the city did have a small, well-established black middle class from the mid-nineteenth century onward. In 1881 a white author published a local history of Springfield and Sangamon County that included about two dozen brief biographical sketches of prominent black Springfield residents. These sketches are notable, not just because they provide information on some of Springfield's black elite in this period, but also simply because they were included at all. The early 1880s marked the beginning of a steady deterioration of race relations in the city. After the 1881 history, no compiler or local historian saw fit to include mention of the black community or biographies of its leading citizens, however wealthy or well established they were. The 1881 history was optimistic about blacks' future in Springfield. After discussing the "men from the best class of the colored race," the author ended on a sympathetic note, which even just a decade later would strike most whites as antiquated: "It is a fact worthy of mention that the transition from slavery and consequent ignorance to a condition of citizenship and comparative education stands without a parallel in either modern or ancient history, and the unprejucial [sic] observer of events must predict, for the future of the African race, a grand and glorious future."[31]

The 1881 history omitted some better-off blacks, but it does give a partial view of the lives of middle- and upper-class blacks in the late nineteenth century. The economic profile of this group in the 1880s resembled that of the elite in the 1900s. Of twenty-five men mentioned in the biographical sketches, five were small shop owners; three worked for the state government in minor positions; three were waiters at Springfield's most elegant hotel, the Leland; and two were ministers in the two churches that drew most of the city's black elite, the Zion Baptist and African Methodist Episcopal Churches. Small businesses, especially barbershops and restaurants; positions at the better hotels as headwaiter or waiter; employment with the state government as a janitor or messenger; jobs with the post office; and opportunities within the ministry provided the basis for Springfield's black elite from the 1880s to the 1900s. By 1908 this elite included two black physicians, two newspaper editors, an undertaker, and two black attorneys. Several blacks, including William Florville, Jr., made a respectable living from dealing in real estate. Since they faced little competition from foreign-born whites, black barbers, waiters, and others involved in personal service occupations kept most of their white clientele after the turn of the century.[32]

Compared to a city like Boston, for example, where many northern-born blacks could trace their descent from antebellum freedmen, and where there was a small but impressive circle of "black Brahmins," Springfield's black elite appears rather modest.[33] Four-fifths of those mentioned in the 1881 history of Sangamon County were of southern origin, many were former slaves, and most had arrived in Springfield after the Civil War. In 1908 many of them were still counted among the city's black elite, but in comparison to older black communities farther east, they seemed newly arrived. Margaret Ferguson reflected upon the occupations of the black middle-class in Springfield in the 1900s: "One of the most elite jobs you could have here was to work in the state house; and if you had a job [there] you really had it made." Government work was desirable because it was relatively secure and steady, and it was clean, safe, and respectable employment. Ferguson observed, however, that "you couldn't be anything except a messenger or a janitor. You didn't get higher jobs." As for black businesses, she said that they were "little things like barbershops and saloons and pool-rooms," but not, as she put it, "real business." Ferguson concluded—and what she said was true of many northern cities in the early twentieth century—"truly Springfield was not a fertile place for black business."[34]

Springfield's black elite lived in a markedly different and more comfortable social world than that of the black working class. Like Margaret Ferguson's family, wealthier Springfield blacks lived in large, comfortably furnished homes. The women in these families did not work and had the leisure time to engage in a variety of social and charitable activities. This leisure was evident in Ferguson's description of her family's social activities: "I remember my mother belonged to two bridge clubs [which] met in the afternoons and they had real fancy parties. You had picnics and the men fished, and they had boats and they'd ride around on the Sangamon River." On Sundays after church, Ferguson said that as many as twenty or thirty visitors might stop by at her parents' home. And there were hayrides into the countryside as well as dances and balls. Some of the latter were simple affairs at nearby schools, while others were more formal and substantial, held at such places as the large Masonic hall downtown. Her family often entertained at home, aided by the new wind-up victrola in the parlor.[35] Another daughter of a black middle-class family, Edith Carpenter, also recalled entertaining at home. Friends and neighbors—some white—"would come to our home to hear us perform because we all played a piano. The older girls sang, and there were some rather wealthy people on our street at that time. And they would come to our home."[36]

The social world of the black elite was sometimes viewed by the black working class with a mixture of envy and resentment.[37] Alice Hopkins, a child in a black working-class household early in the century, hinted at some of the class resentments that existed in Springfield's black community. Her father labored at odd jobs, usually as a yardman, when he could get the work, and her industrious mother helped supplement the family's income by taking in washing and by raising and canning fruits and vegetables for the family table. Hopkins's parents managed to purchase a small house near the edge of town, but they faced a constant struggle to maintain a minimum level of comfort and respectability. Hopkins commented on the more prominent of the city's black elite, those working for the state government: "[Their] jobs weren't too good. Those people who had those state jobs, they didn't want to talk to people who didn't have them. Those janitors, when they would come out, they would feel like they were bigger than anybody, felt like they were the governor, and they was just janitors! Walking over the other [black] people!"[38] The social circle of more successful blacks was further closed by their tendency to socialize and intermarry with those of similar status. The 1881 history reveals, for example, that many among the middle and upper classes belonged to the same fraternal orders. Also, by 1881 at least eight of the families mentioned had intermarried. As newcomers to Springfield's elite appeared after the turn of the century, they in turn formed marital ties with the older well-established families.[39]

Residential Patterns

From the late nineteenth to the early twentieth century the location and boundaries of Springfield's black neighborhoods changed very little. With one exception, the black enclaves that existed in 1908 had been established many years earlier, and, as time passed, the proportion of blacks in each increased. Nearly 90 percent of Springfield's blacks lived in two large enclaves in the eastern half of the city (see Table 2.3).[40] In the Badlands of the northeast First Ward, the housing stock was among the oldest and most rundown in the city, and as whites steadily moved off to better homes, the city's poorest blacks gradually replaced them. Working-class blacks especially, but

Table 2.3. Black Population by Ward, Springfield, Illinois, 1910

Ward	Number	Percent
1	1,186	40.1
2	60	2.0
3	218	7.4
4	249	8.4
5	91	3.1
6	1,469	49.6
7	131	4.4
Total	2,961	100.0

Compiled from U.S. Bureau of the Census, *Thirteenth Census, 1910, Population* (Washington, D.C.: Government Printing Office, 1913), 2:516.

also some of the middle- and upper-class blacks, settled in a second
large enclave in the city's southeastern Sixth Ward, where a modest
home—or the land on which to build one—was less expensive than
in areas closer to downtown Springfield. This area, along with the
easternmost edge of the Badlands, also was closer to several of the
coal mines near city limits, and thus it was more convenient for
black miners. Including the Badlands and the large Sixth Ward settlement, there were seven identifiable black residential clusters scattered over the city (see Map 1.1). Smaller enclaves dotted the Third
and Fourth Wards, and a number of blacks rented rooms over shops
and businesses in the downtown Levee. Finally, a small concentration of homes belonging to better-off black residents stretched over
several blocks of Adams Street, just south and east of the central
business district. Over time more and more blacks settled within the
established boundaries of the two largest black neighborhoods on
the east side, which did not expand much geographically in the
1900s but became blacker. This process is visible in the Badlands
(see Maps 2.1 and 2.2).[41]

Homes were in good supply in Springfield early in the century,
and, as researchers for the Russell Sage survey of the city indicated,
the condition of its housing was relatively satisfactory. Except for
some buildings downtown with multiple dwellings over shops, the
city had little overcrowding. Springfield's location on flat prairie
land with no natural barriers blocking its expansion made for low
population density. The Russell Sage investigators reported that
"the single family house with a good sized yard or lawn [was] the
rule" for most citizens.[42] Even in the poorest black neighborhood,
the Badlands, most buildings were single family dwellings with large
yards, though most of this housing stock was substandard: "Houses
are more dilapidated, water supply and toilets more inadequate, everything in a more rundown, shabby condition than in other sections." The 1914 survey concluded that Badlands landlords did not
care about the condition of the houses they rented to blacks and
were "inclin[ed] to give less and charge more [than] in the case of
white tenants."[43] For most of Springfield's residents, however, adequate, inexpensive housing was ample, and the survey gave the capital high praise for its abundance of single family homes and spa-
cious yards.

Russell Sage investigators noted that the eastern half of Springfield was markedly poorer than its western and south-central sections. Their public health survey revealed that the east side had less
than its share of city services—water and sewer service in particu-

lar—and more than its share of infectious diseases.[44] The area east of Ninth Street was Springfield's major working-class district. Much of the city's industry was concentrated in the northeastern First Ward because "prevailing winds are from the southeast. A factory district to the leeward of the city would be therefore far less objectionable from the standpoint of smoke, gases and noises."[45] American-born whites and those who were financially better off gravitated to the cleaner, healthier west side of the capital, where the housing stock was newer and neighborhoods more modern and park-like. The wealthiest wards were the "aristocratic" Fourth and Fifth, south and southwest of the central business district, far removed from the factories, foreigners, and blacks on the other side of town. A 1951 study of Springfield indicated that the first half of the century saw a steady movement of wealthy whites to the west side, further away from the city's center. They were followed by middle-class whites whose less pretentious homes formed a sort of buffer zone between the wealthier districts and the downtown and working-class districts.[46]

Over half (about 56 percent) of Springfield's foreign-born whites lived in the eastern First and Sixth Wards and the downtown Seventh Ward (see Appendix, Table 2.6). Most of the recently arrived "new" immigrants settled in east-side or downtown locations. Over two-thirds of the Italians and four-fifths of all the "Russians" lived in these three wards. Many non-Jewish "Russians,"—Lithuanian, Polish, and true Russian coal miners—clustered on the eastern edges of the First and Sixth Wards, near the mine tipples. Italians and Russian Jews favored housing in and near center city since many of them were involved in small businesses or peddling, though a few Italians settled in locations closer to the mines. Still, no large or clearly discernible ethnic neighborhoods emerged in the capital. The "older" immigrants, the Germans and Irish, had long since abandoned most of the less desirable housing in the downtown Seventh Ward and by 1910 had scattered all over the rest of the city. Here and there on the east side and downtown appeared a few very small concentrations of single ethnic groups, an occasional block or two that had a preponderance of Italians or "Russian" immigrants. But the clustering was not great enough to create a large or dense neighborhood of one ethnic group. In the case of many newer immigrants, one major reason they did not settle in distinct neighborhoods was that their workplaces were scattered. The several coal mines that ringed the city each attracted a share of the new immigrant miners. One finds, for example, several small concentrations

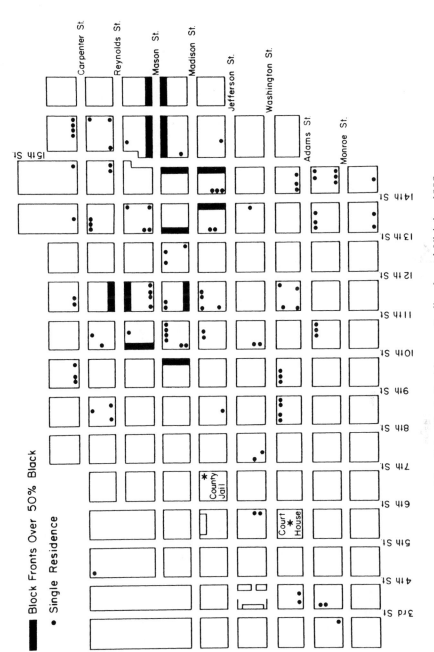

Map 2.1 Black Residences: Badlands and Vicinity, 1892

Map 2.2 Black Residences: Badlands and Vicinity, 1907

■ Block Fronts Over 50% Black

• Single Residence

County Jail

Court House

Carpenter St.

Reynolds St.

Mason St.

Madison St.

Jefferson St.

Washington St.

Adams St.

Monroe St.

15th St.

14th St.

13th St.

12th St.

11th St.

10th St.

9th St.

8th St.

7th St.

6th St.

5th St.

4th St.

3rd St.

of Lithuanians and Poles near coal mines at different points on the city's edge.

The mines had the same scattering effect on black residential patterns, with the result that Lithuanians, Poles, Russians, and blacks often lived in the same neighborhoods and worked in the same places.[47] In general, there seems to have been little hostility between east-side blacks and the new immigrants. Several black Springfielders who grew up on the east side characterized relations between blacks and immigrants as civil but distant early in the century. Reverend Henry Mann, a black minister who lived in the large black enclave in the Sixth Ward, recalled that blacks and immigrants "were all mixed up in there together." He occasionally overheard conversations between whites and blacks over subjects like politics and the weather, but "every group had its own way as far as personal socialization was concerned."[48] Alice Hopkins remembered her family's move to a new house in the sparsely settled area on Washington Street near city limits. "It was all foreigners out there," she said—their new house was adjacent to one of several clusters of Lithuanian miners. At first white neighbors seemed alarmed by the prospect of a black household in their midst. "They didn't want us to buy the house," Hopkins explained. But as time passed, the neighbors became more cordial.[49] Other east-side blacks remembered having peaceful relations with the whites on their streets, and none said they felt threatened by their white neighbors when the riot broke out.[50] Some blacks claimed that immigrant whites even offered assistance during the worst of the violence. Madge Jackson, for example, whose father worked at the Leland Hotel in 1908, said that his white friends, "most of whom were Italians, would escort him to and from work to ensure his safety." She also told of a "friendly Jewish woman who hid blacks in her basement" during the riot.[51]

From the 1890s to 1907 most established black neighborhoods expanded very little, and only a small number of black families ventured into new, predominantly white areas. However, one small but significant change in black settlement did occur in those years along East Washington Street downtown, particularly in the Levee between Seventh and Ninth Streets. Poorer blacks began to rent flats and rooms over shops, stables, saloons, and small manufactories in this area. The black presence there was not large by 1908; indeed, the whole Seventh Ward, including most of downtown Springfield and the Levee district, contained only 131 black residents in 1910 (see Table 2.3). Nonetheless, it was a new black settlement, one that had not existed in the early 1890s (see Maps 2.1 and 2.2). Housing in the converted space over businesses, stables, and small workshops downtown was substandard. Russell Sage investigators who surveyed Springfield's housing after the riot criticized the rundown condition of the units rented to blacks (and to some poor whites) in the Levee. The rooms over stores and manufactories were dark ill-ventilated firetraps, they reported, and often lacked proper sanitary facilities. In one building they cited, tenants could reach garbage barrels only by going downstairs, out of the building, and around to a back lot. As a result, the tenants "adopted the simple expedient of throwing their garbage from the windows at the barrels. Perhaps it is because women are notoriously bad shots that so much of the garbage lies scattered about on the ground." On East Washington Street the investigators also found a dwelling that had been transformed into an "apartment" by dividing one room into two with a flimsy folding screen. Three blacks occupied the two gloomy and ill-ventilated "rooms."[52]

Roughly coincident with the appearance of black renters downtown was the establishment of black businesses in the Levee. It had but one black saloon in 1892, for example, but by 1907 six stood on two blocks of East Washington Street alone, along with other new black enterprises.[53] The arrival of new black residents and businesses in and near the Levee must have meant that blacks became much more visible downtown. By 1907 the Levee was home for many poor blacks, and some of the new black businesses, especially the saloons and small restaurants, must have attracted at least some of their clientele from the Badlands, which lay only several blocks to the northeast. Thus, more blacks were on the streets of one of Springfield's major public spaces in the 1900s, and many of those frequently seen, apart from black businessmen, would have been those from the most desperate and impoverished segment of the city's black community.

This new visibility of blacks in part of downtown Springfield is probably more relevant to the growth of anti-black hostility locally than the number or percentage of blacks in the city as a whole. As some black leaders worried, white attitudes toward the race could be adversely affected by the character and behavior of blacks in public places, despite the fact that, in terms of actual numbers of residents and businesses, the black presence downtown was small. This helps explain the repeated warnings and scoldings in the city's black newspaper, the *Forum*, which complained, for instance, that downtown "there are too many too noisy Negroes too uncouth and trifling."[54]

The *Forum*'s editor warned again and again that the sins of the few would be cast on the many, and that the whole black community might be held accountable for rowdiness downtown.

Riot as the Wages of Urban Sin

Prior to the race riot, the city's white press had virtually nothing to say about changes in the racial composition of Levee residents and businessmen. One finds little indication that Springfield's whites paid any attention at all to developments in this seedy and rundown district before 1908. Nonetheless, by looking at the wholesale condemnation of the Levee and Badlands after the riot in the press and in speeches and sermons, it is possible to infer what many better-off whites' attitudes were. White editors and other influential whites *did* emphasize blacks' behavior—drinking, gambling, drug use, criminal acts, and general disorderliness—as one cause of the violence. It is noteworthy, though, that they did not limit their criticism to blacks downtown. The Levee district as a whole, including its white residents, was denounced.

In analyzing what was wrong with Springfield, influential whites claimed that the riot represented a recrudescence of a more general civic illness. The behavior of Levee blacks was but one symptom. Their criticism reflected widespread anxieties Americans shared about their cities in this period, anxieties having to do with the existence of poverty, crime, and disorder—in particular, the problems posed by the lower, "dangerous classes." In Springfield and elsewhere in the North, the riot sparked nervous speculation about the problem of imposing social control and order in urban areas. Reflecting on the Springfield rioters, one national magazine editor wrote: "It is a fearful thing to think of, that such a stratum of society can exist in a city, who can thus create a mob to overturn law. It shows how much yet remains to be done to civilize our people." Addressing "the better, the law-abiding, the decent elements of society" in cities, the editor warned that they had to "reform, to civilize and Christianize the pagans in their own midst."[55] Influential Springfield whites harshly condemned the character of the new and highly visible black settlement downtown after the riot, but in such a way as to make Levee blacks emblematic of larger civic problems they wished to reform: poor blacks were just one group of "pagans" downtown who needed to be "civilized."

For many better-off Springfield whites, then, the riot provided a stimulus and occasion for criticism of the city's ills and for the expression of a variety of reform concerns. As they searched for the causes of the riot, they generally minimized the importance of interracial hostility and instead traced the violence to civic weaknesses that supposedly fostered lawlessness among the so-called dangerous classes. Both Springfield's press and its ministers (and some later students of the 1908 riot) blamed the city's corrupt government and the presence of saloons, gambling dens, and brothels for the outbreak. The riot, they argued, was the inevitable product of bad government and its toleration of drinking and vice because these attracted a lawless, dangerous element to the city. It was this criminal class, the argument ran, that had run amok, looting, burning, and killing.

That Springfield's city government was a reformer's nightmare was not exactly news in 1908. Vote fraud, graft, ballot-box stuffing, bribery, and other political infirmities were well entrenched long before the riot, and they rested upon the stable and enduring foundation of the apathy and disinterest of many Springfield citizens and voters. Abraham Lincoln poked fun at the city's low social and political morals in the mid-nineteenth century. One of his favorite anecdotes begins with a pious man who asks a government official for permission to deliver a series of religious lectures in the statehouse. When asked what the theme of his speeches will be, he answers, "The second coming of our Lord." The statehouse official replies, so the story goes, "It is of no use. If you will take my advice, you will not waste your time in this city. It is my private opinion that if the Lord has been in Springfield once, He will not come again."[56]

One has only to flip through Springfield's newspapers in the years before the riot to get a sense of the prevailing political atmosphere. Just before a November election in 1898, for example, these headlines appeared in a Republican newspaper: "Resort to Larceny: Common Thievery is Part of the Democratic Campaign"; "Democrats Accused: Register Says They Are Guilty of Registration Frauds."[57] The Democrats were accused of "raising a big fund" to "spend liberally in behalf of their candidates," and the paper raised the possibility of bribery, saying, "envelopes for the party workers are already made up and they have been filled with more than the customary Democratic liberality."[58] The Democratic press held its own, running headlines such as "Rascality and Fraud: Startling Schemes of Republicans to Debauch Ballot." They accused their opponents of padding voter registration rolls with "names registered from vacant lots and batallions of men from single rooms."[59] Springfield's politics were controversial, questionable, and colorful well before the twentieth century.

Political symbiosis between politicians, saloons, and vice interests in the capital was both powerful and conspicuous. Although one historian who studied saloons found that in general "barkeeps were not that numerous in municipal chambers" in this period, Springfield in 1908 was one city where the jokester's famous cry "Your saloon's on fire!" really *would* have substantially reduced attendance of aldermen at a city council meeting.[60] At least four of Springfield's fourteen aldermen had ties to the "saloon interest": a newspaper listed two as saloonkeepers, one as a barkeep's brother, and a fourth as a former brewery employee who aspired to open his own drinking establishment.[61] The "dry" organization in town, the Local Option League, charged that a number of saloonkeepers—including two aldermen—illegally kept their places open on Sundays. But the League's reform efforts were largely in vain. Saloons continued to break liquor laws with virtual impunity and rewarded city officials' indulgence of their infractions with votes and cash.[62]

The marriage between city government and liquor and vice interests was further cemented by the economic importance of these establishments to the city. Many citizens and businessmen felt that saloons and vice were good for business and indispensable to a city that attracted tourists, visiting politicians, and traveling businessmen. Also important was the revenue the city derived from the sale of liquor licenses to the more than two hundred saloons in the city in the 1900s. The price of a liquor license was high: $500 per drinking establishment.[63] In 1908 the city comptroller reported for the public's edification (there was an election on local option pending, and the city administration favored a "wet" outcome) that "it would be impossible to conduct the business of the city without the $102,900 paid in annually by the saloons." Springfield's annual budget stood at about $300,000. Not only would the loss of liquor license revenues deliver a terrible shock to the treasury, but, the comptroller added, the city would "be compelled to hand back to 204 saloonkeepers $15,299.82 for unexpired licenses." That revenue loss, he warned, would mean a cutback in police and fire department personnel in a city that all knew needed more, not less, patrolling.[64] The city comptroller did not bother to mention one obvious implication of banning saloons, one that probably carried considerable weight with Springfield's voters: the loss of liquor license revenue would mean higher taxes. He merely predicted that "the treasury will be depleted and the dog fennel growing in the streets in nine months" if the city voted out the saloons.[65] In the subsequent local option election, the voters, by a generous margin, "declined to ride on the water wagon."[66]

The city administration and much of Springfield's public looked benignly upon gambling, prostitution, and saloons; and the confinement of vice to a segregated, closely monitored district in a shabby neighborhood made popular acceptance easier. Springfield, according to the Russell Sage survey, had "some conspicuous features of a 'wide open' town." The segregated vice district was "very evident, marked by glaring red lights, house names, and women soliciting from windows." Before 1913 "public gambling flourished," and the Sunday saloon closing law, according to the chief of police, "was a dead letter."[67]

The capital's vice district, which included much of the Levee and nearby blocks to the north and east, had flourished long before the riot and, after a brief, but largely cosmetic, police "cleanup" in 1908, continued to thrive in brazen disorder. During 1913 the Illinois Senate Vice Committee conducted investigative hearings in Springfield and interviewed the mayor, the chief of police, prostitutes, and women factory operatives. It quickly became obvious that vice was still widespread, even under the new reformed city government that had been instituted in 1911. The mayor readily admitted the existence and official toleration of a segregated vice district and revealed, under questioning, that since 1911 "immorality and prostitution" probably had increased.[68] Well into the twentieth century, Springfield had an "undainty municipal personality," as one journalist put it. His description of the capital in the 1940s could easily have been written at the turn of the century: "Politically, the capital is as murky with intrigue as a medieval border state. Springfield's vice may be no worse than that of many American cities, but it is more obvious."[69]

Profits from vice operations were substantial. Russell Sage investigators ventured a conservative estimate based upon the average earnings of 143 white prostitutes in thirty-three recognized brothels and came up with a figure of $185,000 per year in total income for the "houses of ill fame."[70] An overabundance of saloons in the city, combined with the high price of a liquor license, added to the prostitution problem, for competition for customers was keen. To keep ahead of competitors, some saloons introduced gambling and prostitution to lure patrons. Consequently saloons added their political influence to the effort to protect vice in the city.[71] It was not without cause that one prohibitionist fumed that vice existed "with a full knowledge of the Governor, the Mayor, the Chief of Police, the Prosecuting Attorney, and the whole miserable mess of time servers who hold their honor below par and sell the manhood of the state and city to the saloon and brothel in exchange for a miserable mess of political pottage."[72]

However much reform-minded critics of Springfield's civic affairs claimed that the race riot was logical retribution, visited Gemorrah-like upon the city for its sins, the capital was not unique in having vice, saloons, and governmental laxity. Illinois never reached the level of reform fervor in the Progressive era that some other states did, and bossism, "boodling," and public apathy often hindered reformers' efforts there.[73] Springfield's vice activities may have been more visible than those of other Illinois cities, but other communities had the same kinds of civic weak spots, including police corruption, gambling, and prostitution. The Illinois Senate Vice Committee, for example, uncovered segregated, tolerated vice districts in Peoria, Rock Island, Alton, "and over a dozen other cities," many of which were much smaller than Springfield.[74] Municipal untidiness and illicit, tawdry businesses were far from uncommon in early twentieth-century cities.

Especially vocal in their criticism of conditions in Springfield after the riot were the small numbers of citizens committed to and active in reform. The reformers promoting local option, who were offended by saloons and drinking, lost no time in exploiting the violence for their own ends. They traced the riot to the evils of liquor. In the wake of the violence a flurry of articles appeared such as "Riot Laid at Liquor's Door," which claimed that Springfielders had rioted because they were inebriated. The Prohibition party candidate for vice president made a speech in Springfield several weeks after the riot and "declared liquor was responsible for at least a portion of the rioting and that prohibition [the mayor had temporarily "put the lid on"], by closing the saloons, easily restored order."[75] One minister claimed that, under the influence of drink, "the disorderly element became uncontrollable, and on a pretext precipitated a bloody riot," which would, he predicted, "undoubtedly hasten the total destruction of the saloon in the interest of public safety."[76] Billy Sunday, a famous evangelist of the day, mentioned the riot when he preached in a nearby town and echoed the sentiment voiced by Springfield's "drys." "The people who committed those crimes in Springfield," he said, "are the worst class of people—people who were whiskey-soaked."[77] Another prohibitionist even suggested that racism itself originated in drunkenness. "Wipe out the saloon," he claimed dramatically, "and you settle the race question. . . . Any number of black and white men can live peaceably in this country sober."[78]

During the rioting some mob members probably did imbibe liquor looted from saloons and restaurants. Still, the obvious anti-black intent of the violence cannot be explained away by rioters' indulgence in alcohol. Even at the time, such explanations struck some observers as farfetched. One pro-saloon newspaper, the Democratic *Record*, ridiculed prohibitionists for their assessments of the violence, terming them "foolish and yellow utterances." The *Record* had sent a number of its staff to the streets during the riot, who reported seeing an occasional drunk man but said most rioters "showed no evidence of intoxication other than the intoxication of excitement [and] the drunkenness of blood-lust." Several citizens interviewed by the *Record* also denied witnessing any traces of "booze" in the crowd. The *Record* accused anti-saloon workers of "libeling" the character of the city and sarcastically reminded its readers of the recent conviction of a leading Kansas prohibitionist on bribery charges.[79] That perhaps was a low blow, but pro-saloon Democrats quickly recognized their opponents' attempt to turn the riot into political capital.

A second, more insistent argument used by reformers traced the riot to bad city government. They claimed that municipal laxity had bred a dangerous, lawless class in Springfield. "The seeds of mob violence," said one observer, "were sown when municipal rottenness fertilized the lower strata of society." The mob was "made up almost entirely of law-breakers," whose presence in town Springfield city officials had encouraged.[80] Ministers, too, blamed the city government for the rioting. One declared: "The weight of this occurrence rests hard on the city administration. The authorities have criminally permitted the most brazen violation of the law by the saloons and dives. One kind of lawlessness breeds another. It is not strange that the mob laughed in the mayor's face when he tried to plead for law and order. Think of the consistency! The total inefficiency of the city government was held up to ridicule by this affair. The administration has sown the wind and reaped the whirlwind."[81]

This minister, and other citizens who sought to blame city officials for the riot, called loudly for the election of reform-minded candidates at the next opportunity. But like the prohibitionists, who had hoped to see the winds of political change blow more briskly because of the riot, those who promoted government reform were doomed to disappointment. The character of Springfield's politics would remain unsavory for decades to come.

Race and Politics

Springfield blacks did influence local politics, but it is difficult to assess either the extent of their participation or its impact on the city's race relations. In theory enough black voters existed in the First and Sixth Wards, which contained the city's two largest black neighborhoods, to influence the outcome of elections for the two aldermen chosen to represent each ward in the city council (see Table 2.4). The black vote in the remaining five wards was negligible. Republicans and Democrats competed strenuously in aldermanic elections, and, in the First and Sixth Wards at least, sometimes the black vote may have provided the margin of victory. Unfortunately, it is impossible to confirm this possibility. Lists of voters are unavailable, and election returns did not break down vote tallies by race. Moreover, neither before nor after the 1908 riot did the press ever mention the black vote as a decisive factor in any election.

The complexity of Springfield's politics early in the century makes the task of determining the extent of blacks' political influence even more difficult. Both the Republican and Democratic parties were split into bitterly feuding factions, and by 1908 the Prohibition party also competed for the votes of reform-minded citizens.[82] For the most part, blacks in the North in this period voted for the party of Lincoln, but in Springfield they also were divided between the reform and "machine" wings of the Republican party. Like black voters in Chicago and Philadelphia, the majority of

Table 2.4 Males of Voting Age by Ward, Springfield, Illinois, 1910

Ward	Total Males of Voting Age		Black Males of Voting Age	
	Number		Number	Percent of Voters
1	2,598		423	16.3
2	1,822		23	1.0
3	2,586		74	2.9
4	2,893		71	2.5
5	1,931		44	2.3
6	2,979		315	10.6
7	1,281		71	5.5
Total	16,090		1,021	6.4

Compiled from U.S. Bureau of the Census, *Thirteenth Census, 1910, Population* (Washington, D.C.: Government Printing Office, 1913), 2:516.

Springfield's black voters shunned reform candidates and supported
the Republican faction committed to protecting the "liquor interest," which also dangled the possibility of city jobs as rewards for
loyal party service. The election of reform candidates might have
endangered black employment, for the saloon district and downtown
demimonde provided work for some blacks, and a "cleanup" would
have put many out of a job.[83]

Springfield's black Republicans tended to favor city "boss" Richard
M. Sullivan, who had been influential in local politics since 1902. In
a special election in 1907 Sullivan successfully managed the mayoral
campaign of his former business partner, Roy Reece, who had the
misfortune of holding office when the riot broke out.[84] Sullivan
courted and won the support of the majority of Springfield's black
Republicans. Even the usually reform-oriented *Forum* had nothing
but praise for the "boss." Its editor reminded his readers that "as to
the colored constituency, Mr. Sullivan will be remembered as the
first high official to recognize them from a meritorious standpoint."
In 1904 during his tenure as county treasurer, Sullivan hired a black
clerk and stenographer.[85]

White city newspapers occasionally linked black political activity
with the riot. But the problem, as they saw it, was not with the number of black voters or their role in the outcome of any particular
election per se, but with the character of black political participation and some whites' reaction to it. Whites who blamed the riot on
lax and corrupt city government, for example, sometimes condemned black vote selling during elections, particularly in the First
and Seventh Wards. Here again, though, these critics saw black political misbehavior as emblematic of long-standing, more pervasive
civic shortcomings.

Vote buying and selling apparently became common in Springfield in the 1880s and continued after 1908.[86] From the start, many
voters, poor whites and blacks alike, were eager for the two to five
dollars their vote might fetch on election day in downtown precincts.
Before the turn of the century, according to one politician, it was
well known "that hundreds of voters will not approach the polls until they have received cash in hand for alleged party services." Of
the First Ward, which contained the Badlands, he claimed that "the
illegal registration of negroes would fill companies of militia."[87]
During the 1908 Republican gubernatorial primary, the reform-
minded black editors of the *Forum* witnessed "business as usual" at
the polls and were outraged: "We saw young and old men stand
back waiting for money or pay before they would vote—some failed

to vote at all because they did not get their price—a shame! Yet these same people boast of their political freedom. We also saw aldermen and city officials at the polls, doing crooked business—voting nondescripts and repeaters. We want men nominated who stand for something, not vagabonds, pimps, and transients."[88]

Whether the black vote was a decisive factor in local elections or not, it was large enough in two wards that white politicians dared not ignore it. Both parties wooed black voters, though the Democrats in general were not very successful in severing blacks' loyalty to Lincoln's party early in the century.[89] Shortly after the riot, one Democratic newspaper complained about the political situation in the First Ward, with its Badlands voters: "The male citizen of the black belt in late years has come to pose as a political factor in Springfield. No candidate for office has dared overlook the lords and barons of this vassalage who were the owners of the gin joints and cocaine alleys. One faction affiliated with the republican party and the other with the democratic. Pretense to fierce warfare and political partisanship has been made at each city and county election, but after the campaign was over both sides were found to be doing business at the same old stand."[90]

Not only did political parties court, and sometimes pay for, black votes on election day, they doled out a variety of modest rewards to black ward leaders and some of their followers. Historian David A. Gerber has pointed out that, in northern cities in this period, black politicians were usually subordinate to the larger white political machines. This was also true in Springfield. Unable to influence politics for the benefit of the race as a whole, black politicians tended to settle for limited rewards: appointments to lower-status, lower-paying city jobs and protection for saloons and less legitimate enterprises.[91] One white newspaper alleged, for example, that "the black vote of the first ward has been more catered to and cuddled than the decent citizenship of the entire remaining portion of the city," and accused black Levee saloons of enjoying "privileges that were denied to the white saloons."[92] White politicians also rewarded black political workers with appointments to city positions, many of them lowly: janitor, cook, or turnkey in the city jail, or city dogcatcher. On the other hand, by 1907 blacks received a relatively generous share of jobs on Springfield's police force. In that year there were forty-one patrolmen and detectives in the city and four of them were black—nearly 10 percent of the city's police. In addition, the city fire department had one all-black engine company, which was staffed by six black appointees.[93]

While influential Springfield whites viewed blacks' misbehavior—disorderliness, involvement in "machine" politics, and vote selling—as symptomatic of larger civic illnesses visible downtown, they also implied that any substantial black influence in politics was, in and of itself, a threat to the peace of the city. Lawlessness bred lawlessness, they said again and again, but black political success spelled further trouble because some whites (they never specified whom) would take it as an intolerable affront. The press blamed the Democrats, Republicans, and the city administration alike, not only for corruption, but for conferring jobs and recognition upon a despised segment of the community. Giving blacks access to power, prestige, and upward mobility, however modest, was tantamount to social leveling, and would anger whites. "The politicians who have truckled for their votes have told the Negroes again and again that they are the white man's equal, and have given them places on the police force and other city jobs," one writer noted. The result, he said, was that blacks manifested an "arrogant bearing" and "pretensions," which "created a strong feeling against them among our [white] citizens."[94]

Setting aside for the moment the question of what kinds of whites felt compelled to punish black "arrogance" (political or otherwise) with violence, and reading between the lines of post-riot commentary on black political behavior, one gets the clear impression that the problem was not simply that blacks were active in city politics. After all, blacks had been a political factor since the late nineteenth century. Further, vote selling and doling out rewards to the black party faithful were well-established practices by 1908. Though the evidence is admittedly impressionistic, it seems that part of the problem was that black political participation downtown (and the rewards it brought to some) became more visible over time, as did the presence of black businesses and residences there. And it was more than a just matter of blacks being more in evidence at downtown polling places. There were other new kinds of political visibility. First, black political captains for both parties maintained headquarters in Levee saloons. Second, by 1908 blacks occupied an unprecedented number of the most highly visible patronage jobs as policemen and firemen, working either in or near the downtown district. After the riot, one white writer tried to sum up the social consequences of black Springfielders' political success. "The Negro of Springfield is not the Negro of the South," he explained. "He is usually ready to open up an argument that he is just as good as a white man. . . . A Jap would create just as much hatred and opposition if he should take such an aggressive attitude."[95]

Aside from the increased visibility of blacks in downtown Springfield, there is one final factor that may have contributed to whites'
sense that blacks were becoming "aggressive" or "arrogant": black
resistance to discrimination in the city. Since this resistance involved
very few blacks, it is an open question as to whether or not whites
ever paid it any attention, especially since it generally went unremarked in the city's white newspapers. On the other hand, it was yet
another sign that some Springfield blacks were in fact ready to open
an argument that they were "as good as a white man." Much of the
leadership in combatting discrimination came from the black Republican newspaper, the *Forum*. In 1907 its editor, E. L. Rogers,
launched a sustained attack against white businessmen who denied
service to black customers. He announced "a crusade against those
merchants who are averse to [doing business] i.e., so far as the Negro is concerned," and said that the paper would "call the attention
of our people" to offending businesses "in strong and emphatic language." Rogers proceeded to print the names and locations of businesses that discouraged black trade, including restaurants, saloons,
amusement parks, and dry goods stores. These businesses received
bitter condemnation in the *Forum*, which urged the public to boycott
them until they mended their ways. The editor also asked his black
readers to take copies of the *Forum* to the accused white businessmen and "ask them as to the veracity of this charge." At the same
time, he guaranteed that the white businesses that advertised in the
Forum welcomed black customers.

When a white restaurant refused to serve Rogers one morning in
the winter of 1907, he castigated the owner in the next issue. He
had entered Logan's Cafe on Monroe Street for a quick sandwich
and coffee and was told he would have to pay a much higher price
for the food than that listed on the menu. Such overcharging was
one popular tactic whites used to discourage black customers. Rogers pointed out that Logan had gotten his start in business on Washington Street catering to black patrons. Now that he was successful,
the editor said, "he had the gall and temerity to refuse people who
helped him when he was barely able to pay for the [restaurant] license." Advising blacks to shun Logan's place, the editor stated "we
are not going to allow such backwoods unlettered fellows to dominate over us unprotested."[96] It may be only a coincidence, but Logan turned up on the streets as a rioter the next year.[97]

In addition, a few local blacks sued white businessmen who discriminated against them, even though the fines eventually levied
against the offenders often were as low as the law allowed. After a

white attendant at the White City amusement park refused to sell tickets to rides to a black customer, for example, the outraged patron immediately took the owner to court. To the delight of the *Forum*, the offended black won his case. The man "only gets $25," said Rogers, "but the principle is the same. Many other places may be sued if they don't change their tactics." After a similar lawsuit the *Forum* editor applauded, "Learn these 2 by 4 upstarts a lesson."[98]

Riot as Reform

Springfield's race riot was one of the more dramatic symptoms of the vulnerability and insecurity of northern blacks in late nineteenth- and early twentieth-century cities. In Springfield's case, the generation of anti-black hostility had little to do with large-scale social strain. Its troubles were not due to a sudden, large increase in the number of its black residents. The available evidence indicates an absence of the kind of heated competition for employment and housing, or the tensions caused by labor strife, that characterized some northern cities during the next decade. Furthermore, local patterns in housing, employment, and politics remained largely stable from the 1890s to the eve of the riot. Ecological changes in downtown Springfield in black residential, business, and political activity, however, did represent a possible new source of interracial conflict, even though the actual number of blacks involved was small. Influential white observers after the riot suggested that the visibility of blacks' political activity and success downtown was particularly troublesome, for it made them "pretentious" and "arrogant," attitudes that would, in turn, outrage some whites.

Most contemporary assessments of the race riot come from Springfield's more influential and wealthy citizens: the press, ministers, reformers, politicians, and businessmen. Their remarks reveal a great deal about what the city's better-off whites thought about the riot, its participants, and local race relations, but very little about the attitudes of the rioters themselves. Before we turn to an analysis of riot participants, however, two general observations about influential whites' responses to the violence are in order. First, regardless of whether or not they had a stake in any particular reform, by emphasizing civic weakness rather than anti-black hostility as the cause of the riot, they avoided and distorted the real meaning of the origins and nature of the outbreak. By blaming drink, vice, municipal corruption, and political chicanery for the riot, better-off Springfield whites in effect denied that their city had a problem with race relations. Likewise, their insistence (after the second night of riot-ing) that the riot was solely the work of criminals or riffraff further revealed their inability or unwillingness to confront the existence of deep and bitter anti-black hostility in the city. Such arguments in some degree represented civic face-saving and, finally, enabled re-spectable whites to distance themselves from responsibility for the violence and to deny or mask their own anti-black sentiments.

Second, although influential whites generally seemed to lack any pressing or acute sense of grievance against blacks in the city and did not themselves take an active part in the violence, their beliefs and opinions nonetheless had important implications for the way conflict in their community was handled. A rough but apt term for their view of the riot is "reformist." For example, better-off whites' tendency to see the black presence downtown as one symptom of serious civic disease led them to legitimate the violence in its early stages. Both the press response after the first night of rioting and William English Walling's trenchant observations of public opinion suggest that many of the wealthier spectators and bystanders, who by their sheer numbers and vocal support emboldened the rioters, might have thought they were witnessing the purge of some great social evil from the city. The evidence suggests strongly that initially they viewed the riot as a regrettable but effective "reform" measure: the removal of "bad Negroes" and their "dives" might produce a safer, purer, more moral Springfield. Admittedly, one cannot pre-cisely measure the impact of this initially indulgent attitude toward the violence, but it might well have contributed to the continuation of rioting in the capital. At any rate, insofar as influential whites defined the violence as "reform," they both excused and lent legiti-macy to the rioters' actions.

By the second night of rioting, of course, it became clear that moral reform was not a major item on the rioters' agenda. As the press and other influential whites perceived this, they abruptly re-defined the situation. The rioters had now become part of the prob-lem of social control downtown, not the solution that had been hoped for earlier. Influential whites might accommodate forced re-moval of supposed black lowlifes in the name of "reform," but not an urban "pogrom." Indeed, by initially imagining that rioters shared their views of the city and its problems, better-off whites re-vealed again, in part, their lack of understanding of the real sources of anti-black hatred in Springfield. Thus, continued rioting made no sense to them. Finding the rioters bent on something other than reform—and faced with a clear challenge to their own authority—

the city's white elite had no choice but to rewrite the script. Overnight the rioters themselves became the object of "reform," the so-called urban pagans—criminals, drunks, and hoodlums.

NOTES

1. On Springfield's settlement and early years, see Paul M. Angle, *"Here I Have Lived": A History of Lincoln's Springfield, 1821–1865* (Springfield, Ill.: The Abraham Lincoln Association, 1935); *History of Sangamon County, Illinois* (Chicago: Inter-State Publishing Company, 1881); Joseph Wallace, *Past and Present of the City of Springfield and Sangamon County, Illinois,* vol. 1 (Chicago: S. J. Clarke Publishing Co., 1904).

2. Cullom Davis and James Krohe, Jr., "Springfield: An Evolving Capital," in Daniel Milo Johnson and Rebecca Monroe Veach, eds., *The Middle-Size Cities of Illinois: Their People, Politics, and Quality of Life* (Springfield, Ill.: Sangamon State University, 1980), 193–94; *History of Sangamon County, Illinois,* 198. For a detailed discussion of the sources of migration into Illinois in the nineteenth century, see Daniel J. Elazar, *Cities of the Prairie: The Metropolitan Frontier and American Politics* (New York: Basic Books, Inc., 1970), 155–205.

3. U. S. Bureau of the Census, *Thirteenth Census of the United States Taken in the Year 1910: Mines and Quarries, 1909* (Washington, D.C.: Government Printing Office, 1913). See also Illinois Bureau of Labor Statistics, *Twenty-First Annual Coal Report, 1902* (Springfield, Ill.: 1903), 1–5; Harry Mitchell Dixon, "The Illinois Coal Mining Industry," (Ph.D. diss., University of Illinois, Urbana, 1951).

4. James Krohe, Jr., *Midnight at Noon: A History of Coal Mining in Sangamon County* (Springfield, Ill.: Sangamon County Historical Society, 1975), 2–5; Frank R. Fisher, "Coal Mining and Production," in Newton Bateman and Paul Selby, eds., *Historical Encyclopedia of Illinois and History of Sangamon County,* vol. 2 (Chicago: Munsell Publishing Company, 1912), 823–25; A. R. Crook, "Mineral Resources," in Bateman and Selby, eds., *Historical Encyclopedia of Illinois,* vol. 2, 820.

5. Quote from Krohe, *Midnight at Noon,* 23. See also Illinois Bureau of Labor Statistics, *Twenty-Seventh Annual Coal Report, 1908* (Springfield, Ill.: 1909), 138, 299; Fisher, "Coal Mining and Production," 824–25; Lee Franklin Hanmer, *Recreation in Springfield, Illinois* (New York: The Russell Sage Foundation, 1914), 3; U.S. Bureau of the Census, *Thirteenth Census, 1910, Population* (Washington, D.C.: Government Printing Office, 1913–14), 4:274–75. For production statistics and the decline of coal mining in Sangamon County, see U. S. Bureau of the Census, *Mines and Quarries, 1909,* 22–27, 74; Krohe, *Midnight at Noon,* 41; Illinois Bureau of Labor Statistics, *Twenty-Seventh Annual Coal Report, 1908,* 70–71; *Nineteenth Annual Coal Report, 1900* (Springfield, Ill.: 1901), 3.

6. J. C. Power, *History of Springfield, Illinois: Its Attractions as a Home and Advantages for Business, Manufacturing, Etc.* (Springfield, Ill.: Illinois State

Journal Print, 1871), 28–37. On the history of Springfield's railroads, see also J. H. Lord, "Railroads," in Batemen and Selby, *Historical Encyclopedia of Illinois*, vol. 2, 770–78; Angle, *"Here I Have Lived,"* 100, 144–53, 162–67; John H. Keiser, *Building for the Centuries: Illinois, 1865 to 1898* (Urbana: University of Illinois Press, 1977), 151–79; Clarence Woodrow Sorensen, "The Internal Structure of the Springfield, Illinois Urbanized Area" (Ph.D. diss., University of Chicago, 1951), 43–44. On the removal of the capital to Springfield, see Angle, *"Here I Have Lived,"* 55–58, 83–84; Davis and Krohe, "Springfield," 192–93; Power, *History of Springfield*, 15–21; Wallace, *Past and Present*, 10–15.

7. Louise C. Odencrantz and Zenas L. Potter, *Industrial Conditions in Springfield, Illinois* (New York: The Russell Sage Foundation, 1916), 1–3; *Thirteenth Census, 1910*, 4:274–79. *Industrial Conditions in Springfield, Illinois* was one of many volumes produced by an exhaustive investigation of Springfield that covered areas ranging from public health and recreation to housing and government. A condensed version of the various reports may be found in Shelby M. Harrison, *Social Conditions in an American City: A Summary of the Findings of the Springfield Survey* (New York: The Russell Sage Foundation, 1920).

8. Odencrantz and Potter, *Industrial Conditions*, 3; Ernest L. Bogart and John M. Mathews, *The Centennial History of Illinois: The Modern Commonwealth, 1893–1918* (Chicago: A. C. McClurg & Co., 1922), 103.

9. Odencrantz and Potter, *Industrial Conditions*, 3–4; *History of Sangamon County, Illinois*, 574; Bateman and Selby, *Historical Encyclopedia of Illinois*, 2:783.

10. Bureau of the Census, *Thirteenth Census, 1910*, 4:274–79; Odencrantz and Potter, *Industrial Conditions*, 2–3.

11. *ISJ*, 16 August 1908.

12. The 1910 census listed 2,489 coal mine operatives and 5,670 males working in manufacturing and mechanical industries. *Thirteenth Census, 1910*, 4:275.

13. Art Gramlich Memoir, SSUO.

14. *SN*, 20 August 1908.

15. Illinois Bureau of Labor Statistics, *Twenty-Ninth Annual Coal Report, 1910* (Springfield, Ill.: 1911), 6–7; *Thirteenth Census, 1910*, 4:452. A total of 58,738 coal mine operatives were listed in 1910.

16. CD, 1907.

17. James Crouthemal, "The Springfield Race Riot of 1908," *Journal of Negro History* 45 (July 1960): 165; James Krohe, Jr., *Summer of Rage: The Springfield Race Riot of 1908* (Springfield, Ill.: Sangamon County Historical Society, 1973), 4; Augustus W. Low, ed., *Encyclopedia of Black America* (New York: McGraw Hill Book Company, 1981), 232; John H. Keiser, "Black Strikebreakers and Racism in Illinois, 1865–1900," *Journal of the Illinois State Historical Society* 65 (Autumn 1972): 326.

18. On the complexity of race relations in coal mining and the UMW, see Herbert G. Gutman, "The Negro and the United Mine Workers of Amer-

ica," in Julius Jacobson, ed., *The Negro and the American Labor Movement* (Garden City, N.Y.: Doubleday & Company, 1968), 49–127; Stephen Brier, "The Career of Richard L. Davis Reconsidered: Unpublished Correspondence from the *National Labor Tribune*," *Labor History* 21 (Summer 1980): 420–29; Ronald L. Lewis, *Black Coal Miners in America: Race, Class, and Community Conflict, 1780–1980* (Lexington: University Press of Kentucky, 1987), 39–57, 79–118.

19. *ISJ*, 11 October 1898. During the 1898 Illinois coal mine labor troubles, blacks were not the only group used as strikebreakers. One Virden mine operator tried "to cause division in the ranks" of strikers by announcing that, if they attacked the stockade protecting the mine, "the Polocks and other foreign miners will be put in front" of the defending force (*ISJ*, 9 October 1898). See also Lewis, *Black Coal Miners in America*, 83–84, 94–97, and Victor Hicken, "The Virden and Pana Mine Wars of 1898," *Journal of the Illinois State Historical Society* 52 (Summer 1959): 263–78, for accounts of the strikes and strikebreaking at Pana and Virden. Lewis and Hicken do not address the role of black UMW members in these conflicts. Neither does Lewis provide any substantial discussion of race relations among black and white union miners in the period from roughly 1900 to the early 1920s.

20. *SR*, 18 August 1908. Scarcely a week before the Springfield riot broke out, a combined force of black and white Alabama miners attacked a train carrying nonunion strikebreakers. See *ISJ*, 17 August 1908; Lewis, *Black Coal Miners in America*, 51–57; Darold T. Barnum, *The Negro in the Bituminous Coal Mining Industry*, The Racial Policies of American Industry, Report No. 14 (Philadelphia: University of Pennsylvania Press, 1970), 20.

21. *SN*, 17 August 1908.

22. *ISJ*, 19–20 August 1908.

23. Krohe, *Summer of Rage*, 4; Bruce Alexander Campbell, *200 Years: An Illustrated Bicentennial History of Sangamon County* (Springfield, Ill.: Phillips Brothers, Inc., 1976), 199–200.

24. *ISJ*, 13 October 1898, 15 October 1898.

25. W. T. Casey, "History of the Colored People in Sangamon County," in *Directory of Sangamon County's Colored Citizens* (Springfield, Ill.: Springfield Directory Co., 1926); Bateman and Selby, *Historical Encyclopedia of Illinois*, 1:482–83. See also Elazar, *Cities of the Prairie*, 181–83; Angle, *"Here I Have Lived,"* 29.

26. Casey, "History of the Colored People in Sangamon County"; *History of Sangamon County, Illinois*, 736–37; Elazar, *Cities of the Prairie*, 181–84.

27. *SN*, 20 August 1908.

28. Margaret Ferguson Memoir, SSUO.

29. Odencrantz and Potter, *Industrial Conditions*, 68–104.

30. See, for example, Sterling D. Spero and Abram L. Harris, *The Black Worker: The Negro and the Labor Movement* (New York: Columbia University Press, 1931); W. E. B. Du Bois, *The Philadelphia Negro: A Social Study* (Philadelphia, 1899), 97–146; Alexander Saxton, "Race and the House of Labor,"

in Gary B. Nash and Richard Weiss, eds., *The Great Fear: Race in the Mind of America* (New York: Holt, Rinehart and Winston, Inc., 1970), 100, 102–7, 117–20; Walter Licht, *Working for the Railroad: The Organization of Work in the Nineteenth Century* (Princeton: Princeton University Press, 1983), 223–24; Philip W. Jeffress, *The Negro in the Urban Transit Industry*, The Racial Policies of American Industry, Report No. 18 (Philadelphia: University of Philadelphia Press, 1970), 21–25; Mark Karson and Ronald Radosh, "The American Federation of Labor and the Negro Worker, 1894–1949," in Julius Jacobson, ed., *The Negro and the American Labor Movement*, 155–87; William H. Harris, *The Harder We Run: Black Workers since the Civil War* (New York: Oxford University Press, 1982), 29–50.

31. *History of Sangamon County, Illinois*, 736–44.

32. Ibid., 736–44; CD, 1907.

33. Elizabeth Hafkin Pleck, *Black Migration and Poverty: Boston, 1865–1900* (New York: Academic Press, 1979), 92–105, 109–10. See also Adelaide Cromwell Hill, "The Negro Upper Class in Boston: Its Development and Present Social Structure" (Ph.D. diss., Radcliffe College, 1952).

34. Margaret Ferguson Memoir.

35. Ibid.

36. Edith Carpenter Memoir, SSUO.

37. On blacks and class divisions see, for example, Du Bois, *The Philadelphia Negro*, 309–21; Kenneth L. Kusmer, *A Ghetto Takes Shape: Black Cleveland, 1870–1930* (Urbana: University of Illinois Press, 1976), 91–112; Pleck, *Black Migration and Poverty*, 92–105; David M. Katzman, *Before the Ghetto: Black Detroit in the Nineteenth Century* (Urbana: University of Illinois Press, 1973), 135–74; Olivier Zunz, *The Changing Face of Inequality: Urbanization, Industrial Development, and Immigrants in Detroit, 1880–1920* (Chicago: University of Chicago Press, 1982), 378–80, 393–98.

38. Alice Hopkins Memoir, SSUO.

39. *History of Sangamon County, Illinois*, 736–44; CD, 1907; manuscript schedules of the population census for Springfield, Illinois, 1900 and 1910; *Directory of Sangamon County's Colored Citizens*. Only extensive and time-consuming genealogical tracing—beyond the scope of this work—would reveal the true extent of intermarriage among Springfield's black elite over time.

40. *Springfield Duplex City Directory, 1892–1893* (Chicago: United States Central Publishing Co., 1893); U. S. Bureau of the Census, *Thirteenth Census, 1910*, 2:516. An examination of the 1893 city directory street section revealed that six of the seven black enclaves that existed in 1908 were present sixteen years earlier.

41. By 1980 blacks were even more scattered over the city than earlier in the century, but increasing black settlement on the east side and white flight from the area over the years eventually melded the Badlands and Sixth Ward settlements into one large black neighborhood. See *The Eastside Social Justice Reporter*, Spring 1983. Seventy-five percent of the city's black population lived in this large east-side area in 1980; the remainder were scattered

over the rest of the city: "for the first time in Springfield's history, blacks were found living in all 31 of the city's census tracts."

42. John Ihlder, *Housing in Springfield, Illinois* (New York: Russell Sage Foundation, 1914), 1–3, 8–10.

43. For examples of the practice of charging blacks high rents for inferior housing, see Du Bois, *The Philadelphia Negro*, 295–96; Kusmer, *A Ghetto Takes Shape*, 46–48, 166; Gilbert Osofsky, *Harlem: The Making of a Ghetto, Negro New York, 1890–1930* (New York: Harper & Row, 1966), 136–41; Robert B. Grant, *The Black Man Comes to The City: A Documentary Account from the Great Migration to the Great Depression, 1915–1930* (Chicago: Nelson-Hall Company, 1972), 50–58; Allen H. Spear, *Black Chicago: The Making of a Negro Ghetto, 1890–1920* (Chicago: University of Chicago Press, 1967), 23–24; Zunz, *The Changing Face of Inequality*, 375–78, 392–93.

44. Franz Schneider, Jr., *Public Health in Springfield, Illinois* (New York: The Russell Sage Foundation, 1915).

45. Sorensen, "The Internal Structure of the Springfield, Illinois Urbanized Area," 151.

46. Ibid., 81–82, 138–50.

47. Manuscript schedules of the population census for Springfield, Illinois, 1910.

48. Reverend Henry Mann Memoir, SSUO.

49. Alice Hopkins Memoir.

50. Margaret Ferguson Memoir, William Hubbard Memoir, SSUO; Edith Carpenter Memoir.

51. *People's Press*, Spring 1978, Vertical File, SVC.

52. Ihlder, *Housing in Springfield, Illinois*, 8–16.

53. *Springfield Duplex City Directory, 1892–1893*; CD, 1907. In 1892 only 2 of a total 108 saloons listed were operated by blacks; in 1907 blacks ran 11 of a total 226 saloons in Springfield.

54. *Forum*, 26 January 1907.

55. "Atlanta Outdone," *The Independent* 65 (20 August 1908): 442–43.

56. Elise Morrow, "The Cities of America: Springfield, Illinois," *Saturday Evening Post* 220 (27 September 1947).

57. *ISJ*, 27 October 1898, 2 November 1898. Republicans charged that Democrats had padded voter registration lists with illegal voters, among them so-called "tombstone voters" (names taken from cemeteries). A second accusation involved the theft of a Republican registration list by Democratic party workers at a polling place in November. The light-fingered Democratic ward heelers landed in jail.

58. *ISJ*, 31 October 1898. The Republicans themselves were not averse to passing out such envelopes to cooperative voters.

59. *ISR*, 25–26 October 1898.

60. Perry R. Duis, *The Saloon: Public Drinking in Chicago and Boston, 1880–1920* (Urbana: University of Illinois Press, 1983), 141.

61. *SN*, 22 August 1908.

62. *ISJ*, 29 August 1908. Shortly before the riot, the chief of police was caught dunning city saloonkeepers to help defray the costs of the upcoming

Republican campaign. A brief flurry of outrage in the press followed, but in the end the police chief escaped the incident unscathed. See *ISR*, 2 August 1908.

63. *ISJ*, 5 April 1908; Bateman and Selby, *Historical Encyclopedia of Illinois*, 1:339–40. See also Duis, *The Saloon*, 115, for the importance of saloon license revenue to city governments. Duis notes that by 1906 this revenue had come to comprise nearly a quarter of Chicago's city income. He concluded, "Little wonder that some barmen thought they owned city hall."

64. *ISJ*, 5 April 1908. According to the Russell Sage survey conducted several years later, Springfield's police force was smaller than most cities its size. Also, pay for police work in the capital was too low to discourage patrolmen from entering "into alliance with law-breaking elements." Zenas L. Potter, *The Correctional System of Springfield, Illinois* (New York: Russell Sage Foundation, 1915), 145–59.

65. *ISJ*, 5 April 1908.

66. Ibid., 8 April 1908. An act of the legislature in 1839 gave counties, towns, and cities in Illinois the right to outlaw liquor within their boundaries by popular vote. The Springfield Local Option League was composed of a small band of citizens who attempted to convince the city to vote itself dry in a number of elections. For background on the local option movement in Illinois, see Duis, *The Saloon*, 12; Bogart and Mathews, *The Modern Commonwealth*, 385–87.

67. Potter, *The Correctional System of Springfield*, 1–2.

68. Davis and Krohe, "Springfield: An Evolving Capital," 201–10; D. O. Decker and Shelby M. Harrison, *City and County Administration in Springfield, Illinois* (New York: The Russell Sage Foundation, 1917), 9–10. Information on the history and structure of Sangamon County's government can be found in Works Progress Administration, *Inventory of the County Archives of Illinois, No. 83, Sangamon County* (Chicago: The Historical Records Survey, 1939), 4–35. See also Illinois General Assembly, Senate Vice Committee, *Report of the Senate Vice Committee, Created under the Authority of the Forty-Ninth General Assembly* (Chicago: State Printers, 1916).

69. Morrow, "Springfield, Illinois." See also Davis and Krohe, "Springfield: An Evolving Capital," 211; Jerry Wallace, "Treating Symptoms or Dealing with Principles?" in James Krohe, Jr., ed., *A Springfield Reader: Historical Views of the Illinois Capital, 1818–1976* (Springfield, Ill.: Sangamon County Historical Society, 1976), 159–64.

70. Potter, *The Correctional System of Springfield*, 164.

71. Ibid., 162–63; *SR*, 22 August 1908.

72. William Lloyd Clark, *Hell at Midnight in Springfield; Or a Burning History of the Sin and Shame of the Capital City of Illinois*, 4th ed. (Milan, Ill.: 1914), 18; *ISJ*, 25 February 1913.

73. For an overview of Illinois politics in the Progressive era, see Donald F. Tingley, *The Structuring of a State: The History of Illinois, 1899–1928* (Urbana: University of Illinois Press, 1980), 150–95.

74. *Report of the Senate Vice Committee*, 42, 333–35. Some of the cities mentioned were East St. Louis, Aurora, Bloomington, Champaign, Danville, El-

gin, Freeport, Kankakee, Ottawa, Pekin, and Jacksonville.

75. *ISJ*, 4 September 1908.

76. *Chicago Record-Herald*, 16 August 1908.

77. *ISJ*, 19 August 1908.

78. Clark, *Hell at Midnight*, 61.

79. *SR*, 30 August 1908.

80. "The So-called Race Riot at Springfield, Illinois," *Charities and the Commons* 50 (19 September 1908): 709.

81. *ISR*, 17 August 1908; *SR*, 22 August 1908.

82. On factionalism in Illinois politics in this period, see Tingley, *The Structuring of a State*, 150–95.

83. Spear, *Black Chicago*, 121–22; Du Bois, *The Philadelphia Negro*, 372–84; *Chicago Record-Herald*, 9 August 1908.

84. *Forum*, 18 July 1908; CD, 1902.

85. *Forum*, 18 July 1908.

86. "The So-called Race Riot at Springfield, Illinois," 709.

87. *ISJ*, 27 October 1898, 17 November 1898; John Peter Altgeld, *Live Questions* (Chicago: George S. Bowen & Son, 1899), 713–15. In Springfield during the fall of 1896, Altgeld complained that the registration "was so phenomenally large as to arouse suspicions that frauds were attempted." On election day he reported that 182 unregistered men had voted illegally in the First Ward. "They were mostly negroes, many of them simply gave their name as 'Jones' and they have since nearly all disappeared."

88. *Forum*, 15 August 1908.

89. There is no way to tell how successful the Democrats were in courting Springfield's black vote; however, they did reward the black party faithful with jobs (*Forum*, 9 March 1907). Edith Carpenter remembered that her father went over to the Democrats, even though most blacks the family knew voted Republican. Her father worked for the election of a white Democratic candidate. Later, along with three other black Democratic party workers, he received a job as city policeman. Edith Carpenter Memoir.

90. *SN*, 17 August 1908.

91. David A. Gerber, "A Politics of Limited Options: Northern Black Politics and the Problem of Change and Continuity in Race Relations Historiography," *Journal of Social History* 14 (Winter 1980): 235–55. See also Roger Lane, *The Roots of Violence in Black Philadelphia, 1860–1900* (Cambridge, Mass.: Harvard University Press, 1986), 56–81.

92. *SN*, 17 August 1908, 22 August 1908.

93. CD, 1907.

94. "The So-called Race Riot," 711.

95. Ibid.

96. *Forum*, 4 May 1907, 1 June 1907, 4 January 1908, 9 May 1908.

97. CD, 1907; *ISR*, 16 August 1908; *ISJ*, 18 August 1908.

98. *Forum*, 11 May 1907, 13 March 1908.

CHAPTER 3

The Rioters

THE engine crew on the "north local" of the Chicago, Peoria and St. Louis Railroad got word of the rioting in Springfield early in the evening of Friday, 14 August, just after they pulled into the station at Petersburg, a small town about twenty miles north of the Illinois capital. A black migrant worker who had been earning his passage south by loading freight, when he heard the news, gathered his belongings and abandoned the train. The engine crew's white fireman (stoker), William Lee, had the better part of a twelve-hour workday behind him, but, tired as he was, he was eager to see what all the excitement was about downtown when he got home to Springfield.

It was growing dark by the time the north local arrived at the capital. Lee hastily changed from his workclothes into a light-colored summer suit and a brand new Stetson hat. Walking west a short distance, he soon came upon the noisy throng in front of Loper's restaurant on North Fifth Street. Lee had missed the earlier confrontation at the county jail, but acquaintances in the crowd surely told him the story. The fireman must have pushed and shoved his way to the front ranks, for his prized new hat was knocked off and trampled. Most likely he heard Kate Howard challenge the rioters to storm the restaurant. Very quickly Lee changed from a passive spectator into an active rioter. When interviewed many years later for a local oral history project, Lee was in his eighties, but he recalled the scene at Loper's well: "Of course, I seen a lot that went on. I see old Barney Lang, one of the dry goods merchants, or clothing merchants out on the street picking bricks out of the street and throwing 'em through Loper's restaurant. And, of course, I went down into Loper's and between I and another guy I was raised with and went to school with . . . he drove a laundry wagon; I run into him at Loper's. And [he] and I went down and knocked the cash register over and got the change out of it."

William Lee stayed with the mob long into the evening. After the rioters finished wrecking Loper's place, Lee joined the march north and east to the Levee and witnessed the destruction of the black business district. He arrived at the corner of Eighth and Washington Streets just in time for the gunfight between the rioters and black snipers at "Dandy Jim" Smith's saloon. The unarmed fireman thought it safer to watch the battle from a distance: "I was alone and I had on a light suit of clothes and I was a good target for anybody, being tall. And up above the building [the saloon] it had an advertisement brick wall built up above the building. Well, they were in there behind there, the colored was, with these old Springfield rifles. Well, I was standing across on the west side of Washington Street with my hand up on a telegraph pole, and zing! zing! and the slivers just flew above my fingers, and I left." Lee did not mention whether or not he took part in the looting on East Washington Street.

As the evening wore on, Lee drifted from the business district north and east into the Badlands, where he joined about ten other men in an attack on a black residence. The rioters pelted the house with bricks and stones: "We knocked all of the window light out of that house and everything else," he recalled. Lee neglected to explain what "everything else" meant, nor did he elaborate further on his adventures in the Badlands. Sometime early Saturday morning he made his way back home to the room he rented from a family in the north end of town.[1]

William Lee's interview is the only surviving first-hand voluntary account of a rioter's participation in that Friday night's violence. A few rioters—under duress at police stations or during trials—offered short descriptions, which were printed in the city newspapers, but their stories were fragmented and distorted. Unfortunately, Lee had nothing to say about why he participated in the riot. He seemed to view both anti-black hostility and violence as somehow natural, as something to be taken for granted, and which therefore needed no explanation. His account is useful, though, for it illustrates the diverse roles played by many of the rioters. Lee's shift from bystander to looter to vandal shows the varieties of behavior characteristic of the bulk of Friday's mob.

However united the rioters may have been in their anti-black sentiment, they did not all behave in the same fashion. At times during
the rioting, several distinct mobs acted simultaneously, and each
crowd often had a marked division of labor. Arrested after boasting
too loudly of his part in the attack on the Badlands, teenager Roy
Young confessed to the police that he had spent most of the evening
pouring oil and setting fire to black residences. At the same time,
Young managed to collect "sox, suspenders, underwear, shoes, coats,
trousers," and other items. Many rioters who were arrested—including some of the few women who were active in the crowds Friday
evening—followed in the wake of the violence, systematically looting
Levee shops and Badlands homes. William "Fingers" Lotherington,
who had "an [un]enviable reputation as a thief" in the vice district,
was one such scavenger. City police arrested him and Madge Clark,
a "keeper of a resort," when they discovered stolen goods at Clark's
brothel at Ninth and Mason Streets. Apparently the two had pilfered shops along East Washington Street, making off with armfuls
of women's clothing. The police also discovered that Lotherington, a
sometime coal miner, had secreted a thirty-five-pound miner's drill
he had stolen, still in its original wrappings, on the roof of Clark's
house.[2] Finally, some lent important moral and vocal support to the
more violent rioters, who beat and lynched blacks, even though they
were themselves reluctant to lay hands on their victims. While they
approved of the violence and were perhaps willing to take part in
theft and vandalism, some must have felt as the fireman William
Lee did: "You know, there's guys that don't give a damn what they
do or who they do it to. That stuff [lynching] didn't suit me; I
couldn't have knocked a guy in the head or hung him or anything."[3]

The composition and size of the crowd changed over time during
the rioting Friday evening. It was largest at the county jail and at
Loper's restaurant, where it reached its maximum size—probably
around five thousand people—then dwindled in numbers as the
evening wore on and as active rioting moved through the Levee and
the Badlands. One middle-class observer who watched the rioters
that night later said that "the personnel of the mob changed mate-
rially in its course from the time it left the jail until the troops dispersed it" early Saturday morning. The crowd at the jail early in the
evening, he said, was made up of serious, determined men, but that
at Loper's consisted of "very young men, lawless and bent on any
kind of mischief."[4] This judgment was overly harsh. Newspaper accounts during and immediately after the weekend's violence reported that the crowd at Loper's was extremely varied and included

more than lawless young men. Some boys and adolescents did participate in vandalizing the restaurant, but many of the determined older men who had earlier menaced the jail were present, too.

Early Friday night the crowd contained an ample cross-section of the city's white community. A minister who mingled with the throng at Loper's restaurant reported that "it seemed to me a rollicking, jovial, joking crowd, more like a carnival crowd than anything else."[5] Murray Hanes, a young man at the time of the riot, returned from a day of fishing in time to join the crowd at Loper's. Unlike William Lee, the railroad fireman, Hanes came from one of Springfield's elite families. His father was a successful architect whose office was in the same building where Abraham Lincoln had had his law firm. The elder Hanes had married the daughter of a prominent local judge, George W. Murray. Murray Hanes later took up his father's profession as an architect. Hanes's observations support those made by William English Walling and others that many from the business and professional classes watched the early stages of the riot.

As was the case with William Lee, Hanes saw a number of friends and acquaintances at Loper's restaurant. "The crowd," he said, "contained many whom I knew, many whom I knew well." Murray Hanes confessed that he was swept up in the excitement of the attack on Loper's place and reflected later: "What is it in youth that makes destruction an exhilaration! I cannot deny that I felt the exhilaration. The urge to join one's friends, the surge of the crowd, in an imagined righteousness growing by the minute into a monstrous thing. Long buried resentments mount into a fevered excitement, and there comes a thrill and an indignant justification for the digging of a brick from the pavement and throwing it into a plate glass window. I have always known that I felt the fever."[6] Hanes's fever quickly subsided when he discovered his grandfather, county judge George W. Murray, standing just behind him, watching him critically.

Hanes never threw a brick, and he and the judge left before the crowd moved off to the Levee for further plundering. They and most of the other solid burghers of the city went home early, leaving to others the work of arson, pillage, and murder. "By the time the troops arrived on the scene [in the Badlands]," remarked one eyewitness, "the better element had almost entirely disappeared from the ranks of the mob."[7] Newspaper accounts also claimed that most of the "better element" were absent during the hit-and-run attacks during the second night of rioting and William Donnegan's lynching. By that time, of course, better-off whites were beginning to view the rioting as senseless mayhem. The evidence on the identity of participants in the hit-and-run attacks after Friday night's rioting is scanty, but it does suggest that better-off whites had little if any part in the continued violence.

Identifying Riot Participants

We have seen that the city's newspapers changed their assessment of the typical riot participant over the course of the weekend's violence. They and other influential whites eventually concluded that the riot was solely the work of riffraff, and, as the prosecution of a handful of alleged ringleaders began, they must have felt their opinion vindicated. Although over seventy persons received indictments, the newspapers gave ever-increasing coverage to those singled out as riot leaders. Among them were Abraham Raymer, a young Russian Jew from St. Louis who had worked at different times as a waiter and peddler; the redoubtable Kate Howard, a widow and the proprieter of a cheap Levee boardinghouse, who, according to one newspaper, had "repeatedly figured in police circles" before the riot; and, finally, Ernest "Slim" Humphrey, a struggling young vegetable huckster who had recently moved to Springfield from Pawnee, a small village in Sangamon County.[8] These three indictees certainly fit the community's conception of typical riffraff or "undesirables," but were they representative of the mob?

There is reason to suspect that they and many other indictees somehow served as scapegoats to salve the conscience or quiet the anxieties of more respectable elements of the city. Spokesmen for the nation's Jewish community, for example, suspected that Springfield's authorities were trying to pin the blame for the riot on outsiders like Raymer. Though Raymer was probably guilty of at least some of the many charges against him, some Jews felt that he had been deliberately singled out for abuse because of his origins. "The local chief of police," claimed one writer, "attempted to fasten upon the Jews the responsibility for the lynching of negroes."[9] More than a grain of truth lay in such suspicions that blame for the riot was somehow being shifted. As it turns out, these three ringleaders were not typical rioters.

In order to better understand the Springfield rioters' motivation and the underlying tensions in the city that fostered the violence, it is necessary to examine the membership and composition of the mob. Who was the typical active rioter? It is possible to identify at least part of the Springfield mob's membership, for the city's newspapers published the names, and sometimes the addresses, of persons arrested for rioting and those of whites who were injured during the two-day outbreak. Names of other rioters also appeared in short news articles in the days after the riot as the police continued to make arrests. Finally, the press also eventually printed lists of those facing indictments, which could be checked against the records of the circuit court for completeness.[10] These two sources—newspapers and court records—yielded the names of 190 rioters.

Admittedly, it is impossible to tell how large a share of the active mob these 190 might represent, for estimates of crowd size at the height of the rioting vary. The military's estimate of five thousand early Friday evening is probably the most accurate count, and the newspapers generally agreed with this figure. Most of those in the crowds at the county jail and at Loper's restaurant that first night were probably spectators, but in fact there is no precise way to determine the proportion of active rioters. One man who witnessed some of Friday night's rioting did report: "I am positive that the mob proper numbered, at no time, more than four hundred lawless men and women. The crowd, at one time numbering ten thousand people, was composed of mere onlookers, attracted by curiosity."[11] Even so, analysis of those rioters named does enable some rough calculation of the type of person likely to be actively involved in the rioting. To compile data on the background of each rioter—age, sex, ethnicity, occupation, and residence—each riot participant was traced in Springfield city directories and in the manuscript schedules of the 1900 and 1910 United States Census. County birth and marriage records provided supplemental information on age and birthplace. These sources yielded information on 134 rioters, of whom 112 were located in both the censuses and city directories.[12]

Any analysis that deals with persons arrested and indicted for participation in crowd violence must grapple with the important question of whether or not these people are representative, or typical, members of that crowd. Leonard L. Richards, for example, in examining the composition of anti-abolition mobs in the Jacksonian era, noted that those who felt the full brunt of the criminal justice system for their part in the New York City riot of 1834 tended to be either well-known criminals or transients. Richards concluded that "there are ample grounds for believing that status and influence played their usual roles in determining whose name got on the police blotter."[13] The data on the Springfield rioters can be used to assess whether the city's law enforcement officials systematically tended to overlook the "better sort" of rioter. Accordingly, those arrested and those indicted were treated as separate categories of rioters in order to check the possibility that those who were caught but released without further punishment might differ in some important way from the less fortunate, whose cases went all the way to the circuit court.

Apart from the possible selectivity of Springfield's criminal justice system, a second factor influenced who felt the heavy hand of the law and who eluded justice: the willingness of citizens to volunteer evidence and to testify against rioters. Without enough witnesses, those arrested might never face indictment, and those indicted might escape punishment. After the riot it was clear that many white citizens were unwilling to give evidence, some for fear of reprisal, and others because they shared the rioters' anti-black hostility, though one cannot say for certain which influenced reluctant eyewitnesses the most. The smoke had scarcely cleared from the ruins of the Badlands before difficulties in gathering evidence appeared. Governor Charles Deneen sought to loosen reluctant tongues by offering a reward of $200 for the apprehension and delivery to the county sheriff of any persons involved in the weekend's lynchings.[14] No takers appeared. The city coroner also experienced frustration during inquests held to determine who had been responsible for the deaths of the four white and two black casualties of the riot. The coroner's jury had to deliver the verdict that Scott Burton, the black barber, for example, had met his death at the hands of "parties unknown," since four witnesses who had earlier agreed to testify failed to appear at the inquest. With the investigation into William Donnegan's lynching pending, the coroner decided to intensify his search for sources of testimony. He publicly offered fifteen dollars for "witnesses who would come before the jury and swear to the identity of persons who were in the mob who lynched the aged negro." One enterprising man, hearing the coroner's offer, decided to try to make some money by locating witnesses. After canvassing the city for a whole day, he gave up in disgust.[15] In the end, the coroner's juries could locate no one responsible for any of the riot deaths.

Few white eyewitnesses would talk about whom they had seen rioting. The *Chicago Tribune* mentioned the trouble that the state's attorney's office had in finding witnesses willing to aid the grand jury's investigation. "Many people who are known to have been eyewitnesses of the mob's work declare that they did not see it, or else they do not wish to testify for fear that something dreadful will happen to them."[16] Many rioters were eventually indicted, but most of the incriminating testimony came from the militia and a few extremely diligent city detectives. A handful of riot victims also testified.[17] Since most of the militia were not residents of Springfield and therefore were not as familiar with its inhabitants, their testimony was sometimes shaky. In at least one instance an indictment had to be dropped because military witnesses had trouble identifying a rioter.[18]

Given the climate of fear that persisted immediately after the riot, it is understandable that some citizens would be afraid to give evidence against rioters. City officials and employers of blacks, for example, received anonymous "black hand" letters that threatened reprisals if they did not fire their black workers. Acts of retaliation were infrequent, but the potential cost of defying the will of the rioters was clear. Joseph Burtle, a white civil engineer, was accosted on the street by an angry man who threatened to murder him and destroy his home. The threat, delivered in broad daylight, was made because the man mistook Burtle for a member of the grand jury. More than a month after the riot someone shot at Mrs. Sam Polk while she was home alone one evening, ostensibly because she had testified against one of the indicted rioters. Mrs. Polk was not injured, but this story and others like it printed in the newspapers all too clearly pointed to the dangers of being a witness. Murray Hanes, the architect's son who had gotten caught up in the excitement at Loper's restaurant, commented on the climate in the city. He recalled that he "lost a friendship for life" simply for refusing a companion's offer of silverware—souvenirs, in effect—looted from Loper's.[19]

Fear of retaliation was not the only factor impeding the effort to identify and prosecute rioters in the days and weeks following the outbreak. Once the military restored law and order, many citizens reverted to what one newspaper termed "passive sympathy" for the rioters. Influential whites argued that, since only "bad Negroes" had been attacked and driven from the city, some good might come out of the violence. Those "men who would be horrified at the thought of taking part in a lynching and who never would incite others to violence," but who viewed the results of the violence as salutary, were unlikely to be concerned about whether or not justice was done to black victims.[20] Both fear of retaliation and indifference to the plight of black riot victims helped discourage potential witnesses and, in some cases, led some witnesses who had given evidence earlier to make themselves scarce for the duration of the riot trials.[21]

The reluctance of white witnesses to testify, combined with the selective tendencies of the criminal justice system, helped ensure that those who eventually received indictments represented the poorer and less powerful elements of the mob. The rioters for whom the most damning evidence was forthcoming were people like Kate Howard and Abraham Raymer, the rootless Jewish huckster. They and other "Levee characters" indicted, of course, were also better known to city detectives. In general, the police were more familiar with the faces of those who lived in or frequented the downtown district than with those of more "respectable" rioters, who normally did not get in trouble with the law. Further, it was easier to induce witnesses to testify against outsiders and marginal people like Raymer and Howard, since these defendants not only would be less able to retaliate, but would be less likely to have a substantial—and therefore potentially dangerous—network of family and friends who might exert unpleasant social sanctions. Finally, however "passively sympathetic" many whites in the community were toward the rioters in general, fewer would feel outrage over the prosecution of obvious "undesirables."

There was, however, a third group of rioters whom law enforcement officials never scrutinized and for whom the question of availability of witnesses was irrelevant: those whites injured during the riot. It seems reasonable to assume that most of those injured were not merely innocent bystanders, partly because most of the injuries occurred during the more violent rioting in the Levee and the Badlands, and partly because those in the front ranks of the mob were in the most danger of being shot or struck by bricks. During the gun battle at "Dandy Jim's" saloon in the Levee, for example, "a sharp fire of guns and revolvers was kept up and every few minutes a small crowd of sympathizing friends would be coming from the front or the thickest part of the flight to the outskirts of the crowds carrying a man injured, bleeding and from there he was hurried to the nearest drug store or hotel where medical attention was given him."[22]

Nearly all of the riot-related injuries to whites took place during Friday night's rioting. Since many who were hurt did not got to the hospital for treatment, newspaper lists of casualties are incomplete. Many preferred to hide their wounds for fear of becoming "entangled in the grand jury meshes."[23] All but a handful of those listed as injured by the newspapers had sustained gunshot wounds, either during the rioting in the Levee or during the confrontation with the militia early Saturday morning in the Badlands. Some of the rioters hit with buckshot probably were in the forefront of the attack on Scott Burton, the black barber, for he got off at least one round before his assailants overwhelmed him.[24] Of a total of fifty-three injured rioters mentioned in the newspapers' casualty lists, all but eleven had gunshot wounds; the rest had been wounded either by flying bricks or broken window glass. In a few cases the press mentioned that an individual had been "shot in [the] leg by troops" or "shot in left foot by militia."[25] The lists show a surprising number of rioters with gunshot wounds to the lower extremities. Though newspapers often did not mention who fired the shots, the militia probably inflicted most of these foot and leg injuries Saturday morning when they fired a low volley of multi-ball cartridges to disperse the crowd. Not all the soldiers aimed low, however, for some of the rioters "shot by militia" sported wounds to the thigh or arm.[26] After William English Walling visited the wounded whites in St. John's Hospital, he concluded that most of them had been riot participants. While there Walling met the notorious Kate Howard, who proudly displayed her buckshot wounds to him. The riot's so-called "Joan of Arc" told him that "she relied confidently on her fellow citizens to keep her from punishment." This, Walling observed, "was the feeling of the half hundred whites in the hospital."[27]

It is unclear why those who were wounded during the riot—except for two who were later indicted—were not arrested or prosecuted. Nothing indicates that either the police or the military ever looked into the involvement of the injured rioters. Even though it was clear from the newspapers that several rioters had received their wounds at the hands of the militia, the authorities were unwilling or unable to prosecute. Locating witnesses was probably the largest stumbling block. Most wounded rioters had been carried off by friends to the hospital before the militia and police could apprehend them. And since the police and militia provided most of the witnesses, those rioters who had evaded contact with them, wounded or otherwise, were relatively safe from prosecution.

The newspapers, in the few instances in which they mentioned the circumstances surrounding a particular injury, could be very misleading. No one who appeared in their casualty lists was described as a rioter per se, but several were said to be bystanders who had been hit by stray bullets, the implication being that these persons were innocent. One newspaper, for example, reported that John Colwell, a white miner fatally injured during the attack on the Levee, "was merely an onlooker, suddenly stricken down" by a "bullet fired by an unidentified negro." Another newspaper told a different story: "Colwell was in the mob marching east on Washington street. After the man was shot several of the mob trampled him before his body was noticed."[28] Frank Delmore, another white miner killed during Friday night's rioting, reportedly was "struck by a stray bullet." Delmore also was supposedly a spectator, but Dr. John Salyers, the city physician who attended him at St. John's Hospital, cast doubt on this interpretation. Salyers claimed that he heard Delmore's deathbed speech. "I had the satisfaction of seeing one nigger shot," Delmore allegedly boasted, "and if I live to get out with the bunch I will see some hung."[29]

Although full information on the background of only twenty-six of the fifty-three persons listed as injured in the newspapers was available, it is still useful to treat these people as yet a third category of rioter. Unlike arrestees and indictees, the injured rioters (with the exception of two who eventually received indictments) were never processed by the criminal justice system. Insofar as bullets and bricks were more "democratic" in selecting rioters than law enforcement officials, these injured rioters may be somewhat more representative of the mob's membership than those who were singled out for arrest and prosecution.

Age and Sex

Regardless of whether a rioter was arrested, indicted, or injured, it was most likely that the person involved was a male in his mid-twenties. Only nine of the total 190 identified rioters were women, and all but one of the women were indictees. Except for Kate Howard, who faced murder charges, all the women had been arrested for crimes against property—burglary, larceny, and vandalism. Like Madge Clark, the owner of a "disorderly house," most of these women were looters caught stealing food, clothing, and household articles.[30]

All three categories of rioters were very similar in their age characteristics, and, compared to Springfield's population as a whole, were relatively young (see Appendix, Tables 3.1 and 3.2). Some of those arrested were very young. The youngest was Harold Alkire, a boy about thirteen years old, who had been in the crowd at Loper's. Alkire had helped wreck the interior of the restaurant, and the police later picked him up carrying home "a shovel and a bottle of beer."[31] Like most of the rioters under eighteen years old, Alkire was arrested but released without further punishment. Roy Young, a sixteen-year-old laborer, was not so fortunate. His loud boasting in public about his exploits the first night of the riot attracted the attention of the police. Under severe questioning the boy broke down and confessed to plundering and burning houses in the Badlands. The authorities packed Young off to a reformatory, but not for long; by 1909 he was back in town and attending school.[32] Only six rioters over the age of fifty appeared among the indictees, arrestees, and injured. One of these, a real estate and horse dealer in his early seventies, died of a gunshot wound he received while watching the attack on "Dandy Jim" Smith's saloon in the Levee.[33] It is well to keep in mind that, although a striking number of boys and young men were present in the mob, at least half of the rioters examined were twenty-five years old or older. Most of those among the older half of the rioters were forty-five or younger.

Birthplace and Ethnicity

One of the more persistent notions about Springfield's race riot is that it was somehow more a "southern" than a "northern" outbreak. Implicit in this view is the assumption that either southern-born whites played an important role in the riot or that some southern cultural predisposition to anti-black violence persisted over the years to dominate the outlook of Springfield's whites.[34] Such an interpretation first appeared in William English Walling's influential article in *The Independent* in 1908. Because he heard so many Springfield whites express the same types of racist sentiments then widespread in the South, Walling speculated that a "Southern element in the town" might have been responsible for the violence. "Many of the older citizens are from Kentucky or the southern part of Illinois," he noted darkly. He concluded, however, that it was more likely that northern whites were inspired by examples of the South's virulent racism—stories of lynchings and segregation reported in the press, for instance. Walling accused the South of infecting and corrupting a previously benign North with anti-black hostility, and, to illustrate this process of cultural contamination from the South, he cited the experience of Kate Howard, the Levee boardinghouse keeper: "Even the famous Kate Howard had received her inspiration, she told us, from the South. While travelling with her brother in Texas and Arkansas she had observed enviously that enforced separation of the races in cars and public places helped to teach the negro where he belonged. Returning home she had participated in the alarm that 'no white woman was safe,' etc., and in the demand for negro blood."[35] Springfield's riot was one sign, Walling warned, that southern demagogues like "Vardaman and Tillman will soon have transferred the race war to the North."[36]

The identification of actual riot participants helps clarify this question about the allegedly "southern" nature of Springfield's violence: Was there an important "southern element"—southern-born whites or descendants of southerners—active in the mob? Was this a "northern" riot or merely another southern lynching party writ large? Of all the contemporary newspaper and magazine discussions about who in Springfield was responsible for the rioting, only Walling's piece mentioned southerners. There may be a very simple reason for this omission: southerners had no conscpicuous or disproportionate part in Springfield's riot. Only 3 of the 115 rioters for whom information on birthplace was available had been born in the South (including Texas and the northern tier of southern states—Tennessee, Kentucky, Maryland, and Delaware). An additional 15 rioters had at least one southern-born parent; the two groups—southern-born and those with a southern parent—comprised 15.7 percent of the 115 rioters examined.[37] Important both numerically and culturally in the early nineteenth century, when many of them settled in southern Illinois and parts of central Illinois, by 1900 southern-born Springfielders had dwindled to a small fraction of the city's population. In that year census enumerators counted 1,184 white southern-born residents—4.3 percent of the total native white population. Further, some of these southerners carried north a mixed cultural heritage, for nearly one-fifth of them had at least one foreign-born parent.[38] One can make only a crude estimate of the number of southern-born whites in Springfield in 1910, since the census that year did not distinguish southern-born individuals by race. But even by the most generous estimate, white southerners made up only about 4.5 percent of the city's total native white population in 1910 and but 3.9 percent of all 48,699 whites as compared with 2.6 percent of the identified rioters (3 out of a total of 115).[39]

Of course, one might suspect, as Walling did, that even if southern-born whites were not involved heavily in the riot, perhaps many of the native American white rioters were from southern Illinois—an area that did keep its southern character into the twentieth century. Information on rioters' birthplaces, however, suggests that this was not the case. Altogether, 82 of 115 rioters whose birthplaces were available were born in Illinois. After eliminating those with a "mixed" background (foreign or southern parents), one finds that the vast majority of Illinois-born rioters came from cen-

tral or northern parts of the state. Also, most were born in Springfield, the surrounding Sangamon County, or nearby towns and
counties.[40]

Just as the northern press, including Springfield's, did not mention the involvement of a southern element in the riot (Walling's
article being the exception), neither did they single out immigrants
as a source of the trouble. City newspapers did give several foreign-
born indicted rioters unflattering attention, but they did the same
with some of the American-born rioters as well, most notably Kate
Howard. One foreign-born indictee who received extensive press
coverage was the recently arrived Russian Jew, Abraham Raymer.
Immediately after the riot, when the city's elite worried about the
possible persistence of "mob rule," the press anxiously wondered
whether Raymer was an anarchist, a "party to a plot to kill, and to
wreck business property and residences of Springfield." But the authorities failed to uncover a radical conspiracy. Under strenuous
questioning by the police, punctuated by beatings, Raymer confessed that his only political interest was Zionism.[41]

Another foreign rioter who received substantial press coverage
was Fergus O'Toole, an Irish-born bartender and "a well known
levee character." Springfield's newspapers treated O'Toole in a less
serious vein than Raymer, who had temporarily raised the specter of
imported anarchism. O'Toole appears in press accounts as the ste-
reotypical disorderly and violent Irishman, quick to curse and ready
to resort to fisticuffs at the drop of a hat. The newspapers re-
counted with relish that, when the police nabbed him for "inciting a
riot" during the first night of violence, it had taken a "whole bunch
of bluecoats" to subdue the bartender. A month and a half later, the
press was still poking fun at O'Toole, who, on his wedding day,
ended up in a street brawl with his bride-to-be. Both landed in jail.
Released and married the same day, the O'Tooles returned to
Springfield where, one newspaper sarcastically observed, they were
"snugly ensconced in their happy home—just across the street from
the county jail."[42] Despite their occasional evocation of stereotypes
of the sinister Russian anarchist and the fighting Irishman, however,
the city's newspapers said virtually nothing about the ethnic or cultural background of the rioters.

The birthplaces of the 115 rioters for whom data from censuses
and local records are available suggest that foreign-born individuals
were not overrepresented in the mob.[43] Foreign-born rioters as a
whole, for instance, made up 14.8 percent of those arrested, injured, or indicted—virtually the same as their share (14.2 percent)

of the city's total white population (see Appendix, Table 3.3). When
the three categories of rioters are compared, no important differences in the ethnic backgrounds of those groups appear. In other
words, if a rioter was singled out for arrest or indictment, foreign
birth did not figure as a significant factor influencing the selectivity
of the criminal justice system.

When one examines rioters from each ethnic group, however, a
few important differences appear. Some groups seem to have been
disproportionately involved—or uninvolved—in the rioting. Despite
the large and increasing presence of Lithuanians and Poles (catego-
rized with many Jewish immigrants as "Russians" in the 1910 census) in the city, only one turned up among the 115 identified
rioters.[44] Their absence is even more striking when one considers
that most non-Jewish "Russian" immigrants were heavily concentrated in the city's one industry—coal mining—in which blacks had
a significant foothold. On the other hand, another group of recent
immigrants, the Italians, are overrepresented among the 115 rioters.
Four Italians ran afoul of the law during the outbreak, but it is not
entirely clear what sort of riot behavior they engaged in. Two Italians were shot during the rioting, which suggests that they were active either in the Levee or Badlands attacks. Another, Joe Rose, was
arrested when police discovered goods looted from Fishman's pawnshop at his home.[45]

Other important patterns of differential ethnic involvement in the
riot appear. Germans, for example, are underrepresented. While
they made up 4.4 percent of the city's white population, they account for less than 1 percent of the 115 rioters. Canadians and English, on the other hand, account for more than their "share" of the
rioters. The number of rioters in each of these ethnic groups is
small, but it is possible to calculate the number of American-born
rioters whose parents were both foreign-born for three major
groups—American-born with two Irish parents, American-born
with two German parents, and so forth. Adding the foreign-born for
each of three groups—Germans, Irish, and English—to the rioters
with parents from each, yields sufficient numbers of, say, those of
"Irish descent" or "German descent" to make comparisons with 1910
census data (see Appendix, Table 3.4).

When thus combined and compared, a clearer focus on the rioters' ethnic background emerges. Those of Irish descent, though
much fewer in number in the city than their German counterparts,
appear much more riot-prone than any other ethnic group. The
Germans and their offspring, Springfield's largest ethnic group,

were strikingly underrepresented among the 115 rioters. They, along with Lithuanians and Poles (none of the 115 rioters were American-born children of "Russians"), were much less likely to take to the streets to attack black residents and businesses. The English were present in only slightly greater numbers than one would expect.

Other evidence indicates the same discrepancies in German versus Irish involvement in the riot. In addition to those who were either born in Ireland or who had two Irish parents, five other rioters had one Irish parent, and one English-born rioter had two Irish parents. Furthermore, nine other rioters had surnames that were clearly Irish—Ryan, Rourke, Brennan, Sullivan, O'Brien, for example—but no information could be found about them. When all are added together, they total twenty-eight rioters of "Irish descent." If the same procedure is applied to the Germans (adding those for whom data are lacking but who have German surnames), the total is only six rioters of "German descent." Clearly, the Germans were "stay-at-homes" during the riot.

The conspicuous presence of the Irish in the Springfield riot underscores earlier findings on their relations with black Americans. From the early nineteenth century on, the Irish and blacks clashed, often violently, over jobs and politics in urban America.[46] William Tuttle, after tracing Chicago's long history of black-Irish conflict, which broke out anew in the 1919 race riot in that city, indicated that by the early twentieth century, "mutual antagonism between Irish and blacks was legendary."[47] The same kind of long-standing antagonisms between the two groups likely operated in Springfield. For example, many local elections in the capital were decided by slender margins, and the Democratic Irish-Americans may have perceived competition for power and patronage from the largely Republican blacks.

Unfortunately there is no substantial body of scholarship on immigrant groups other than the Irish that traces relations with blacks. German immigrants did not seem to have a tradition of bitter political and economic grievances against blacks, perhaps in part because they lacked the ethnic cohesiveness that characterized the Irish. As one historian put it, unlike the Irish, the Germans "were so diverse socially, economically, culturally, and politically that there was no common interest strong enough to bind them together."[48] The political loyalties of Springfield's German-Americans were divided, for example, with many favoring the Republican party. Thus they were far less likely than the predominantly Democratic Irish to view the black Republican vote as competition. Moreover, in part because of the diversity among Germans, they were generally more apathetic about politics than the Irish, who viewed it as a major source of upward mobility in American cities. Again, this apathy would have muted any tendency to resent blacks' modest political gains in Springfield. Finally, German immigrants tended to be more skilled and more occupationally diversified than the Irish and thus lacked the latter's long history of competition with blacks for jobs on the lower end of the economic ladder.[49]

Putting aside the issue of Irish-Americans' traditional anti-black hostility and their possible resentment of black political activity in Springfield, the data on rioters' birthplaces (and occupation, as we shall see) do permit further generalizations about the role of ethnicity in the city's race riot. Social strain theories suggest that those most likely to riot are those who experience or perceive a black threat to the status quo, particularly in the areas of employment and housing. Conventional wisdom on the Springfield riot holds, for example, that a major source of interracial hostility was direct and heated competition between foreigners and blacks for less skilled work, especially coal mining.[50] The identity of Springfield's rioters, however, suggests that those immigrants who shared both workplaces and neighborhoods with blacks were in fact *less* likely to riot than those who lived and labored apart from or distant from blacks.

Lithuanians and Poles—the vast majority of the "Russians," who comprised Springfield's second largest foreign-born group by 1910—lived and worked in closer contact with blacks than other recent immigrants. If any group faced direct competition for jobs and living space, it was these new Russian miners, yet only one Lithuanian miner appeared among the 115 riot participants identified. One might argue that, as new arrivals, these Eastern Europeans had not yet had time to absorb American anti-black prejudices, or that, as "birds of passage" who planned but a brief stay in America, they saw little reason to support or help maintain the interracial status quo. Yet the Italians, equally newcomers to Springfield and equally transient, appeared to be more active in the rioting, even though they were far less likely to live near blacks or to compete with them for employment. In the state as a whole and in Sangamon County, Italians were the largest ethnic group involved in coal mining.[51] But few Italians lived in Springfield (276 in 1910), and, though some did work as miners in or near the city, no Italian miners turned up among the rioters injured, arrested, or indicted. Data on birthplace are available for fifteen of the eighteen rioters identified as miners. All but one were "old stock" miners, those of American or Northern European descent, mostly Irish, English, and Welsh. From the 1890s on these old stock miners witnessed a sharp decline in their status, security, and wages in the face of the Eastern and Southern Europeans' massive "invasion" of America's coal mines. "The new immigrants," noted historian Richard J. Jensen, "seemed obnoxious to the old miners."[52] These old stock miners who rioted lived apart from blacks, and though they did often share the same workplace with them, they likely viewed blacks, along with the new immigrant miners, as part of a larger threat to their security. As local newspapers and oral histories from Springfield suggest, social ties and sympathy were greater between blacks and new immigrants in the mines, while old stock miners tended to distance themselves from both.

Class and Occupation

A second major feature emerges from the data on participants in the violence: it was, above all, a working-class riot. An examination of the occupations of 133 indicted, arrested, and injured rioters reveals that most (over four-fifths) were recruited from the ranks of blue-collar workers. Semi-skilled and unskilled whites accounted for more than half of the total. The occupations of the 133 rioters were found in the 1908 Springfield city directory (see Appendix, Table 3.5). Three rioters, like William "Fingers" Lotherington, the thief, were identified by the city newspapers as criminals. The rioters were placed in five broad occupational categories: high white-collar, low white-collar, skilled, semi-skilled, and unskilled workers (see Table 3.1).[53] Over 80 percent of the rioters were from the working class—skilled, semi-skilled, or unskilled—but this estimate errs on the conservative side. Two of the clerks assigned to the low white-collar group, for example, likely had very small incomes; one worked in a

Table 3.1 Occupational Distribution of Springfield Rioters (N = 133)

	Number	Percent
High white-collar	3	2.3
Low white-collar	17	12.8
Skilled	34	25.6
Semi-skilled	42	31.6
Unskilled	34	25.6
Criminal	3	2.3

small grocery store, and the other was a "saloon clerk." Another two low white-collar workers were strangers who happened to be in the city the weekend of the riot.

Three occupational groups account for over one-third of the 133 rioters examined: miners, railroad and streetcar workers, and laborers. Miners were more numerous than any other group, but this is not surprising, for the many mining concerns in and near Springfield employed thousands of hands. In 1910 miners made up about 15 percent of 17,014 male wage earners; in 1908 they were about 13 percent of the identified rioters. Neither were laborers overrepresented among the 133 rioters. However, nearly twice as many railroad and streetcar employees appeared among the rioters than one would expect—they were but 5 percent of the male work force in 1910, yet accounted for one-tenth of the rioters.[54] One reason so many railroad men turned out during the riot probably had to do with their acquaintance with Clergy Ballard and William Hallam, the husband of the woman whom George Richardson allegedly raped. Ballard had been an engineer for the Chicago, Peoria and St. Louis Railroad just a few years before his murder and apparently had been a very popular man. Nearly all of the railroad workers among the 133 identified worked for the C.P. & St. L., even though there were five other major rail lines in Springfield. William Lee, the fireman who described his part in the riot, worked for this railroad, though he did not mention whether he knew Ballard. Likewise, the four city streetcar employees who were either injured or arrested in the riots probably knew William Hallam, a motorman who ran the cars in the evening. Thus, in the case of railroad and streetcar workers, friendship ties may help account for their overrepresentation among the rioters.

When the three categories of rioters are compared, differences in their socioeconomic status emerge. Indictees appear to be lower on the occupational ladder than either arrestees or injured rioters (see Appendix, Table 3.6). Indictees were more likely to be semi-skilled and unskilled workers than injured rioters, with the arrestees falling between these two categories. Not only were all three "criminals" among the indictees, but almost two-thirds of those indicted came from the lower ranks of the working class. On the other hand, fewer than half of the injured rioters were semi-skilled or unskilled workers. Nearly 30 percent of the injured rioters were skilled workers, as opposed to one-fifth of the indictees. The number of rioters in each category is admittedly small, but these figures suggest that indicted rioters were poorer than those arrested or injured.

The contrast in the relative status of indicted and injured rioters is particularly important, for the injured were never processed by the city's criminal justice system, and therefore the question of selectivity is irrelevant. It was the chance bullet or brick that "selected" the injured rioters, not the police, witnesses, or the courts. The point is not that poorer whites were more riot-prone, but that they were somehow more likely to be arrested and prosecuted. In other words, if the city's criminal justice system operated impartially, one would expect the status of all three categories of rioters to be relatively similar. One would expect, for instance, to find more "Levee characters" and impoverished rioters on the lists of those injured during the first night of violence and more skilled workers facing indictments. But it was the poorest rioters who received the harshest treatment at the hands of the law.

To a significant extent, the relative vulnerability of poorer rioters to arrest and prosecution must remain a matter of speculation. Yes, the police probably were better able to identify downtown rioters whom they saw more frequently on a day-to-day basis. And it does seem plausible that white witnesses would be more willing to testify against marginal men and women, whom they viewed as riff-raff. One could also speculate that these poorer rioters' behavior during the violence may have somehow been more outrageous, flagrant, or deviant, and therefore more visible to police and witnesses alike. But the higher status of the injured—those who arguably were in the front ranks of the most active violence—casts doubt on this suggestion.

There was one important distinguishing characteristic of indictees: they were usually caught with stolen goods and pilfered items that directly linked them to the riot. On the one hand, it is possible that, being relatively poor, indictees were more likely to loot and get caught red-handed with incriminating evidence. The police did snare several indictees on the periphery of the rioting who were carrying home armloads of clothing, hardware, and liquor. On the other hand, the police did actively generate arrests downtown that they would not, or could not, have generated elsewhere in the city. Newspaper accounts strongly suggest that Springfield's lawmen systematically searched brothels, cheap boardinghouses, and seedy hotels downtown for evidence of riot participation. Once they found stolen goods, of course, a suspect would receive the scrutiny of the police, the military, the grand jury, and any riot witnesses willing to testify, thus dramatically increasing the chances of an indictment. The police did not subject citizens in more residential or more affluent neighborhoods to such intensive and intrusive searches, but concentrated their efforts in the one area they must have felt would be most productive of arrests and least likely to stir public criticism of their tactics. Thus, the relatively low status of the indictees may reflect, in part, a greater tendency among poor rioters to steal, or their relative vulnerability to intrusive police searches, or both.

Other more impressionistic evidence illustrates the more humble and marginal status of the indictees as opposed to the other two categories of rioters. Springfield's press, for instance, took pains to portray Abraham Raymer and Kate Howard as undesirable characters. Raymer, for example, had "loafed about pool rooms and dram shops." Another paper unearthed the news that Kate Howard's son had, like his mother, "repeatedly figured in police circles"; in fact, several months before the riot he had been arrested for drunk and disorderly conduct after tussling with both his mother and police. "Overindulgence in alcoholic stimulants" caused the youth's "nerves to become totally deranged," and the police transferred young Howard to a hospital to dry out. The press intimated that prostitutes frequented Kate Howard's hotel and declared that Kate herself was "semi-notorious." "Mrs. Howard's connection with the race riots," stated one newspaper, "became a synonym for shadiness."[55]

Raymer and Howard aside, the press revealed the marginal status of another nineteen indicted rioters. Some had been in trouble with the law before the riot; others came from families that had other members in prison. Some of these nineteen may have been professional criminals, even though they were listed as holding legitimate jobs in the city directory. One indictee, for example, had been charged with "obtaining goods under false pretenses" a month before the riot. The charges, the newspaper explained, had something "to do with the mortgaging of a horse." Other indictees, like Fergus O'Toole, the press identified as "well known characters," or "levee characters." The police netted one of these in a "hop joint" (opium den) in the Levee two weeks after the riots. Yet another indictee was mentioned as a resident of Madge Clark's brothel.[56]

One of the more unusual indictees discussed in the press after the riots was Edward Ferris, an eccentric loner "off his mental balance." The police eventually identified Ferris as one of the men who had helped demolish Harry Loper's automobile on the first night of rioting. When they visited him to search his rented room, the authorities found an assortment of riot souvenirs: a policeman's club, silverware from Loper's restaurant, and some oversize underwear looted from Reuben Fishman's pawnshop on East Washington Street. When questioned, Ferris admitted he had been at Loper's, but explained that he had been "gathering material for a book he [was] writing on 'both sides of the liquor question.' " The police indeed found "a large amount of manuscript" in Ferris's room, but they refused to reveal its contents to a curious press.[57]

Besides the nineteen indictees that the press implicitly or explicitly identified as either unstable or from the lower rungs of society, ten others informed the court that they were unable to afford lawyers for their defense. With the addition of the three known criminals among the indictees, then, it seems that over half of the indicted rioters were either poor or had been in some kind of trouble with the law before the riot. The newspapers painted them as a rather unsavory lot. At least in terms of their socioeconomic standing in the community, the press came close to the truth. But these were not necessarily typical rioters. Most indictees were those who were left after better-off rioters had been sifted out by the criminal justice system.

Two indictees were notable exceptions. Two teenage boys, indicted for their part in sacking Loper's restaurant, were white-collar workers. Eugene Bradley, a clerk in a dry goods store in the small town of Chatham in Sangamon County, was caught with bottles of liquor stolen from Loper's. The other boy, eighteen-year-old Fred Willhite, worked as a collector for the local telephone company. He was charged with "riot" at the restaurant. It is likely that the two boys were friends and that they were together during the rioting at Loper's, because a year after their arrest Willhite married Bradley's younger sister and moved into his father-in-law's residence in Chatham. There is no evidence that the two were involved in the Levee and Badlands rioting. Eugene Bradley's father, Milton Bradley, was a physician with a successful practice in Chatham. Milton Bradley surely was not pleased to find his son and Fred Willhite in trouble with the law in Springfield, especially since both boys' names appeared in the newspapers several times. However, the boys' involvement in the riot does not seem to have either damaged their standing in Chatham or to have hurt their chances for respectable careers. The doctor, after all, did give his daughter in marriage to Willhite and housed the newlyweds at his home. His son Eugene continued as a clerk in Chatham. Willhite began working for the *Springfield News* in 1909 as a solicitor and advertising manager. The *News*, ironically, was one of the loudest in denouncing the riot indictees as riffraff and "undesirables."[58]

Many of the rioters were in their early twenties or younger and still resided with their parents at the time of the riot. Information on parents' occupations for forty-two of these young rioters underscores the working-class character of the riot. Since these young men were just beginning their working careers, it is not surprising to find that many of them had parents in higher-status, working-class jobs. Just as indictee Eugene Bradley, the low white-collar dry goods clerk, lived in a physician's household, many of the unskilled and semi-skilled rioters lived with fathers who were at least one step above them on the occupational ladder. Exactly half of the forty-two rioters living at home had parents at the same or higher occupational levels; seven held jobs of higher status than their parents. All but three of them lived in households headed by blue-collar parents. Eugene Bradley, the doctor's son, was the only rioter who lived in a household headed by a high white-collar worker.[59]

One final point is that most of the rioters' occupations involved no contact or competition with blacks. In fact, in only seven of the sixty occupations rioters held—miner, elevator operator, domestic, laborer, barber, and teamster—was there any substantial possibility of interracial competition. These seven trades accounted for about 30 percent of the rioters. Blacks were excluded from over two-thirds of the rioters' occupations, and those blacks who were small proprietors (barbers excepted) catered to black customers not welcome in white establishments. For example, those rioters who were either barkeeps or employees of white-owned saloons were not in direct competition with blacks in similar establishments because both largely served their respective races. A few blacks worked in the building trades, but their opportunities were limited, in most cases, by union policies that discriminated in favor of whites. Moreover, white workers had a near-monopoly in jobs in industry and transportation. In short, most of the rioters examined faced no black threat to their employment security and had no black co-workers or customers—contrary to earlier social strain interpretations of the riot that have cited economic competition as a major source of interracial tension. The actual distribution of occupations among the rioters suggests quite the opposite: those who rioted were not those most directly threatened economically.

Homeownership and Residence

The evidence on homeownership, though less ample than that on occupation, also indicates that indicted rioters were less well off then those arrested or injured. Arrested and injured rioters usually owned their own homes or lived with their parents; the indictees were more likely to have been renters or boarders in households headed by nonrelatives (see Appendix, Table 3.7). Only one-fifth of the indictees owned their homes or lived with parents who were home-owners, as opposed to nearly half of the injured rioters. The arrest-ees again fell between the other two groups of rioters—about 28 percent of them owned their own homes or lived with home-owning parents. This rate of homeownership makes a rather poor showing when compared to the rate for Springfield's population as a whole: in 1910 about 45 percent of all heads of Springfield households owned their homes. In the First Ward, in the northeast corner of the city, and the Sixth Ward, in the southeast—the wards that con-tained most of the city's poorest inhabitants—40 percent and 48 percent of household heads, respectively, owned homes.[60] Even Springfield's blacks had a higher rate of homeownership than the indictees—about 36 percent.[61] Since the age distribution of the three categories of rioters was nearly identical, differences in the rates of homeownership were not due to the relative youthfulness of indictees as opposed to the other two groups. Those rioters who faced indictments were simply less well-off than arrestees and in-jured rioters.

Among the 42 rioters living at home with their parents, a surpris-ing number lived in households headed by widowed mothers—12 of the 42 cases. All but one of the rioters in these female-headed households worked at semi-skilled or unskilled work to help support the family. Some of these young men, like arrestee George Ham-mon, were forced to find work at an early age to help keep the household running after their fathers died. Hammon's father George, a moulder, had died two years before the riot, leaving be-hind his Irish-born widow, Bridget, two sons, and four daughters. The large Hammon family, which occupied a rented house a few blocks north and west of the Badlands, must have had serious finan-cial trouble after the father died, for Bridget had to take work as a washerwoman to help support her children. Her son George was fifteen years old in 1908 and worked as a waiter in a downtown sa-loon. Given his impoverished background, it is not very surprising to find that young George was arrested for theft in the course of the riot. The police nabbed the youth carrying off "a box of chalk, a pair of spectacles, poker chips, bicycle saddle springs and a rat trap" from looted Levee stores.[62] Most of the rioters' families headed by widows, however, were not in such desperate straits; some of the fathers had managed to pay for a house before they died, and other bereft families had older sons who were quite capable of shouldering much of the families' support.

An examination of 125 rioters' place of residence in 1908 shows that the majority lived in working-class areas in the northern, central, and eastern sections of the city (see Appendix, Table 3.8). The First and Sixth Wards, the two poorest in Springfield, contained the city's two largest black enclaves. Of Springfield's seven wards, the First Ward alone contributed nearly a quarter of the rioters. The Sixth Ward had fewer rioters than one might expect, given its working-class nature and its sizeable black population. But, since the black community there was not the immediate target of the mob, Sixth Ward rioters had to walk downtown to join in the outbreak. The central business district, largely contained in the Seventh Ward, contributed many rioters. The more "aristocratic" Fourth and Fifth Wards contributed twenty rioters, most of whom, however, lived in or near the central business district and the Seventh Ward, and not in more genteel suburban locations. The overwhelming majority of the rioters came from two areas: the central business district and its immediate environs, and from the more distant working-class areas of the First, Second, and Third Wards. Finally, very few of these rioters lived in the same immediate neighborhood with blacks. Most lived well beyond the boundaries of the Levee, the Badlands, and the large Sixth Ward black enclave.

It is possible to approximate the typical participant in the Spingfield riots. He was an American male, born in the North, in his twenties, and single—nearly three-quarters of 103 rioters for whom marital data were available were unmarried, divorced, or widowed (see Appendix, Table 3.9). He had been born and raised in Illinois. The house he lived in was usually rented, but whether he had his own dwelling or still lived under his parents' roof, his home environment was working-class. He was a semi-skilled worker—not well off, but certainly not riffraff. And, since most of his fellow rioters resided either downtown or in the north end, he probably recognized many of the faces in the Levee and Badlands crowds.

William Lee, the railroad fireman, was very much an average riot participant. Lee was twenty-five and single in the summer of 1908 and lived in the Second Ward in a room he rented from an unrelated family, well away from any black neighborhood. All of his peers and co-workers on the railroad were white. Indeed, the only blacks he usually saw on any workday were either hobos catching free rides or porters and janitors at stationhouses on his route. Lee had no previous criminal record, and his extensive narrative reveals that, except for his part in the riot, he was a hard-working, law-abiding citizen.[63]

It remains, however, to explain further what the riot might have represented to those who were active in the violence. Why were they—unlike Springfield's better-off whites, who initially tended to view the riot as "reform"—determined to drive away all of the city's blacks? We can infer a little about the motives of some rioters: some were angry friends of the Ballards and Hallams; Irish-American rioters, with their long history of anti-black conflict, may have been expressing resentment over increased competition with Republican blacks for political power and patronage; a few "criminals" naturally took advantage of the disorder to steal. But what of the rest? As we have seen, William Lee and many other rioters like him were socially and geographically distant from Springfield's blacks. Their jobs, like Lee's, were secure against black competition. Indeed, the typical rioter usually saw no blacks at all where he worked. He also had no black neighbors and had to walk at least a quarter of a mile to get at those he wished to attack. The origins of this riot, then, cannot lie in white frustrations over any immediate black threat to white material interests or security. Social strain theory does not work. We must turn to an analysis of the victims of the violence—those who were injured or who lost property during the riots and afterward—to help clarify the sources of rioters' aggression and the conditions that led them to wage race war.

NOTES

1. William F. Lee Memoir, SSUO.
2. *ISJ*, 18 August 1908; CD, 1906–7, 1910.
3. William F. Lee Memoir.
4. "The So-called Race Riot at Springfield, Illinois," *Charities and the Commons* 50 (19 September 1908): 710.
5. *ISJ*, 24 September 1908.
6. Murray S. Hanes, "Samuel Jackson Hanes," typescript, n.d., G. Cullom Davis Papers, SSU; CD, 1911.
7. "The So-called Race Riot," 710.
8. CD, 1906, 1908–9; *ISJ*, 16 August 1908; *ISR*, 16 August 1908; also *ISJ* and *ISR*, 17 August to 8 October 1908 passim.
9. Albert M. Friedenburg, "The Year 5669," in *American Jewish Yearbook* 11 (1909–10): 63; James Krohe, Jr., "Not Guilty! The Trial of Abraham

Raymer after the Springfield Race Riots of 1908," *Illinois Times*, 11 August 1978.

10. Rioters' names were found in four newspapers: *Illinois State Journal, Illinois State Register, Springfield News,* and the *Springfield Record.*

11. "The So-called Race Riot at Springfield, Illinois," 709. For other estimates of crowd size see *ISJ*, 15 August 1908; Adjutant General of Illinois, *Biennial Report of the Adjutant General of Illinois to the Governor and Commander-in-Chief, 1907–1908* (Springfield, Ill.: Illinois State Journal Company, 1909) 263, 271, 281.

12. Certain common problems confront researchers who attempt to trace individuals in city directories and the manuscript census. For example, some people cannot be traced because their names are very common. Some rioters had names like John Brown and John Schmidt, making it impossible to tell which of a dozen or so men with these names in the sources was the guilty party. Men with very common names thus were dropped from the list of 190 total rioters mentioned in the newspapers and court records. A second problem resulted from careless or incomplete enumeration in the various census districts. Some of the rioters were left out of either the 1900 or 1910 census, even though it was clear from city directory listings that they still lived in Springfield. Finally, city directories also occasionally overlooked people who, according to the censuses, were still Springfield residents. Thus, in a number of cases, it was impossible to trace an individual through both sources.

13. Leonard L. Richards, *"Gentlemen of Property and Standing": Anti-Abolition Mobs in Jacksonian America* (New York: Oxford University Press, 1970), 150–51. See also Lawrence M. Friedman and Robert V. Percival, *The Roots of Justice: Crime and Punishment in Alameda County, California, 1870–1910* (Chapel Hill: University of North Carolina Press, 1981), 67–134. For a general theory that accounts for and explains variations in the application of law, see Donald Black, *The Behavior of Law* (Orlando, Fla.: Academic Press, 1976).

14. *Chicago Tribune*, 18 August 1908; *SN*, 18 August 1908.

15. *ISR*, 20 August 1908.

16. *Chicago Tribune*, 18 August 1908; *SN*, 18 August 1908.

17. Names of witnesses who brought evidence against indicted rioters were listed in each case's file. See for example, CCF, case numbers 22655, 23285–90, 23309, 23311, 23344, 23408, 23349, 23449, 23402, 23403, 23410, 23421–22, 23424–25. The press occasionally commented on the progress of various cases and provided most of the testimony against the rioters given during trials; see *SR*, 12 October 1908; *ISJ*, 4 September 1908; *SN*, 21 August 1908.

18. *SR*, 12 October 1908.

19. *ISJ*, 1 September 1908, 19 September 1908; Murray S. Hanes, "Samuel Jackson Hanes."

20. *Chicago Tribune*, 21 August 1908.

21. *ISJ*, 29 August 1908.

22. *SN*, 15 August 1908. For another race riot analysis that also treats those injured during riot violence as rioters, see Adrian Cook, *The Armies of the Streets: The New York City Draft Riots of 1863* (Lexington: University Press of Kentucky, 1974), 193–96, 256–68. Though Cook wrote an excellent descriptive narrative of the 1863 riot, he made little attempt to integrate the wealth of data he uncovered on individual rioters into an explanatory framework.

23. *SR*, 17 August 1908; *Chicago Tribune*, 15 August 1908; *ISJ*, 18 August 1908.

24. William English Walling, "The Race War in the North," *The Independent* 65 (3 September 1908): 531–32; *Chicago Tribune*, 16 August 1908.

25. *ISR*, 15 August 1908; *ISJ*, 18 August 1908.

26. Adjutant General of Illinois, *Biennial Report*, 272–73; *ISR*, 16 August 1908; *ISJ*, 18 August 1908.

27. Walling, "The Race War in the North," 531–32.

28. *ISJ*, 16 August 1908; *ISR*, 16 August 1908.

29. *ISR*, 18–19 August 1908, 25 August 1908.

30. CCF, case numbers 23267–70, 23344–46, 23349, 23405, 23407, 23441, and 23443.

31. *ISJ*, 15 August 1908; manuscript schedules of the population census for Springfield, Illinois, 1910.

32. CD, 1909; manuscript schedules of the population census for Springfield, Illinois, 1900; *ISJ*, 18 August 1908, 5 September 1908.

33. *ISJ*, 18 August 1908.

34. For examples of the view that the Springfield riots were more "southern" than "northern" in character, see James Crouthemal, "The Springfield Race Riot of 1908," *Journal of Negro History* 45 (July 1960): 177–78; James Krohe, Jr., *Summer of Rage: The Springfield Race Riot of 1908* (Springfield, Ill.: Sangamon County Historical Society, 1973), 3–4; Cullom Davis and James Krohe, Jr., "Springfield: An Evolving Capital," in Daniel Milo Johnson and Rebecca Monroe Veach, eds., *The Middle-Size Cities of Illinois: Their People, Politics, and Quality of Life* (Springfield, Ill.: Sangamon State University, 1980), 193–95; Bruce Alexander Campbell, *200 Years: An Illustrated Bicentennial History of Sangamon County* (Springfield, Ill.: Phillips Brothers, Inc., 1976), 199; Augustus W. Low, ed., *Encyclopedia of Black America* (New York: McGraw-Hill, 1981), 232.

35. Walling, "The Race War in the North," 532.

36. Ibid., 534.

37. This is a generous and inflated estimate of the size of the "southern element." For example, all those who had only one southern-born parent were assumed to be "southern" in outlook, regardless of whether or not they were born in the North. A number of rioters with one southern parent had a foreign-born parent as well. One might in fact question how "southern" a northern-born rioter with an immigrant parent might be, but for the sake of argument, all were treated as part of the same group.

38. U.S. Census Office, *Twelfth Census of the United States, Taken in the Year 1900: Population* (Washington, D.C.: Government Printing Office, 1901), 1:718–21, 726–29. For a discussion of the various streams of immigration into Illinois over the nineteenth century and speculations on the cultural heritage different groups of migrants carried with them, see Daniel J. Elazar, *Cities of the Prairie: The Metropolitan Frontier and American Politics* (New York: Basic Books, Inc., 1970), 153–93.

39. The total number of Springfield residents born in the South in 1910 was 2,433, or a little over 5 percent of a total population of 44,761 American-born persons of all races in the city. In 1900, 559 southern-born blacks lived in Springfield; taking this as an extremely conservative figure for the number of black southerners in 1910, and subtracting it from the total number of southern-born, one gets a crude and probably inflated estimate of 1,874 southern-born whites at the time of the later census. U.S. Bureau of the Census, *Thirteenth Census of the United States Taken in the Year 1910: Population* (Washington, D.C.: Government Printing Office, 1913), 1:770, 772, 774, 776, 778.

40. The censuses only list the state of birth of an individual, not a particular locality within a state. Sangamon County birth and marriage records, however, do list the town and county of nativity for a number of the Illinois-born rioters; the birthplaces of a few others were found in the obituary columns of Springfield's newspapers. After eliminating those rioters with at least one southern or foreign-born parent, thirty-six rioters were left, whose parents were northern, native Americans. Twenty-five of these were located in the birth, marriage, or obituary records, and all but three of these rioters were born in central or northern Illinois. In the process of searching for Illinois-born rioters with native parents, the birthplaces of a dozen other rioters born in the state, but having a foreign or southern parent, were also found. Without exception, all members of this smaller group were born either in Springfield or the surrounding county. *Index to Birth Records, Sangamon County, Illinois*, vols. 3–7, Office of the County Clerk of Sangamon County, Springfield, Ill.: *Index to Marriage Records, Sangamon County, Illinois*, vol. 1, Office of the County Clerk of Sangamon County, Springfield, Ill.; Obituary Index, Sangamon Valley Collection, Lincoln Library, Springfield, Ill.

41. *ISR*, 17 August 1908; *ISJ*, 17 August 1908, 20 August 1908.

42. *ISJ*, 15 August 1908, 7 October 1908.

43. Percentages for various groups of foreign-born in the city as a whole were calculated from tables in Bureau of the Census, *Thirteenth Census, 1910*, 2:504, 516.

44. Though Lithuanians and Poles were listed as Russians in published census volumes, the manuscript schedules specified their actual nationality.

45. *SN*, 17 August 1908; *ISJ*, 18 August 1908; *ISR*, 16 August 1908, 23 August 1908.

46. Carl Wittke, *The Irish in America* (Baton Rouge, La.: Louisiana State University Press, 1956), 125–26, 219; Dennis Clark, *The Irish Relations: Trials*

of an Immigrant Tradition (East Brunswick, N.J.: Associated University Presses, 1982), 143–58; David A. Gerber, *Black Ohio and the Color Line, 1860–1915* (Urbana: University of Illinois Press, 1976), 7, 29, 104; William M. Tuttle, Jr., *Race Riot: Chicago in the Red Summer of 1919* (New York: Atheneum, 1970), 101–3; Larry Kinkaid, "Two Steps Forward, One Step Back: Racial Attitudes during the Civil War and Reconstruction," in *The Great Fear: Race in the Mind of America*, Gary B. Nash and Richard Weiss, eds., (New York: Holt, Rinehart and Winston, 1970), 47; H. Leon Prather, Sr., *We Have Taken a City: Wilmington Racial Massacre and Coup of 1898* (Cranbury, N.J.: Associated University Presses, 1984), 21, 60, 89; Leon F. Litwack, *North of Slavery: The Negro in the Free States, 1790–1860* (Chicago: University of Chicago Press, 1961), 162–66; David J. Hellwig, "The Afro-American and the Immigrant, 1880–1930: A Study of Black Social Thought" (Ph.D. diss., Syracuse University, 1973); Paul A. Gilje, *The Road to Mobocracy: Popular Disorder in New York City, 1763–1834* (Chapel Hill: University of North Carolina Press, 1987), 160–62.

47. Tuttle, *Race Riot*, 101.

48. Frederick Luebke, "The Germans," in John Higham, ed., *Ethnic Leadership in America* (Baltimore: Johns Hopkins University Press, 1978), 67. See also Paul Kleppner, *The Cross of Culture: A Social Analysis of Midwestern Politics, 1850–1900* (New York: The Free Press, 1970), 37–51, 69–83; Richard J. Jensen, *The Winning of the Midwest: Social and Political Conflict, 1888–1896* (Chicago: University of Chicago Press: 1971); Stephen Thernstrom, ed., *Harvard Encyclopedia of American Ethnic Groups* (Cambridge, Mass.: Harvard University Press, 1980), 421.

49. Luebke, "The Germans," 67; Thernstrom, *Harvard Encyclopedia of American Ethnic Groups*, 421; Litwack, *North of Slavery*, 166–67; Hellwig, "The Afro-American and the Immigrant, 1880–1930"; Gilje, *The Road to Mobocracy*, 160–62.

50. Crouthemal, "The Springfield Race Riot of 1908," 178; Krohe, *Summer of Rage*, 4.

51. James Krohe, Jr., *Midnight at Noon: A History of Coal Mining in Sangamon County* (Springfield, Ill.: Sangamon County Historical Society, 1975), 8–9.

52. Jensen, *The Winning of the Midwest*, 238–62.

53. Occupational categories were derived from those used by Olivier Zunz, *The Changing Face of Inequality: Urbanization, Industrial Development, and Immigrants in Detroit, 1880–1920* (Chicago: University of Chicago Press, 1982), and Stephan Thernstrom, *The Other Bostonians: Poverty and Progress in the American Metropolis, 1880–1870* (Cambridge, Mass.: Harvard University Press, 1973).

54. Proportions of workers in specific occupations were calculated from tables in Bureau of the Census, *Thirteenth Census, 1910*, 4:274–79.

55. *ISJ*, 2 March 1908, 21 August 1908; *ISR*, 16 August 1908; *Chicago Tribune*, 27 August 1908; *SN*, 15 August 1908, 18 August 1908.

56. *ISJ*, 8 July 1908; *SR*, 29 August 1908, 15 August 1908; *ISJ*, 30 August 1908; *ISJ*, 18 August 1908.

57. *ISJ*, 31 August 1908, 2 September 1908, 5 September 1908.

58. Information on Willhite and Bradley was taken from CD, 1906–11; manuscript schedules of the population census for Springfield, Illinois, 1900 and 1910; CCF, 23312 and 23449; *ISR*, 16 August 1908, 23 August 1908; *ISJ*, 23 August 1908; Joseph Wallace, *Past and Present of the City of Springfield and Sangamon County, Illinois* (Chicago: S. J. Clarke Publishing Co., 1904), 1:507–8.

59. Manuscript schedules of the population census for Springfield, Illinois, 1900 and 1910; CD, 1900–10.

60. Bureau of the Census, *Thirteenth Census, 1910*, 1:1356.

61. Bureau of the Census, *Negro Population, 1790–1915* (Washington, D.C.: Government Printing Office, 1918), 473.

62. *ISR*, 15 August 1908; *ISJ*, 15 August 1908; CD, 1900–10.

63. William F. Lee Memoir.

CHAPTER 4

The Victims

The next mob may get me or may get you.
— William J. Butler, white Springfield attorney.
Illinois State Register, 19 August 1908.

I ain't got a thing left in the world but my panama hat.
— James "Dandy Jim" Smith, black saloonkeeper.
Illinois State Journal, 16 August 1908.

IN mid-July, about two weeks after Clergy Ballard's death, Spring-field's *Illinois State Journal* added a new comic strip to its Sunday entertainment section, *Sambo and His Funny Noises*. Sambo's debut was not the first time this newspaper or others in Springfield cari-catured blacks or foreigners. Neither was Springfield's comic-strip population of slow-witted, bumbling Germans or infantile and cow-ardly blacks unusual in early twentieth-century America. Such car-toon creatures were merely one expression of the racial and ethnic stereotypes that pervaded American culture all over the nation.[1] The *Journal's* new character Sambo displays many traits calculated to amuse a white readership. An ink-black child of indeterminate age, Sambo is silly, pretentious, sneaky, and cowardly. He often wears loud or outlandish clothing. He speaks in what his white creator took to be black dialect, and his speech is replete with "yo'alls" and "yassahs."

Sambo embodies comic stereotypes of blacks common in this pe-riod, but another, more covert theme emerges from his antics in the Sunday entertainment section: Sambo is usually a victim, a moving target for white aggression. The comic's other main characters are two white boys, lower-class urchins, whose varied attacks on Sambo provide the dramatic action for most of the stories. In *Sambo and His Funny Noises* one can see a miniature, sanitized, but perpetual inter-racial conflict acted out in the *Journal's* Sunday comics. It is an un-equal battle. Not only are there always two whites against one black, but when attacked, Sambo may not retaliate in kind. While the white boys frequently belabor him with bricks or clubs studded with nails, Sambo has to resort to his wits, or, more frequently, to his heels. An armed black, however tiny, probably would not have impressed white readers as "funny."

Sambo occasionally gets token revenge on his little tormentors by playing pranks on them. For example, knowing that the urchins plan to steal a box of snuff from him, Sambo laces the powder with a generous helping of pepper. Sure enough, the two boys steal the box, and when they open it, they are seized with a bout of uncontrollable sneezing. Sambo watches from under cover, laughing at their well-deserved distress. But in this case and others where Sambo achieves a measure of vengeance, he must pay for it in the end. After the snuff escapade Sambo cannot go home, for the urchins, armed to the teeth, are stationed outside his front door.[2]

Sometimes Sambo's mere appearance on a street is enough to precipitate conflict. But one thing sure to provoke the white boys was the sight of Sambo working. If Sambo has a job at the beginning of a story, ropes and bricks are sure to appear. On the first Sunday following the race riots, Sambo appears as a tidily uniformed delivery boy. The two urchins spot him on the street delivering a large expensive vase. "How dares woik! De very idea!" the two exclaim. "Yous a disgrace to us!" They throw rocks at Sambo and trip him with a rope. Sambo falls, the vase is broken, and the reader may safely assume by the end of the strip that Sambo has lost his job.[3]

However amusing the small-scale battles in *Sambo and His Funny Noises* may have been to Springfield's white newspaper-reading public, the comic strip's underlying hostility toward blacks is clear. The type of black-white conflict that informed the *Sambo* comic made sense to the Springfield white reader because it was based on commonplace, everyday social realities. A successful white Springfield business or professional man and his family, for example, settling down to read their newspaper on Sunday morning in a quiet residence comfortably distant from black districts and the turbulent street life downtown, would have quickly grasped the comic urchins' outrage at the sight of Sambo employed. The appearance of weapons in response to this "disgrace" would not have struck them as odd, for Sambo out of his proper place was somehow naturally a threat to lower-status whites. William English Walling thought he detected similar feelings of resentment among some of the whites (some of them self-admitted riot participants) he interviewed after the race riot. Talking to whites on the streets downtown, Walling said he heard the same justification for the riot repeated many times: "Why, the niggers came to think they were as good as we are!"[4]

The Limits of White Consensus

Many white Americans in all walks of life early in the twentieth century held in common a set of stereotyped beliefs about blacks, which constituted a consensus that variously characterized blacks as buffoonish or criminally inclined—lazy, incompetent, and irresponsible—in short, generally unfit for life in a civilized nation. This consensus, or shared anti-black viewpoint, cut across class lines, but the unity it seemed to imply was only superficial. Most whites in the socially diverse crowd that watched the destruction of Loper's restaurant early in the rioting likely felt that the violence was justified and that the mob was expressing outrage and concerns shared by the larger white community. As the violence persisted, though, better-off whites perceived that the riot was not a communal event. The limits of consensus had been reached, and underlying differences in white relations with, and views of, blacks became increasingly visible. The consensus fractured along class lines.

Working-class rioters clearly intended to purge the city entirely of blacks and attempted to coerce the city's elite into supporting that goal. From the rioters' point of view, whites with economic ties to blacks helped encourage and sustain a despised segment of the community. They were traitors. If blacks were deprived of jobs and if all stores refused their trade, then perhaps the remainder not driven away by violence would be forced to abandon Springfield—literally starved out of the city. Rioters demanded that middle- and upper-class whites who had black employees or who sold goods to black customers sever those economic ties or suffer injury or property damage. Hence, Springfield's more affluent whites soon discovered that blacks were not the sole potential targets and victims of the mob's anger. Abruptly faced with a challenge to their authority from below, many better-off Springfield residents who had initially approved of the violence as reform to rid the city of "worthless blacks," Levee saloonkeepers, or Badlands "denizens," sorely resented rioters' attempts to dictate whom they might hire or how they might conduct their businesses. Furthermore, since many did have profitable and convenient economic ties with blacks, they rejected the mob's goal of creating an all-white city. When the rioters menaced their social betters, Springfield's elite closed ranks to fight "mob rule" and "rebellion" by "riffraff" and "undesirables."

In the days after the riot, whites who employed blacks were "being threatened by a flood of anonymous letters." For several days it was thought that "the letters were the work of boys or irresponsible individuals," but the growing number of mailed threats soon alarmed Springfield authorities enough that they requested the intervention of federal postal investigators. Mayor Roy Reece received several letters demanding that he discharge all blacks on the city's payroll, including patrolmen, firemen, and janitors.[5] The state's attorney's office reported that many local merchants were complaining of letters that threatened arson if they did not get rid of their black workers or stop selling to black customers. In at least one case, such threats were carried out. Several days after the riots ended, an unidentified person telephoned W. E. Smith, the white part-owner of a butcher shop downtown on North Sixth Street. Smith said that the caller "told him the firm must stop delivering meat to negroes. 'He told me that if we didn't stop selling to blacks, something would happen to our place.'" After eight o'clock that evening, a woman who roomed over the butcher shop shouted to two soldiers on patrol nearby that the building was on fire. The fire department arrived and promptly extinguished a small blaze in the basement. The authorities concluded it had been a case of arson, for someone had entered the building by forcing open a back door.[6]

City officials and businessmen were not the only targets of such threats. White families who had black help—house servants, drivers, yardmen, and the like—also received menacing notes and phone calls. The threats even reached beyond city limits. A wealthy white farmer who lived just outside of town was told that if he did not discharge his black farm hands, his house and barn would be burned. At the joint meeting of Springfield's business and professional associations after the riots, attorney William J. Butler disclosed that he had received a threatening note demanding that he dismiss his black servant. Butler's statement, according to the press, "brought out 'so did I's' from a number" of other men in the hall.[7] Edith A. Butler, daughter of the white owner of the Merchant's Transfer Company, recalled the difficulties her family experienced after the riots. Her father employed several black teamsters, and when the riot broke out, he sheltered them and their families in his warehouse until the trouble died down. Somehow the news got out that he had protected his workers, whom he kept on as employees.

"After that, for a long time," Butler said, "Papa had to have someone guard us at home." The family was the target of threats for
some time. "I tell you," she said, "you just didn't dare go out."[8]

Many other better-off whites, whom the rioters did not threaten—
businessmen in particular—suffered losses because of the city's disorder, which again fostered the white elite's repudiation of the
rioters and their goals. Curfews and early closing times imposed by
the authorities hurt many businesses, and continuing tensions in the
city made shoppers reluctant to venture downtown. Moreover, as the
city's white newspapers emphasized, most of the vandalized Levee
buildings and razed Badlands houses, though inhabited by blacks,
were owned by whites. It is possible that the rioters did not realize
that whites owned the small frame houses that they so methodically
set ablaze, but even if they had, that knowledge probably would not
have prevented them from burning the Badlands.

Of the forty damaged or destroyed Badlands buildings, all were
white-owned, except the barbershop belonging to Scott Burton, one
of the two blacks lynched during the riot. Over a quarter of the
houses belonged to Isadore Kanner, a Russian immigrant of high
standing in the city's Jewish community. The remaining white Badlands landlords owned from one to three buildings.[9] The Levee also
saw extensive damage to white-owned property leased to black shopkeepers or saloonkeepers. "This maudlin sentiment that the mob
disturbed only negroes is ridiculous and flimsy," complained a white
editor. "The mob attacked and destroyed white man's property and
white man's property alone, from the time it threw the first brick at
Loper's until it fired the last building on Madison Street." This sober accounting of economic losses contributed to middle- and
upper-class whites' rising clamor for law and order after the second
day of rioting. "Now that the excitement has ceased, property owners and businessmen are taking a little stock of results."[10]

Attorney William J. Butler conveyed the essence of the better-off
whites' concerns after the riot: fear and resentment of the rioters'
challenge to their authority, the economic toll, and the widening
gulf between more affluent whites and the rioters over the meaning,
function, and goals of the rioting. To Springfield's assembled white
businessmen and professionals he said: "A few men could have
stopped that mob last Friday night. Look what you and I have paid
for this temporizing. Of the dead three are white and 80 per cent of
the wounded are white. They say this is regulating the color question, that this is teaching the negro his place. See what we have paid
for it in blood. See what we will have to pay for it in property taxes

to meet damages to property, our own fair city's name tarnished and our property values depreciated. The next mob may get me or may get you."[11]

Black Victims

The rioters' major targets, of course, were Springfield's black citizens. Even those who escaped injury or property losses experienced considerable hardship and distress during the outbreak. Hundreds fled the city temporarily and endured a variety of discomforts and inconveniences. Some faced insult, and even danger, as whites in surrounding communities responded to black riot refugees with fear and alarm. Arthur Brittin, the nine-year-old son of a white Sangamon County farmer, later recalled that residents in the predominantly white countryside surrounding Springfield were nervous in the days after the violence in the capital. Young Brittin went out for the mail shortly after the riot and spotted two black men seated at a nearby creek eating corn stolen from a neighbor's field. "Scared like the dickens," the boy ran home to tell his parents what he had seen. His parents decided to ignore the trespassers, but Brittin remembered being afraid because the blacks "might be mad at white people for the way they were being treated out at town."[12]

Whites' fear that riot refugees might be in a retaliatory mood was not the only source of anxiety in the countryside. As the *Illinois State Register* noted, "At Auburn, Thayer, Virden, Girard, Pawnee, Spaulding, Buffalo, Riverton, Pana, Edinburg, Taylorville, Pleasant Plains and a score of other places in central Illinois a negro is an unwelcome visitor and is soon informed he must not remain in the town." Such banning of blacks by custom and unwritten law from rural and small-town communities was not a phenomenon limited to Illinois and was not peculiar to the early twentieth century. One historian has estimated that at least fifty-two places in Illinois in the late nineteenth century excluded blacks, and that in some coal-mining communities the practice may have reflected white miners' desire to ensure their dominance in local pits. Many towns and villages near Springfield prohibited blacks from living within their boundaries, and in some cases refused even to allow them to remain overnight.[13] As a result, white residents in more rural areas often denied riot refugees even a temporary sojourn in their communities.

Safe refuge was hard to find. Pawnee, a village about nineteen miles southeast of the capital, was reportedly "antagonistic towards the blacks and no negro is allowed to stop there and vigorous measures are resorted to if the warnings are disregarded." The *Chicago Tribune* mentioned that "race hatred [had] reached a high pitch" in the town of Buffalo, fifteen miles from Springfield. In front of the interurban station there, whites had set up a large sign that read: "All niggers are warned out of town by Monday, 12—sharp. Buffalo Sharp Shooters." In Pleasant Plains, another small Sangamon County town, whites ordered all blacks out, excepting only an elderly couple who were "old and law abiding citizens."[14] When a lone Springfield refugee appeared on the streets of the village of Spaulding eight miles from the city, he was greeted by a menacing mob of nearly one hundred whites. Deputy sheriffs arrived before any harm was done and saw to it that the man moved on. Black refugees sparked hostility outside of Sangamon County, too. At Bloomington, "a crowd of irresponsible young men jeered at a company of inoffensive colored people, applying the epithet of 'nigger,' and finally showered them with small stones." When a small band of Springfield blacks appeared in the village of Greenridge in Macoupin County to beg for food, "the residents of the place denied them anything and stoned them out of town."[15]

During the two days of rioting, two blacks died, at least twenty-one black businesses sustained damage, and over forty black families were left homeless after their houses were burned. Most of the destruction occurred during the first night of violence. Research yielded the names of a total of 83 black victims, including the two men who were lynched and twelve others who were injured. Fifty-seven individuals (about two-thirds) were traced through the censuses and city directories.[16] Sixty-nine of the 83 victims were men; fourteen were women who suffered property losses. In terms of socioeconomic status, the black riot victims fell roughly into two groups: white-collar workers and unskilled workers, reflecting the fact that the black business district and the poorest black residential neighborhood bore the brunt of the rioting. Of 62 black victims, nearly one-quarter held white-collar occupations (including small proprietors), while over two-fifths labored in unskilled positions (see Appendix, Table 4.1). Those in between—skilled and semi-skilled workers—accounted for 21 victims. Though listed as skilled workers, the seven black barbers whose businesses rioters attacked enjoyed a higher status in the black community than their white counterparts did in theirs. With their white clientele, generally well-established shops, and steady employment, Springfield's black barbers usually were solid members of the city's black middle class. The extent of homeownership among the victims was substantial, though most lived in the Levee and Badlands as renters. The 1910 census revealed that almost 33 percent of Springfield's black heads of household owned their homes, and, similarly, 15 of the 52 black riot victims for whom homeownership data were available were homeowners.[17]

Aside from the two lynched blacks, William Donnegan and Scott Burton, the press listed the names of twelve injured blacks who had either been shot or beaten during the two days of rioting. The number of black casualties was relatively low because most Levee and Badlands residents had been able to flee before the mob arrived. Nevertheless, just as many injured rioters' names never appeared in the newspapers' casualty lists, so did an undetermined number of black victims' injuries go unreported, partly because of the carelessness of city authorities. If an injured black went to the police or to a hospital for help, usually no one would bother to record the victim's name or attempt to follow up on the case. During the violence Friday evening, for example, rioters surprised a black fireman at a powerhouse near the State Arsenal and beat him until he was unconscious. Someone called the police, who carried the wounded man, not to the hospital, but back to his room at the edge of the Badlands, even though the riot was still underway. There they left him, and apparently "no effort was made to get his name. He is one of the unknown wounded." The city dispensary also treated an undetermined number of blacks for head injuries and stab wounds, but the names of these victims also went unrecorded.[18]

Patterns of Targeting: The Levee and Badlands

After sacking Loper's restaurant, the rioters selected black Levee businesses as their first target. In part this choice was a simple matter of geography—the Levee was the closest target at hand. Even so, it was a significant choice. Not only did it contain the city's small but vigorous black business district, but it also was the center of much of the capital's black political activity. From the turn of the century, both black business and political behavior became increasingly visible in this section of downtown Springfield, and both generated white resentment. In a sermon after the riots, Reverend E. B. Rogers of the (white) Central Baptist Church asserted that black political participation ran counter to many whites' beliefs about blacks' "proper place" in society. One could take for granted, Rogers said, that many Springfield whites felt that "the negro is too fresh." "Grant it," he continued, "and what gave the black man this exalted notion of his own importance?" More than anything, the minister decided, it was the ballot. On election day the black voter "mingles with white men on a common level. He hasn't sense enough to look beyond the bribe in dollars and drinks to see why the political aspirant wants his vote. The negro feels that he holds the balance of power and so he feels his importance."[19] The minister's proposed remedy for black "freshness" and the racial conflict he said it engendered was a restriction of the right to vote to those able to pass "educational tests."[20]

In destroying the Levee, rioters were not just wrecking businesses, but attacking the political headquarters of First and Seventh Ward black political leaders who operated chiefly out of saloons. Given the paucity of sources directly expressing working-class opinions about the riot, it is, of course, impossible to measure exactly the rioters' level of resentment of blacks' modest political achievements. The city's press, however, did occasionally single out black politics as a source of outrage to some whites, and thus as a major cause of the violence. Moreover, shortly after the riots, someone distributed bright yellow leaflets throughout the city that contained inflammatory anti-black statements. The leaflet listed white grievances and was aimed at a working-class audience. One item, for example, warned: "Niggers are Johnny on the spot at all labor troubles. Observe it." Another item in the leaflet asked: "Do you want niggers to make white men's laws? If not, get busy. Have the men who have made our laws for the past thirty years been elected by the intelligent white vote or by the majority of an ignorant, vicious negro vote?"[21]

Two leading black political captains, one a Democrat and the other a Republican, saw their businesses attacked during the riot. The mob's attack was nonpartisan—they thoroughly wrecked both places. One of these black power brokers was Republican C. C. Lee, a Virginia-born businessman in his mid-thirties. With the aid of his wife, Lee had succeeded in several ventures in Springfield. A saloonkeeper in 1900, by 1902 he ran a small hotel as well. In 1907 Lee launched a more ambitious scheme and combined a theater, saloon, poolroom, and restaurant in a single large building on East Washington Street. A white newspaper described him contemptuously at the height of his career: "Lee is a white coon, short of stature, a flashy dresser on whose bosom there generally sparkles a diamond as big as a hand mirror."[22] Lee's rival, Democrat William Johnson, according to the white press, "conducted a saloon and crap game on the levee between Seventh and Eighth streets." Allegedly, most black voters from the First and Seventh Wards owed allegiance to one or the other of these two men, whose businesses "swarmed with colonies of illegal voters" on election days. Rioters systematically wrecked both Lee's and Johnson's places. Lee's losses alone, which included an electric piano that the mob chopped into kindling, amounted to over $8,000.[23] Though the rioters perhaps had other reasons for sacking the black political captains' businesses, Lee and Johnson, conspicuous with their "flashy" clothes and election-day wads of dollar bills, may have symbolized to these whites the blacks' so-called "exalted notion of importance" that Reverend Rogers so deplored.

Among those whites probably most aware of, and sensitive to, changes in the Levee's social and economic composition were the men who owned or worked in its saloons. White Levee saloons, like black ones, were not simply places for recreation, but served as important centers of working-class social and political life, with saloonkeepers at the hub of interaction. Given the position of saloonkeepers and their employees in the community and the number of them who turned up among the identified rioters, it seems quite plausible that they provided some leadership for Springfield's rioters. Fifteen of a total of 115 rioters identified had saloon-related jobs downtown: eight bartenders, one saloon clerk, three porters, one waiter, and two proprietors. Available information on the ethnic background of ten of them revealed that half were either Irish or had Irish parents. As noted earlier, the Irish had an enduring heritage of bitterness toward blacks, and in Springfield they contributed more than their share of rioters. One of the few studies that has looked at anti-black crowd composition found that during a race riot in Memphis, Tennessee, Irish saloonkeepers and grocers played a critical role in organizing and leading attacks on blacks there.[24] Springfield's white saloons faced no economic competition from black drinking establishments, for both primarily served customers of their own race. Even so, the Irish in particular must not have been very happy about what probably seemed to be a sudden flourishing of highly visible black business and political influence in the Levee after the turn of the century. For them, sacking the Levee and driving away Badlands residents was not just a matter of putting "uppity" blacks in their place—it also meant dealing a serious political blow to their rival, the Republican party. Most blacks voted Republican, and to the predominantly Democratic Irish, for whom politics constituted a major opportunity for upward mobility, the riot offered a means of weakening Republican voting strength and reducing black competition for scarce city government positions.

Though white resentment over black political success downtown most likely did contribute to the violence in the Levee, it was probably not the sole factor influencing the rioters, for they destroyed all of the black businesses there, not just places associated with black politics. Neither were the riots solely an attempt by righteously indignant whites to eliminate crime and vice downtown by wiping out the Levee's "dens and dives," though that was the way the white press early characterized their behavior. Not only did the mob leave virtually untouched white saloons, gambling establishments, brothels, and opium dens, but the majority of the black businesses they wrecked were respectable enterprises: barbershops, restaurants, shoemakers' shops, an upholstery shop, a bicycle store, and the like. Only six of the twenty-one black businesses destroyed were saloons, and not all of these were immoral dives or alleged hotbeds of political corruption. Mayor Roy Reece pointed out that some of these had been just as reputable as any run by whites in the city. "There is the saloon of S. J. Morton," Reece lamented; "Morton has never had any trouble with the police as long as he had been in business. He would not even permit the shaking of the dice in his place for drinks." Morton was not involved in city politics, but by the time the mob finished with his place, the "only thing left unbroken [was a] peanut vending machine."[25]

The city's white press and other influential whites quickly revised their assessment of the rioters, but not of the damage done to the black community. Most clung to the notion that black misbehavior was the cause of the trouble in the first place, and the press continued to print wholesale condemnations of black Levee and Badlands residents. Rare indeed was any recognition that the majority of black businesses destroyed were respectable enterprises, or that most Badlands victims were inoffensive citizens. Instead, the white press emphasized the riot's desirable "reform" by-products (while expressing fear of, and condemnation toward, the rioters) and claimed that respectable blacks had nothing to fear. The wrecking of the black business district—especially its saloons—was generally viewed as a good riddance. The same newspaper that, following Clergy Ballard's death in July, had stridently called for a "cleaning out" of the Levee, later applauded the demise of the black "dens and dives" downtown, conveniently ignoring the more plentiful "shady" white-owned sa-

loons that dotted the central business district. The Levee rioting
seemed a most admirable and salutary reform:

> the negro joints on East Washington street have done more to sink the
> level of that street than any dozen other causes. The negro who runs a
> saloon is generally an undesirable citizen. His saloon is generally dirty
> and filthy. The unspeakable character of the habitués of these dives
> make them very undesirable in any city. Music was permitted and the
> lewd negress was a permanent fixture in all of them. The gins and
> whiskeys that are sold are terrors. Usually they [the drinks] are
> drugged and it is while inflamed with such liquors that they [blacks] go
> out and commit their heinous crimes.[26]

Convinced that the rioting in the Levee had excised a great social
evil, the same paper issued a thinly veiled warning: "The granting
of a license to any negro to run a saloon will be considered an affront by the people of this city."[27]

After the riot Badlands residents also faced sweeping accusations
of depravity in Springfield's white newspapers, which cited their alleged moral lapses, especially violations of the social and sexual etiquette of strict racial separation. The press complained that "the
houses of this black belt were hovels. Whites and blacks lived together. Children ran through the streets of this miserable settlement
who knew not their parents. Their hair indicated one race and their
fair skin the other." Ignoring the facts—that many respectable black
residents suffered losses and that not all, or even a majority, of those
who lived in the Badlands were depraved criminals—the white press
repeatedly insisted that the rioters had attacked only "bad Negroes."
As one newspaper said, "it is not true that against the law-abiding
negro citizens of whom there are many in the city there is a public
sentiment that demands their deportation. A good many of the
blacks who have been attacked are a fine riddance. The negro who
has behaved himself is in danger from none, except the tough and
the ruffian."[28]

Patterns of Targeting: Hit-and-Run Attacks

The rioters' ultimate goal seemingly was to drive away all of Springfield's blacks, and they did succeed in forcing hundreds to flee temporarily. Only the belated arrival of the state militia halted the
mob's progress into other black neighborhoods. Since the increasing
numbers of troops made open mass marches against black enclaves
impossible, rioters switched to hit-and-run attacks against carefully

selected black victims beginning late the first night of the outbreak. In the process, a clear pattern of targeting emerged, which persisted for several weeks after the riot. Whites launched only a few hit-and-run assaults, but, in choosing their victims, they aimed high up the black social ladder. They passed up the chance to attack more accessible but poorer blacks and focused their anger on more affluent targets.

Despite assurances in the white press that law-abiding and well-behaved blacks had nothing to fear, Springfield's black residents knew better. Margaret Ferguson lived in the southeastern black enclave, far removed from the Levee and Badlands, in a middle-class household. At the time of the riot, her father worked for the state government. Ferguson's family owned their home and were wealthy enough later to send her to college, where she would earn a master's degree in education. She remembered that blacks in the large southeast neighborhood felt far from safe during and after the rioting. Even though the militia established constant patrols in the south end, Ferguson's father sent his wife and children to a farm owned by black friends for safety. Ferguson explained why her parents and other black families in the southeast feared for their lives and property: "See, the people that they [the rioters] harmed and hurt were not really the no-gooders. The Donnegan that they hung was a very nice man. They were very busy hurting the prominent [blacks], and so, of course we were frightened, you see, because we, also, were affluent. We owned property; many poor whites didn't. There was a great deal of animosity toward any well-established Negro who owned his own house and had a good job."[29]

Margaret Ferguson and other blacks mentioned the grim determination of many residents to defend their homes and property from attack. The middle-class black family that lived next door to the Fergusons apparently was very light-skinned. The wife looked like a white woman, said Ferguson, and the family received anonymous death threats. The husband camped out in his yard armed with a shotgun, ready to shoot any suspicious whites who came near his house. Edith Carpenter recalled that her father, Edward White, a black grocer who also lived in the southeast, armed himself as soon as it became apparent that the mob intended to attack any blacks it could reach. White "sent word out and let everybody know that if anybody bothered him, he certainly had everything to [protect himself with]," according to his daughter. "All day and all night long, he had a gun on each shoulder and he marched from where our store was to our home, and that was back and forth all evening." No one molested White's store or home, but like Margaret Ferguson's father, he sent his family away until the worst was over.[30] Another black southeast resident recalled that the adults, both men and women, kept a regular watch at the edges of the neighborhood, keeping an eye out for invading white rioters. Apparently the men had some kind of plan to muster to repel attacks if their "scouts" reported anything suspicious.[31]

Neither the presence of the state militia nor the glib assurances of the city's white newspapers convinced better-off black southeast residents that they were safe. White neighbors who attempted to help them apparently were in danger, too. Margaret Ferguson told of her mother's return from the family's farm sanctuary to check on her house and property. As she drove her buggy into town along Eleventh Street, whites came to their doors shouting, "We're going to get you tonight! We're going to get you tonight!" She reached home safely and found the house unmolested. Wishing to save some valuable household items from theft, including a cherished set of old Haviland china, Ferguson's mother asked her English neighbors across the street to help her. They agreed to hide her valuables until the rioting was over. After packing the items carefully in a large wicker laundry basket, she delivered them to her white friends. Her daughter remembered what happened next. "Some people who worked . . . with Mr. Farnsworth [their English neighbor] saw us taking it [the basket] over there, so when Mr. Farnsworth came to work, they told him that if he did not bring it back, they were going to burn his house down." The frightened immigrant returned the basket immediately.[32]

The first hit-and-run attack on a carefully selected black target occurred late in the first night's outbreak when whites fleeing the militia in the Badlands chose to sack one last black residence before retiring for the evening. Many black homes lay along the section of North Thirteenth Street through which they retreated, but the rioters targeted only one, a large two-story, wood frame house owned by the Duncans, a very prominent black family.[33] The head of the Duncan clan, Kentucky-born Clarke Duncan, owned not only the house, but a successful grocery store as well. His son, Otis Duncan, was well known in the black community, for he held a desirable position in the state government and served as a major in the black Eighth Regiment of the state militia. Otis Duncan's sister had married one of Springfield's two black physicians. The Duncan's were counted as part of the city's small black elite and were, according to Margaret Ferguson, precisely the kind of blacks whom working-class whites resented most.[34]

The Duncans, like many black families in the area, had evacuated their home earlier. The rioters passed up the other black homes on the street and immediately surrounded their house. After breaking windows and throwing rocks against the outside of the building, the rioters "entered the building, smashed a fine piano into kindling, broke all the furniture downstairs. They then went upstairs, where they smashed furniture, fired a bullet through a large mirror on a dresser in Major Duncan's room." They also looted the place for valuables—money, a gold watch, diamond rings belonging to Mrs. Duncan—and carried off Otis Duncan's militia uniform and dress saber. "To make the looting good," reported one newspaper, "they carried away a birdcage and its occupant."[35] Margaret Ferguson remembered other details: "There was quite a large picture on the wall of his [Otis Duncan's] mother. When the mob broke in his house, they took this saber off the wall and gouged the eyes out of his mother's picture."[36]

After a tense but peaceful day in the city Saturday, crowds of angry whites reassembled at dusk downtown and, after a futile attempt to storm the State Arsenal, headed straight to William Donnegan's residence southeast of the central business district. According to the press, "the mob appears to have had a destination when it started. It kept true to its course. It went directly to the Donnegan residence and selected the old man for the slaughter." There "was nothing haphazard about" the mob's work, which "was done so quickly that it bears all the marks of clever organization and execution."[37] During Abraham Raymer's subsequent trial for his alleged part in Donnegan's murder, witnesses revealed that the attack was planned ahead of time. One witness who had been downtown early Saturday evening related conversations he had heard among some of the men in the crowd that later marched on the State Arsenal. Several times, the witness said, he heard the men mention Donnegan's name and heard someone exclaim, "Let's get him tonight!"[38]

Margaret Ferguson explained how a mob recruited from distant white neighborhoods might have located their intended victim so quickly. Abraham Raymer and Ernest Humphrey, later indicted as ringleaders in the Donnegan lynching, worked as hucksters in the city. Ferguson remembered that Humphrey "sold fresh vegetables and fruits from his huckster wagon, and he sold to blacks. They were really his stock in trade. He came to our house many times.

And he was one of the main leaders of the mob, going around show-ing people where blacks lived, see."[39] William Donnegan's wife also testified during Abraham Raymer's trial that she had "known the defendant for some time" because the Jewish huckster had occasion-ally stopped by the Donnegan home to sell vegetables. As Ferguson explained, the rioters did not know where many blacks lived outside of the Levee and Badlands, "particularly the ones they wanted to harm or hurt." Thus they used men like Raymer and Humphrey as guides.[40]

One explanation Springfield's press offered as to why the rioters singled out William Donnegan was that he had been married to a white woman. Another was that the rioters may have intended "to clean out the Fourth Ward negroes," who, though few in number in this neighborhood, were inadequately protected by the militia that evening.[41] A third speculation was that Donnegan's high status made him a conspicuous and tempting target. Donnegan's niece, who lived close to her uncle's house, did feel that his wealth was what most attracted the mob's wrath: "They say my uncle was killed because he [was] married to a white woman, but they have been married twenty years and own considerable property. And the prop-erty was the cause of his murder. He was even told by some of the ringleaders of the mob that he had too much property for a 'nigger,' and that he would be killed unless he and his family moved away."[42]

William Donnegan had been a Springfield resident for many years, and he and his family, like the Duncans, were well known in the black community. Born in Kentucky in the 1820s, Donnegan mi-grated to the capital in 1845 and got his start there by importing black laborers from the South. Later he took up shoemaking and made several profitable real estate investments. At the time of his death, he was among the wealthiest blacks in Springfield, with an estimated net worth of about $15,000.[43] The combination of having a white wife and owning substantial property made William Donne-gan a prime target for the mob, though it is impossible to tell which "offense"—the property or the wife—was more important to the ri-oters. Like the hit-and-run attack on the Duncans, however, the Donnegan lynching does suggest that the family's affluence was an important factor behind the attack.

Early Sunday evening, 16 August, after the city was supposedly secure in the hands of the state militia, yet another black family was attacked. A little before 6:00, word reached the militia headquarters that a mob had gathered at the home of Samuel Willis on North Fifth Street and that someone had set a fire there. The authorities quickly dispatched troops, who dispersed a crowd of about 1,500 whites and then put out the fire.[44] Samuel Willis, like Clarke Duncan and William Donnegan, was also a long-time resident of Springfield and, like the others, was a member of the black elite. Over the years, Willis had prospered as a restaurant owner and as a popular chef and caterer. Like Donnegan, he owned a large and comfortable home in a predominantly white neighborhood.[45] Sunday night was not the first time whites had menaced his home, Willis reported. The previous day, whites had pelted his house with stones and bricks and made several attempts to burn it down. Willis escaped the crisis with only minor damage to his property.[46]

Had fewer troops been in the city, the number of assaults on isolated black residences undoubtedly would have been greater; however, the urban "guerrilla warfare," as the newspapers put it, persisted until early September. On the first of that month unidentified marauders set fire to the home of Albert Debose, a successful black contractor who owned a large two-story frame house in the southern part of the city on East Cass Street, in a predominantly white, middle-class neighborhood. "Mr. Debose," the press noted, "is one of the wealthiest colored residents of Springfield." His house was nearly a total loss, estimated at about $2,000. Fortunately Debose had insurance.[47]

Since the Donnegan, Willis, and Debose families all lived in white neighborhoods, it seems tempting to conclude that the attacks on them were motivated by white resentment over residential "invasions" by blacks. According to the press, one hit-and-run attack did appear to be the product of such resentment. Early Sunday morning, on 16 August, shortly after the Donnegan lynching, a crowd of whites converged on the home of Clarence Harvey, a black Chicagoan who had moved to Springfield with his family several weeks earlier. The Harveys rented a small house at 1144 North Seventh Street in the heart of an otherwise all-white, working-class district in the northeastern First Ward. The house was owned by a former black Springfield resident who, over the years, had rented the building to both black and white tenants. During the rioting the Harveys had been warned to leave town, but they chose to ignore the threats. The whites who assembled at their house Sunday morning let loose a barrage of bricks and bullets, breaking windows and demolishing weatherboarding. The frightened family escaped harm and took refuge at the county jail. Without even retrieving their belongings, the discouraged family boarded a train for St. Louis later that day, never to return.[48]

The press interviewed several north-end whites, asking for their opinion on the attack. One resident told a reporter: "We will have no more niggers living out here. We are respectable people along here and we have been tormented with niggers long enough. We have tried every legitimate means of keeping them [blacks] out, even offering to pool our money and buy the place, but the proprietor, who is himself a negro, seems to think that he can lord it over us."[49] Another man said that the Harvey family had behaved in an offensive and disagreeable manner, but this claim is doubtful. The previous black tenant, who had supposedly "tormented" whites in the neighborhood, for example, was perfectly respectable: a minister, the Reverend G. K. McDaniel. Harvey reportedly was a "Dandy Coon type" (at the very least, presumably this meant that he dressed well and was not humble or self-effacing), who made "loud and insulting statements" to north-end whites. No record of Clarence Harvey's occupation survives, but the press did mention that he had obtained "a good position" in Springfield. Given the status of the earlier tenant and Harvey's appellation as a "Dandy Coon," it is likely that the family had achieved a comfortable, perhaps even middle-class, standing. If so, that probably made their presence even more irritating to north-end whites. "To have a bunch of insulting negroes placed in our midst," complained one man, "is more than human forbearance can stand." Very likely echoing the sentiments of many in that working-class neighborhood, he added, "If he [the landlord] moves another colored family in here he will have an ash pile instead of a house."[50]

The Social Location of White Vengeance

Following the Harvey incident, one newspaper claimed that "the white neighborhoods have naturally resented the encroaching of the blacks. The purchase of a piece of property by one negro has always caused [resentment] but it has been done many times." As support for this contention, the article pointed to the large "number of blocks in the city in which there may be only one negro family."[51] The number of blacks living on all-white blocks did increase over time, but this dispersion was a modest and gradual process. Taking block-length sections of streets as units, and including both sides of each street, a search of Springfield's city directories gives a fair indication of the extent and location of black residences in otherwise all-white areas (see Appendix, Table 4.2). In 1892, for example, 70 block-length street sections had a single black household, and in

1907 there were 122 such sections. The majority—over half—of these homes lay near the First, Sixth, and Seventh Ward black enclaves and constituted their fringe or periphery. In wealthier areas, especially in the southern Fourth and Fifth Wards, isolated black households often were occupied by servants who were living close to their employers.[52] For the most part, the 122 black households on white blocks had working-class neighbors, though few were quite so isolated in a sea of white residents as the Harveys.

A more likely explanation for the Harvey attack than whites' resentment of the family's status or the residential "invasion" alleged by the press is location. The Harvey home was only a few blocks from that of Mabel Hallam, the white woman whose alleged rape precipitated the riot. It was also not very far from Clergy Ballard's place. The Harveys thus unwittingly found themselves surrounded by those whites most determined to avenge the Ballards and Hallams. They were, in effect, the lone black outpost in the very heart of enemy territory.

Information on the identity of those who carried out hit-and-run forays is scarce, but the newspapers did reveal the names of five men arrested immediately after the Harvey incident. The background of the five suspects resembled that of the typical rioter described earlier: four were born in the North and one was Irish; all were in their early to mid-twenties; and all were skilled workers in occupations from which blacks were excluded. But most significantly, they all had clear ties to Clergy Ballard. Four had been coworkers of his, either on the Chicago, Peoria & St. Louis Railroad or at the nearby Illinois Watch factory, and one had actually boarded in the Ballard household in 1904. All five lived but a short distance— several blocks—from the Harvey residence. The police captured them together, armed and in the midst of "discussing the riot."[53] For lack of hard evidence and willing witnesses, the five men were never indicted. However, their ties to the Ballards and the fact that the police deemed them prime suspects in the Harvey attack suggest that fear of black residential "invasion," at least in this instance, was a lesser concern than revenge.

North-end whites within the extended social network that included the Ballards and Hallams—men such as the five arrested for mobbing the Harvey home—may have shaped Springfield's violence in significant ways. From the outbreak of the riot to the trials that followed, there is evidence, albeit thin, that those motivated in part by a desire for personal revenge contributed significant impetus, organization, and leadership to the city's disorder. Indeed, their determined pursuit of extralegal retaliation may well have served to transform what otherwise might have remained a dispute involving a few individuals, a family, or a small neighborhood into a conflict that called upon the loyalties of an entire race.

The Hallam home and neighborhood were the first focus for angry milling crowds hours before the riot broke out. Later, when the growing mob at the county jail finally commanded entry to the building, Mabel Hallam's husband and several of his fellow streetcar workers were among those delegated to search for the two black suspects. Throughout the mass violence and afterward, the press several times characterized the north end as the area hardest for the authorities to handle. Finally, the gross disproportion among identified rioters of railroad men who were Clergy Ballard's co-workers also points to a desire for personal vengeance, as does the fact that his two sons worked for the same line.

What role those acquainted with the Hallams or Ballards might have played in delivering anonymous threats to whites with ties to blacks, or in the hit-and-run attacks (other than the one against the Harveys), remains unclear. But those allies with the strongest ties to the two white families probably had the greatest interest in sustaining the quest for revenge; these men undoubtedly provided one important and cohesive social nucleus for the collective assault on the city's black community. Even so, neither the mass rioting nor the subsequent small-scale assaults on black individuals or property can be explained simply as an effort to wreak vengeance for wrongs done to the Ballards and Hallams. Most whites who rioted probably knew neither family. And, if the earlier data on identified rioters are any indication, most rioters were not members of the social networks mobilized to avenge them. That these strangers furnished many quick and eager riot recruits reminds us that whites were responding to sources of interracial conflict that transcended any single black "outrage" like the Ballard murder.

As noted earlier, Springfield's rioters typically were socially and geographically distant from blacks. This finding is consistent with a large and diverse body of social science research. Especially pertinent are the observations of sociologist Donald Black that relational distance is a major factor that determines the extent and style of extralegal forms of social control ("any process by which people define and respond to deviant behavior"), including collective violence such as vengeance, feuds, wars, and race and ethnic riots.[54] Black's concept of relational distance refers to the degree of intimacy or involvement between individuals or groups measured by "the scope, frequency, and length of interaction between people, the age of their relationship, and the nature and number of links between them in a social network."[55] He proposes that "vengeance varies directly with relational distance": where social contacts are few, brief, or superficial, the likelihood of violent retaliation between groups increases.[56] For example, in a cross-cultural study, one sociologist reports that the probability of the most violent response to homicide—revenge—"increases directly and dramatically as the principals become less intimate with one another."[57] Anthropologists who examine the handling of conflict and grievances in preindustrial societies describe a similar pattern. So-called "cross-cutting ties"—created when, for example, one marries outside one's lineage, clan, or tribe—result in a division of loyalties that works to reduce the likelihood of violent retaliation in the face of conflict. Cross-cutting ties also occur in non-kin social groupings in modern industrial societies and may have the same effect. Politics, religion, ethnicity, race, region, neighborhood, and more all compete for our loyalty. While such social diversity may breed competition and conflict, it is also true that, as anthropologist Max Gluckman puts it, "divisions of interest and loyalties within any one group prevent it from standing in absolute opposition to other groups and to the society at large." He concludes, "Feud is waged and vengeance taken when the parties live sufficiently far apart, or are too weakly related by diverse ties."[58]

One major factor that influences relational distance, including the formation of cross-cutting ties, is residential proximity.[59] Since the 1950s, many policy-oriented studies have explored what has been termed the contact hypothesis: that anti-black attitudes may be reduced by certain types of contact or interaction with blacks. Much of this research has looked at the effect of interracial contact in integrated housing and neighborhoods. In general, these studies find that white prejudice decreases as residential contact with blacks of similar status and values increases.[60]

One cannot assume, however, that residential contact among Springfield's whites and blacks necessarily accomplished similar changes in white attitudes earlier in the century. Recent studies of the impact of integration on white opinion coincided with the national climate of toleration and disapproval of discrimination that grew in the United States after World War II. As Gordon Allport notes, before interracial contact in neighborhoods and the workplace can reduce white prejudice, it needs the sanction of "institutional supports [such as] law, custom, or local atmosphere"—sources of support that were largely absent in turn-of-century

America. Unfortunately, also absent are comparably rich data for this early period such as the interviews and opinion surveys of recent decades on changes in white racial attitudes in integrated settings.

For example, some scholars have found that equal-status contact in integrated work settings tends to reduce white prejudice. Likewise, Alfred M. Lee and Norman D. Humphrey noted that during Detroit's 1943 race riot, there was no violence in integrated factories.[61] For Springfield, however, detailed information on white attitudes or behavior in integrated work settings is virtually nonexistent. It is noteworthy, though, that the city's one major integrated industry—coal mining—witnessed no disorder during the riot. Also, white miners seemed slightly underrepresented among those rioters whose occupations were identified. Of course, unlike most workers, the miners had explicit institutional support for integration from the United Mine Workers union. Fortunately, enough information is available for Springfield that it is possible to assess the effects of interracial residential proximity, and it is clear that the residential distribution of whites and blacks did influence the location of violence, who rioted, and who was targeted.

Several students of interracial conflict have commented briefly and impressionistically on the apparent lack of violence in integrated neighborhoods during race riots from the 1910s to the 1940s. Even troubled "contested neighborhoods" (areas "previously dominated by whites but undergoing transition" or "in the line of movement of the Negro population and anticipating invasion") remained largely peaceful during these riots. Attacks against blacks in integrated areas seemed to be the work of strangers—"outside fanatics," as one writer puts it.[62] Likewise, Lee and Humphrey note a "homely truth" about Detroit's race riot: "Neighbors—black and white—do not riot against each other."[63] What these few impressions suggest—that residential proximity reduces relational distance between the races and inhibits violence—is borne out by data on Springfield as well.

Most of Springfield's rioters did not live near blacks. Examining block-length street sections (arguably the most intimate residential setting, apart from shared dwellings themselves), out of 127 white rioters only twelve (less than 10 percent) lived in a section where blacks resided. Seven of these lived in the Badlands or Levee district; the other five were from scattered locations in the city and were arrested for disorderly conduct downtown, not in their own neighborhoods. Other rioters lived slightly farther from blacks: on the same block as a black family, but on all-white street sections. Given their greater relational distance from blacks, one would expect them to be more riot-prone—and they were. Over twice as many rioters (25) lived on the same block as blacks, but with whites alone as their closest neighbors. Again, most (13) lived in or near the Levee and Badlands, and the rest rioted well away from their own neighborhoods. The majority of the 127 rioters, over 70 percent, came from all-white street sections and all-white blocks. Altogether, less than one-third of the rioters shared the same street section or block with blacks. In general, then, the greater a white's residential distance from blacks, the more likely he or she was to riot.

In fact, Springfield's whites overwhelmingly refrained from attacking blacks in their immediate vicinity. Despite the newspapers' claim that whites always resented the presence of a single black home on their block, one of the more striking features of this riot is how rarely these isolated black households were attacked. The assault on the Harvey home in the north end was the only clear instance where immediate white neighbors seemed to have turned on nearby blacks. The location of rioters' homes suggests that, while residential proximity may not have improved whites' view of blacks in general, it may have created ties strong enough in interracial neighborhoods to produce white neutrality—and in a few cases limited support—during the violence.[64] It also supports the observations of black residents like Margaret Ferguson that it was strangers and not white neighbors who posed the greatest danger during and after the riot. The whites who had shouted threats at her mother and otherwise menaced her family, Ferguson explained, lived four or five blocks away or farther. The danger, as her family and other blacks knew, lay in the possibility of a concerted attack by bands of armed whites from distant neighborhoods.[65] Moreover, the few rioters whose residences were located on integrated street sections or blocks (outside of the Badlands and Levee) gravitated to the center of violence downtown, passing up the chance to attack black families closer to home.

In the post-riot hit-and-run attacks, whites focused their planning and destructive energies only on sorties against high-status black residents. Though Ferguson and other blacks characterized their relations with white neighbors as "cordial but distant," apparently even that level of contact was enough to ensure white neutrality. Here the Harvey family was at a distinct disadvantage. Not only had they settled in an unfortunate location in the north end, but they had arrived only a few weeks before the riot. As newcomers, they never had the time to cultivate even the weakest ties with their white neighbors, ties that might have made them less vulnerable to attack.

Finally, as noted earlier, at least a few whites offered limited support to their frightened black neighbors: Badlands whites who pleaded with the mob to spare an elderly black woman's home on their block; Ferguson's English neighbors who temporarily agreed to hide her family's valuables; immigrant neighbors who offered to escort a black man back and forth from work to protect him from attack; and a Jewish woman who allegedly hid black neighbors in her basement. Existing records give us only rare glimpses of white neighbors' helpful efforts, but even so, they indicate the capacity of residential proximity to undermine whites' willingness to take part in anti-black collective violence.

It appears, however, that close interracial residential proximity did not significantly reduce relational distance in the Levee and other areas in or near downtown Springfield. Both whites and blacks there were largely renters who occupied boardinghouses, hotels, converted space over shops, and the like. They were more transient and geographically mobile than those in other parts of the city and lacked the long-term, stable, and regular interracial exposure that those in truly residential integrated neighborhoods experienced. As Lee and Humphrey observed of Detroit, the integrated areas that remained peaceful during its race riot were the ones where "whites and Negroes had lived as neighbors long enough to get to know and understand each other."[66] In downtown Springfield, interracial contact was far more likely to be brief, casual, and superficial, with both black and white residents often confronting new faces in this transient "neighborhood." Given the relatively rapid turnover of residents, there simply was not enough time for neighborly ties or stable acquaintanceships to develop. In such a situation, one scholar noted, "the more contact the more trouble": casual contacts can exacerbate interracial mistrust and hostility.[67] Perhaps this is one reason why the downtown area, along with the white, working-class north end, contributed the most rioters.

Black Progress as Deviant Behavior

The locus of Springfield's anti-black hostility lay, first, with the white working class and, second, among whites of that class who were socially and geographically distant from blacks or who lived near them in residentially unstable areas of downtown Springfield. Those who rioted may well have had perceptions of blacks not shared by other whites in the city. It is impossible to know. Even so, we might speculate that, unlike better-off whites and working-class whites with closer and more regular contacts with blacks, the rioters viewed Springfield's blacks as a danger to their sense of dignity and status. Any signs of black success, power, and upward mobility may have angered them. The sacking of black Levee businesses and the deliberate targeting of affluent blacks in hit-and run attacks may therefore have expressed their resentment. The two lynching victims were successful black men. Also, recall that William English Walling felt that many of the whites he interviewed said that they were angry because the city's blacks had behaved as if they were "as good as" whites. Again, however, these can only be matters of speculation.

One of the things most rioters had to lose was precisely what set them apart from, and insulated them from, blacks: the fact that they lived and worked far from the despised race. Despite the virtual absence of interracial competition for jobs and housing in Springfield, they probably knew that their prized social distance from blacks was less then secure. Middle- to upper-class whites did not have this problem: not only had they already achieved a level of material comfort and security that firmly established their prestige in the community, but they had very different kinds of interactions with blacks. What contact they had with blacks largely took place in contexts where blacks' roles were clearly defined as subordinate: as employees, house servants, laundresses, and the like. Also, in an age when most blacks were trapped in low-status, low-paid occupations, more affluent whites did not have to worry about interracial competition for employment. The white working class lacked such security. Though Springfield's economy was healthy in 1908 and no recent labor conflicts had heightened interracial tensions there, working-class whites needed no reminding that blacks could pose a threat when employers desired to break a strike or drive down wages.

The white working class was also at a disadvantage in housing, for it had less control over the quality and composition of its neighborhoods than better-off whites. Short of extralegal, violent tactics, whites in working-class neighborhoods had few effective means to prevent black settlement. And because property values and rents were low enough for many blacks to move in, integration was an ever-present possibility. As mentioned earlier, single black families who settled on all-white street sections usually had working-class neighbors. The sudden appearance of new black neighbors was seldom a concern of Springfield's wealthier whites of the southern

Fourth and Fifth Wards. Real estate prices were high enough in desirable suburban locations to keep out all but the most prosperous black families. And, of course, many of the few blacks who did live in the wealthier wards were there because they were employed by whites as domestics, coachmen, or yardmen. Finally, if whites in a middle- or upper-class area wished to keep unwanted black newcomers out of their immediate neighborhood, they had more resources, financial and otherwise, to do so.

White prejudice often made it difficult for blacks to purchase property outside of their traditional settlements in the city. Sometimes they had to resort to subterfuge in order to buy a house in a predominantly white neighborhood. William Hubbard, a young black man at the time of the riot, remembered one technique blacks used to acquire homes in good residential areas. A prospective black home buyer would "get a chance to buy him a piece of property. Somebody he worked for would buy it for him, and then he'd pay him. They've been tricking them [whites] since I was big enough to know anything, tricking them like that, but they didn't trick them enough."[68] The use of a white friend or employer as a "front" to purchase a home was probably more common in the east and north sections of the city, where homes were generally less expensive. In the wealthier sections of Springfield, especially in those areas where new suburban developments were built, restrictive covenants were sometimes used to prevent black settlement. Margaret Ferguson remembered the establishment of Harvard Park, a new housing development in the southern part of the city. Deeds to its new homes contained restrictive clauses forbidding the sale of property to blacks:

> Friends of ours wanted to buy a house. And when the people went to sell it to them, they found this clause was in the deed that blacks could not [buy]—so many of the people who moved into some of those houses that were being built down there knew that that clause was in their deed, and so they were very anti-black. And knowing we were so close [in southeast Springfield], I guess they were afraid that maybe [blacks] would try to come out there. There was a great deal of prejudice here in property owning.[69]

Such deed restrictions served to provide wealthier whites a measure of security against black residential advances into the new and highly desirable suburban developments.

A few black real estate dealers took profitable advantage of white prejudice. The wealthy black carpenter, William Florville, for example, created a small sensation in 1908 when he acquired a piece of property in a new Fourth Ward suburban tract. Named Hawthorne Place, this development was an attractive, park-like neighborhood "in which handsome houses were to be erected." A white owner there was eager to leave town and sold his place to Florville. The developers were outraged when they discovered the transaction, but they had no choice but to buy the property back from Florville, at a substantially higher price. "The south side," one newspaper reported, "was greatly aroused." Soon after, Florville managed yet a second purchase in the white section of the south end, with the same profitable result.[70] Not surprisingly, as the black newspaper *Forum* noted, Florville was "the richest colored man in the city and owns a vast amount of real estate and has 'plenty' of money."[71] Even if developers failed to use restrictive clauses in deeds, they could, as the Florville example shows, wield their financial resources to remove black interlopers. Needless to say, working-class residents had no such financial leverage. Some may have tried to make formal or informal agreements in their neighborhoods to prevent the sale of homes to blacks. Even so, since far more houses in Springfield's working-class areas were inexpensive, their neighborhoods were relatively more vulnerable to black settlement.

White racism, then, in terms of various anti-black attitudes and riot-proneness in Springfield, was unevenly distributed across the city. Many working-class whites with stable contacts with blacks at work or in their neighborhoods seemed willing at least to tolerate a black presence in Springfield. Better-off whites, as the black scholar Kelly Miller noted early in the century, were "removed by the double barrier of race and class from the plane of competition." The "Negro problem," as Springfield's middle- and upper-class whites tended to see it, involved black crime and disorder in the Levee district. They viewed blacks as "naturally" undisciplined and blamed them in part for such downtown social excesses as drinking, gambling, and prostitution. It was the white worker, Miller said, who "must be ever on the alert to keep up the line of demarcation" between the races. Whenever working-class whites' "sensitive race pride" was affronted by black behavior that implied social equality or leveling, violence might result. Observing the local scene, the editor of the *Forum* agreed, noting that "this color line drawing is done by those of low birth, and not the better class [of whites]."[72] Springfield's riot suggests that such "race pride" was strongest among those in the white working class who lived and worked well away from blacks. Since they were vulnerable to unbidden contact with blacks at work and in their neighborhoods, they watched "the line of demarcation" vigilantly to ensure that their social distance from blacks remained intact.

The violence in Springfield may also be understood partly as a reaction to a special form of deviant behavior—black progress—a visible violation of a previously inferior place in the social order. As Frederick Douglass once noted for an earlier period, whites could accept the black as "a buffoon, as a menial, as a servant," but "resented and resisted" his upward mobility. The acquisition of wealth, power, and property, Douglass warned, invited white repression.[73] And "blacks of property and standing" in Springfield were major targets for attack. In the comic strip noted earlier, the white urchins' assaults on Sambo when he appeared to be rising in the world may have made sense to white readers because the comic contained more than a grain of truth. Regardless of the rioters' motivation, affluent blacks had good cause to worry for their safety. Black success generated social danger.

By 21 August, less than a week after the rioting broke out, most of the state militia had left the city. Some feared that with the withdrawal of the troops, large-scale disorder would resume. Soldiers in the Seventh Illinois Infantry, part of the reduced force left behind, reported that people they encountered in the streets told them, "As soon as you fellows are going we will have to get rid of these blacks. Springfield must be a white town."[74] Mass violence, however, did not recur, though hit-and-run attacks on homes and assaults on blacks caught alone on the streets persisted until September. Blacks who wandered into some white neighborhoods found themselves in danger in the weeks after the riots.

The streets of the north end were particularly perilous for blacks. One white resident there remembered this incident: "I was up here at Ninth and Ridgley and here come a nigger down the road running and about twenty or twenty-five [men] behind throwing and a howling [to] stop that son-of-a-gun. Trying to kill the poor devil, but he outrun and got away."[75] Some blacks were not so fortunate. Three days after the riots, a gang of whites in the north end "put it all over a negro who was fleeing from the city for the reason he was not getting along fast enough." The crowd surrounded the man and pelted him with bricks and stones, knocking him to the ground. By the time the militia arrived, the man was "in a very bad shape." As was the case with many blacks injured during and after the riots, the press failed to mention the victim's name. Neither were any arrests made, probably because the man's assailants had fled at the approach of the troops. The same day, an Arab immigrant who tended animals at the zoo in the north part of town was set upon by a white man who mistook him for a black.[76] On 5 September, a small group of whites assaulted two black men near a train station downtown. The press claimed that the blacks had invited attack because they had "indulged in strong talk." One black escaped, but the second man "was knocked down and severely beaten." Other whites, attracted by the fracas, frightened off the attackers, who escaped in the darkness.[77]

For several days following the riot, a local artist for the *Springfield News* produced a series of five large drawings meant to encapsulate and symbolize the city's return from the anarchy of "mob rule" to a normal state of affairs. The *News* ran one drawing on the top of its front page each day. The first panel, which appeared on 18 August, showed a bloody-handed rioter labeled "the mob" cowering under bolts of lightening labeled "the militia" and "the law." Sloppily clad in tattered and patched clothing, the rioter clearly was meant to suggest riffraff to the viewer. The drawing for 19 August referred to the Springfield business community's emergency meeting. Captioned "Upholding the Arm of the Law," the picture represented a well-dressed man labeled "Springfield Business Men" literally holding up a massive forearm with "The Law" emblazoned upon it. The symbolic businessman also held a large sheet of paper that read— ironically, in the light of subsequent events—"Our assistance and our testimony will be freely given." The last panel, printed a week after the riots, showed a matronly, well-groomed woman, the embodiment of Springfield, striding confidently down a well-appointed street, displaying a banner proclaiming "peace." At the edge of the street was a small sign pointing the way that read "to Springfield stores," and the woman held a piece of paper with the words "shopping list" in bold print.

Aside from an indistinct figure hanging from a tree in the background of the first drawing, no blacks were ever featured. Except for the news surrounding the pictures, one might not even guess that the city's disturbances had had anything to do with race. What mattered to the artist and the press was that law and order had returned. Property was now secure enough for "business as usual," and the curfews and early business closings the violence had necessitated were over. Springfield could go shopping again.[78] Public attention in the capital now increasingly turned to the upcoming court trials, and many believed that the continuation of racial peace in the city depended on their outcome.

NOTES

1. For a discussion of various stereotypes of blacks in American popular culture, see, for example, Rayford W. Logan, *The Betrayal of the Negro: From Rutherford B. Hayes to Woodrow Wilson*, new enl. ed. (New York: Collier Books, 1965); I. A. Newby, *Jim Crow's Defense: Anti Negro Thought in America, 1900–1930* (Baton Rouge: Lousiana State University Press, 1965); George M. Fredrickson, *The Black Image in the White Mind: The Debate on Afro-American Character and Destiny, 1817–1914* (New York: Harper & Row, 1971). See also Joel Williamson, *The Crucible of Race: Black-White Relations in the American South since Emancipation* (New York: Oxford University Press, 1984).

2. *ISJ*, 23 August 1908, 5 September 1908.

3. Ibid.

4. William English Walling, "The Race War in the North," *The Independent* 65 (3 September 1908): 530.

5. *Chicago Tribune*, 17 August 1908, 25 August 1908; *SN*, 22 August 1908.

6. *SN*, 19 August 1908; *Chicago Tribune*, 26 August 1908.

7. *SN*, 20 August 1908; *ISJ*, 20 August 1908; *ISR*, 19 August 1908.

8. Edith A. Butler Memoir, SSUO.

9. *ISJ*, 5 September 1908. City newspapers listed the addresses of forty damaged Badlands buildings along with the names of owners and tenants of all but three homes.

10. *SN*, 19 August 1908.

11. *ISR*, 19 August 1908.

12. Arthur T. Brittin Memoir, SSUO.

13. *ISR*, 17–18 August 1908. The estimate of Illinois towns that excluded blacks is from John H. Keiser, "Black Strikebreakers and Racism in Illinois, 1865–1900," *Journal of the Illinois State Historical Society* 65 (Autumn 1972): 314–15. See also Ronald L. Lewis, *Black Coal Miners in America: Race, Class, and Community Conflict, 1780–1980* (Lexington: University Press of Kentucky, 1987), 84–85; Emma Lou Thornbrough, *The Negro in Indiana: A Study of a Minority* (Indianapolis: Indiana Historical Bureau, 1957), 224–27; and William B. Hubbard Memoir, SSUO. William B. Hubbard, a black laborer who was interviewed in the 1970s, remembered that the practice of banning blacks was still used as late as the 1920s. Hubbard worked on construction projects in some of Sangamon County's small towns. After a day's work, he had to return to Springfield because he was forbidden to spend the night. As he put it, "They'd say, 'Read and Run, Mr. Nigger.' "

14. *ISR*, 17 August 1908; *Chicago Tribune*, 22 August 1908; *SN*, 20 August 1908.

15. *ISR*, 16–17 August 1908.

16. The sources used to locate and identify riot victims are essentially the same as those used to trace the rioters. Newspapers printed long lists of individuals who had lost property. In many instances, the newspapers could

not find the names of blacks whose homes had been burned, since so many
had left town, but they did print the street addresses of burned houses,
whose inhabitants then could be found in city directories. Additional names
of riot victims appeared several weeks after the riot in newspaper lists of
those who initiated lawsuits against the city for damage to property or for
personal injury. A few names of riot victims who sued but whom the newspapers never mentioned appeared in the circuit court files. With respect to
those who suffered property losses, only heads of households were counted
as riot victims, even though, of course, whole families and many boarders
were rendered homeless when rioters burned their dwellings. Riot victims
were then traced though censuses and city directories. See, for example,
CCF, case numbers 23229, 23348, 23403, 23442; *ISJ*, 25 August 1908,
29–30 August 1908, 5 September 1908.

17. U. S. Bureau of the Census, *Negro Population, 1790–1915* (Washington, D.C.: Government Printing Office, 1918), 473; manuscript schedules of
the population census for Springfield, Illinois, 1910. As Kenneth L. Kusmer
noted, rates of homeownership among blacks were often higher in smaller
northern cities. Idem, *A Ghetto Takes Shape: Black Cleveland, 1870–1930* (Urbana: University of Illinois Press, 1976), 90n. Among northern American
cities having a black population of 2,500 or more in 1910, Springfield had
one of the highest rates of homeownership.

18. *ISJ*, 15 August 1908; *Chicago Tribune*, 16 August 1908.

19. *ISJ*, 17 August 1908.

20. Ibid.

21. I am indebted to James Krohe, Jr.'s article, "Not Guilty! The Trial of
Abraham Raymer after the Springfield Race Riots of 1908," *Illinois Times*, 11
August 1978, for drawing my attention to this leaflet.

22. *SN*, 17 August 1908; CD, 1902, 1904–8; manuscript schedules of the
population census for Springfield, Illinois, 1900 and 1910.

23. *SN*, 17 August 1908; *Chicago Tribune*, 18 August 1908; *ISJ*, 16 August
1908; *ISR*, 16 August 1908.

24. Altina L. Waller, "Community, Class and Race in the Memphis Riot
of 1866," *Journal of Social History* 18 (Winter 1984): 233–46.

25. *SN*, 20 August 1908; *ISJ*, 16 August 1908.

26. *SN*, 22 August 1908.

27. Ibid.

28. Ibid., 18 August 1908.

29. Margaret Ferguson Memoir, SSUO.

30. Edith Carpenter Memoir, SSUO.

31. Sharlottie Carr Memoir, SSUO.

32. Margaret Ferguson Memoir.

33. *ISR*, 16 August 1908; *SN*, 17 August 1908.

34. Margaret Ferguson Memoir; *SR*, 16 August 1908; CD, 1902, 1904–
12; manuscript schedules of the population census for Springfield, Illinois,
1900 and 1910.

35. *ISR*, 16 August 1908.

36. Margaret Ferguson Memoir.
37. *SN*, 22 August 1908.
38. *SR*, 21 September 1908; see also *SN*, 22 August 1908.
39. Margaret Ferguson Memoir.
40. *ISJ*, 22 September 1908; Margaret Ferguson Memoir.
41. *ISR*, 16–17 August 1908; *ISJ*, 16 August 1908; *SN*, 22 August 1908; *ISJ*, 16 August 1908.
42. *Chicago Tribune*, 18 August 1908.
43. *ISR*, 17 August 1908.
44. Adjutant General of Illinois, *Biennial Report of the Adjutant General of Illinois to the Governor and Commander-in-Chief, 1907–1908* (Springfield: Illinois State Journal Company, 1909), 275.
45. CD, 1902, 1905, 1908–10; manuscript schedules of the population census for Springfield, Illinois, 1900.
46. Adjutant General of Illinois, *Biennial Report*, 275; *Chicago Tribune*, 17 August 1908; *ISR*, 18 August 1908.
47. *SR*, 1 September 1908; CD 1902, 1905, 1907–8, 1911.
48. *ISR*, 17 August 1908; CD, 1902, 1906–8.
49. *ISR*, 17 August 1908.
50. *ISR*, 17 August 1908; *SN*, 17 August 1908; *Chicago Tribune*, 17 August 1908.
51. *SN*, 17 August 1908.
52. Ibid.
53. *ISR*, 18 August 1908, 21 August 1908; *ISJ*, 17 August 1908; CD, 1900–11; manuscript schedules of the population census for Springfield, Illinois, 1900 and 1910.
54. Donald Black, "Social Control as a Dependent Variable," in Donald Black, ed., *Toward a General Theory of Social Control: Fundamentals*, vol. 1 (Orlando, Fla.: Academic Press, 1984), 1–36; idem, "The Elementary Forms of Conflict Management," in Melvin J. Lerner, ed., *New Directions in the Study of Justice, Law, and Social Control* (New York: Plenum Press, 1990), 43–49. Black first formulated the concept of relational distance in *The Behavior of Law* (Orlando, Fla.: Academic Press, 1976), 40–48.
55. Black, *The Behavior of Law*, 40–41.
56. Black, "Elementary Forms of Conflict Management," 45–47. See also Jonathan Rieder, "The Social Organization of Vengeance," in Black, ed., *Toward a General Theory of Social Control*, 145–48.
57. Mark Cooney, "The Social Control of Homicide: A Cross-Cultural Study" (S.J.D. diss., Harvard University, 1988), 47.
58. Max Gluckman, *Custom and Conflict in Africa* (Oxford: Basil Blackwell, Ltd., 1956), 19–24. The effect of cross-cutting ties upon the handling of conflict was first delineated in Elizabeth Colson's classic study, "Social Control and Vengeance in Plateau Tonga Society," *Africa* 23 (July 1953): 199–212. See also H. U. E. Thoden van Velzen and W. van Wetering, "Residence, Power Groups and Intra-Societal Aggression: An Enquiry into the Conditions Leading to Peacefulness within Non-stratified Societies," *International*

Archives of Ethnography, part 2, 49 (1960): 169–200; Black, "Elementary Forms of Conflict Management," 45–47; Rieder, "The Social Organization of Vengeance"; Cooney, "The Social Control of Homicide," 53–60.

59. The problem of developing precise measures of relational distance and the relative strength of ties formed in the context of work, family, and residence has only recently begun to be addressed. See, for example, Peter V. Marsden and Karen E. Campbell, "Measuring Tie Strength," *Social Forces* 63 (December 1984): 482–501; Mark S. Granovetter, "The Strength of Weak Ties," *American Journal of Sociology* 78 (May 1973): 1360–80; Cooney, "The Social Control of Homicide," 53–60.

60. The literature on the impact of residential proximity on white attitudes is extensive. A few major case studies and overviews of research on the contact hypothesis include the following: M. Deutsch and Mary E. Collins, *Interracial Housing: A Psychological Evaluation of a Social Experiment* (Minneapolis: University of Minnesota Press, 1951); Daniel M. Wilner, Rosabelle P. Walkley, and Stuart W. Cook, *Human Relations in Interracial Housing: A Study of the Contact Hypothesis* (Minneapolis: University of Minnesota Press, 1955); Arnold M. Rose, Frank J. Atelsek, and Lawrence R. McDonald, "Neighborhood Reactions to Isolated Negro Residents: An Alternative to Invasion and Succession," *American Sociological Review* 18 (October 1953): 497–507; D. Garth Taylor, "Housing, Neighborhoods, and Race Relations: Recent Survey Evidence," *The Annals of the American Academy of Political and Social Science* 441 (January 1979): 26–40; Thomas F. Pettigrew, "Attitudes on Race and Housing: A Social-Psychological View," in Amos H. Hawley and Vincent P. Rock, eds., *Segregation in Residential Areas: Papers on Racial and Socioeconomic Factors in Choice of Housing* (Washington, D.C.: National Academy of Sciences, 1973): 21–84. See also Gordon W. Allport, *The Nature of Prejudice* (Reading, Mass.: Addison-Wesley Publishing Company, 1954), 261, 270–74. For a recent overview of black-white residential segregation, its causes, consequences, and the interracial attitudes involved, see Reynolds Farley and Walter R. Allen, *The Color Line and the Quality of Life in America* (New York: Russell Sage Foundation, 1987), 136–57.

61. Allport, *The Nature of Prejudice,* 275–76, 281; Alfred McClung Lee and Norman D. Humphrey, *Race Riot* (New York: Dryden Press, 1943), 17, 130, 133–14, 140. For the effect of interracial contact at work, see, for example, Pettigrew, "Attitudes on Race and Housing," 61; Ira N. Brophy, "The Luxury of Anti-Negro Prejudice," *Public Opinion Quarterly* 9 (Winter 1945–46): 456–66; W. M. Kephart, *Racial Factors and Urban Law Enforcement* (Philadelphia: University of Pennsylvania Press, 1957), 188–89; Barbara K. MacKenzie, "The Importance of Contact in Determining Attitudes toward Negroes," *Journal of Abnormal and Social Psychology* 43 (1948): 417–41.

62. Allen D. Grimshaw, "Urban Racial Violence in the United States: Changing Ecological Considerations," *American Journal of Sociology* 66 (September 1960): 114–15; The Chicago Commission on Race Relations, *The Negro in Chicago: A Study of Race Relations and a Race Riot* (Chicago: University of Chicago Press, 1922), 109–14, 116, 128.

63. Lee and Humphrey, *Race Riot*, 17, 28, 130, 132–33, 140; Pettigrew, "Attitudes on Race and Housing: A Social-Psychological View," 61.

64. Both the concept of neutrality and limited support are derived from Cooney, "The Social Control of Homicide," 56–59.

65. Margaret Ferguson Memoir; Sharlottie Carr Memoir.

66. Lee and Humphrey, *Race Riot*, 140.

67. Allport, *The Nature of Prejudice*, 263–64. Time is clearly essential to the development of ties. See also Black, *The Behavior of Law*, 40–41; Rose, Atelsek, and McDonald, "Neighborhood Reactions to Isolated Negro Residents," 500–502, 506–7; Pettigrew, "Attitudes on Race and Housing: A Social-Psychological View," 65.

68. William Hubbard Memoir, SSUO.

69. Margaret Ferguson Memoir.

70. *SN*, 17 August 1908. See also Olivier Zunz, *The Changing Face of Inequality: Urbanization, Industrial Development, and Immigrants in Detroit, 1880–1920* (Chicago: University of Chicago Press, 1982), 374–75.

71. *The Forum*, 28 December 1907.

72. Kelly Miller, "The Negro as a Workingman," *American Mercury* 6 (November 1925): 310–12; *Forum*, 28 September 1907, 29 February 1908.

73. Quoted in Leon Litwack, "The Ordeal of Black Freedom," in Walter J. Fraser, Jr., and Winfred B. Moore, Jr., eds., *The Southern Enigma: Essays on Race, Class, and Folk Culture* (Westport, Conn.: Greenwood Press, 1983), 13–14. See also Quincy Ewing, "The Heart of the Race Problem," *Atlantic Monthly* 103 (March 1909): 393; Michael J. Cassity, *Chains of Fear: American Race Relations since Reconstruction* (Westport, Conn.: Greenwood Press, 1984); Charles L. Flynn, Jr., "The Ancient Pedigree of Violent Repression: Georgia's Klan as a Folk Movement," in Fraser and Moore, *The Southern Enigma*, 194–95.

74. *Chicago Tribune*, 25 August 1908.

75. Frederic Fliege Memoir, SSUO.

76. *ISR*, 19 August 1908.

77. *ISJ*, 6 September 1908.

78. *SN*, 18–22 August 1908.

CHAPTER 5

The Aftermath

About two weeks after the riot, Springfield's citizens received the startling news that Mabel Hallam, the white woman whose alleged rape had sparked the violence, had dropped all charges against George Richardson. She swore out an affidavit exonerating him, then claimed that another black man named Ralph Burton had raped her. Armed with this new evidence and a modified description of her assailant, Springfield's authorities searched the city and put police departments elsewhere on the alert. Meanwhile, rumors began to circulate that Mrs. Hallam had never been assaulted and that she had invented the story to conceal some wrongdoing. These rumors were further fueled by the news that medical examinations had revealed that she had contracted a venereal disease but that Richardson was perfectly healthy. Some speculated that perjury charges against Hallam might be forthcoming. After several days of searching, the police could find no trace of anyone fitting the new black suspect's description. The Hallams abruptly and without explanation announced that they would no longer talk to the press.

Not publicized was Mrs. Hallam's admission to a special grand jury in early September that she had not been attacked by a black man at all. Word got out nonetheless, and, several months later, the editor of the *Forum* mentioned her confession in an article about the riot he wrote for an out-of-town magazine. The man she saw the night of her alleged rape, the editor said, was "her white sweetheart," and, "seeking to escape blame and shame and outcast," Mrs. Hallam had invented the story of a black rapist. She admitted to the grand jury that she had not been raped, but under questioning refused to reveal her paramour's identity.[1] Commenting on the silence of the city's white press in the face of Mrs. Hallam's testimony before the grand jury, the *Forum's* editor fumed, "When the papers found out all they tucked their tails and never once editorially condemned the woman. O but how these papers had lauded her in Headlines. 'Negro assaults high-tone Lady in a most Prominent Neighborhood' exclaimed the Register in a two column, front page article."[2]

After the events of August and September 1908, life in Springfield probably became rather uncomfortable for the Hallams. Within several months, Mrs. Hallam, her husband, and her in-laws left the city for good. Despite their troubles, Mabel and William Hallam apparently did not divorce. In 1910 they lived together in Chicago with William's parents, and Mabel gave birth to their first child.[3] As for George Richardson, shortly after Mrs. Hallam dropped the charges against him, he was released from the jail in Bloomington where he and Joe James had been awaiting their trials. Richardson returned to a peaceful life in Springfield.[4]

As the Hallam-Richardson case reached its decisive resolution, the upcoming trials of Joe James and the white rioters claimed increasing public attention in the capital. During the first week of September the special grand jury completed its riot investigation and, relying heavily on police and military testimony, returned a total of 107 indictments against nearly eighty people. Most of those indicted were white rioters, but, much to the embarrassment of the city authorities, four patrolmen faced charges of "failure to suppress riot." The grand jury also published a special report roundly condemning the conduct of some of the city policemen who had "brought a blush of shame to every law abiding citizen of the city." Several officers, they said, "not only failed to use a club, handle a pistol, or raise a voice against the mob, but some of them [were] shown to have assisted by act and word in doing the work that has brought destruction." The grand jury suggested a thorough investigation of the police department, but the authorities seem to have ignored their recommendation.[5]

The department's inability to suppress the riot and its subsequent criticism by the grand jury and by some white newspapers prompted it to attempt to salvage its reputation. For a few weeks city police and detectives conducted a series of well-publicized raids in the Levee and vice district, designed to provide a convincing display of activity to satisfy the press, prominent citizens, and the business community, who were clamoring for law and order. The raids also reflected the belief among influential whites that the riot was the work of lower-class white riffraff and not the product of more widespread anti-black attitudes in the city. Accordingly, shortly after the riot the chief of police announced that "undesirables, all that element which apparently lives high and never labors," would be rounded up and ordered out of town. A colorful series of raids on saloons, bawdy houses, opium dens, and squalid rooming houses followed, in which the city's bluecoats rounded up dozens of "women of spotted reputation and men of vicious customs." The press enthusiastically applauded this burst of virtuous activity by the police, cheered by the seemingly imminent demise of the vice district and the expulsion of its resident "fiends." Some waxed overly optimistic and praised the raids as "the greatest moral awakening experienced by a Springfield police department."[6] In reality, by the time the "crusade" ended, few "shady" joints had been troubled, and the number of "undesirables" ordered out of town was modest. The cleanup crusade was short-lived and more cosmetic than real.

The Trial of Joe James

The riot trials began in mid-September, and first on the docket was Joe James, the black drifter accused of murdering Clergy Ballard in July. Though the press and city authorities worried that his acquittal might spark yet another riot, his conviction appears to have been a forgone conclusion for many in Springfield. From the beginning the city's newspapers assumed that James was guilty and often distorted the facts of the case to his detriment, even after the trial was over.[7] James was in an extremely vulnerable position since he was a stranger to the community, a vagabond with no standing and no kin. His habits, as enumerated in press accounts of his life during his short time as a free man in the city—his drinking, gambling, and stint in jail for vagrancy—meant that he would receive little sympathy or understanding from either the white or the black community. The evidence against him was circumstantial, but it was enough, in light of his freewheeling ways, to convince most that he was guilty. At least some of the members of James's all-white jury probably subscribed to the pervasive negative stereotype of black men as brutal, passionate, and uncontrollable savages. In this case, it was all too easy for white jurymen to fit the black vagrant into this category.

After weeks of tension and conflict, in which the community had divided along lines of class as well as race, most of Springfield's citizens—both black and white—hoped that James's trial and conviction would finally secure peace. For those of the white working class

still eager to avenge Clergy Ballard's death and still determined to
see the city's blacks put in their place, James's conviction was crucial.
Small but highly visible threatening demonstrations before and during the trial expressed their concerns. Better-off whites, who had
little interest in keeping blacks in their place, had other reasons for
desiring a conviction in the James case. They viewed the riot as the
work of "undesirables" downtown, and Joe James seemed a typical
product of the Levee. Thus his conviction would provide an edifying
moral lesson, not just to black wrongdoers, but to the whole mass of
hard-drinking, dope-taking, promiscuous degenerates who inhabited the downtown district.

Black Springfielders had mixed feelings about the James trial.
How much sympathy they felt for James cannot be determined,
though a few individuals tried to raise money for his defense. Most
of the black community—especially better-off blacks—tried to put
as much distance as possible between James and themselves. For one
thing, he was an outsider with no kin or friends in the city. Moreover, many blacks probably believed he was guilty and viewed him as
a troublesome stranger who had helped bring disaster upon them
all. His conviction posed no danger and little insult to Springfield's
blacks, but his acquittal might. If those whites who had been with
the mob, in spirit if not in person, clamored for James's head, then
well and good, as far as most blacks were concerned. Springfield's
blacks must have felt compassion for James's plight, but they had
little reason to mourn his loss.

Just how much of a climate of fear in Springfield persisted into
September, and what influence it may have had on the conduct and
outcome of James's trial, is difficult to assess. Even though anti-black
violence had declined by September, symptoms of white anger were
frequent enough to remind Springfielders that the city was not yet
at peace. The same day the newspapers published Mabel Hallam's
confession, for example, the public was informed that unidentified
persons had set fire to the home of a wealthy black contractor in the
southwest part of the city. Over the next few weeks, two citizens involved in the prosecution of white rioters were harassed. Unknown
parties continued to string up effigies of blacks in various parts of
town. It was also clear that blacks faced danger on city streets and in
public places during the month before James's trial. Usually, the
white troublemakers involved eluded arrest. The police did apprehend one man in late September, however, for assaulting a black
passerby. The offender was an employee of the Chicago, Peoria, and
St. Louis railroad—Clergy Ballard's line—an ominous indication

that the desire to wreak vengeance remained strong in the murdered man's social network.[8]

One incident just before Joe James's trial prompted both the white press and the police to question whether or not the "mob spirit" was still afoot. Early one morning the police were startled by reports that someone had hung an effigy of a black man in the heart of the business district near the courthouse. Pinned to it they found a sign reading "Nigger, don't let the sun go down on you." The phrase, the press reminded its readers, was "much used in the south when blacks are lynched." Later the same day, a threatening letter, "crudely ornamented with skulls and cross bones, cut from druggists' labels," turned up in the yard of the county jail. The police stated that it "reflect[ed] the views of certain citizens as to what the outcome of the [James] case should be." It read: "Springfield, Ill. If Joe James don't hang we are going to kill him and run every nigger out of town. You can't stop us as we will do it when you are not thinking about it. Signed, The Black Hand."[9] Certainly the publicity surrounding such threats, combined with a vivid memory of the rioting, meant that locally selected jurors might easily be intimidated. Throughout the riot trials, extra police were stationed at the courthouse, and large escorts accompanied prisoners as they were moved to and from their hearings.

Those who hoped Joe James would get a speedy trial were not disappointed. The proceedings were brief. As one white newspaper remarked, "the rapidity with which the case was handled was greater than the usual progress in murder trials."[10] Much of the court's haste no doubt was due to the widespread belief that the city's peace and security depended on a quick conviction. The first critical question in the case was where the trial was to be held. O. V. Royall, a local black attorney who agreed to defend James for free, petitioned the court for a change of venue. His argument was simple: James could not receive a fair trial in Springfield, where it would be extremely difficult to find unbiased jurors. Royall mentioned that "a large number of people have stated that he [James] should be hanged and that the sheriff should have given him to the mob." Given the amount of press coverage James had received since July, it would have been difficult to find local jurors unfamiliar with the case. Elsewhere in his petition, Royall referred to the continuing threat posed by some of Springfield's white working class. The Brotherhood of Locomotive Engineers, to which Clergy Ballard had belonged, for example, was one likely source of public intimidation,

if not actual violence, Royall claimed. Finally, he argued that James
had not had access to a lawyer since the authorities moved him to
Bloomington's jail in August.[11]

Circuit Court Judge James A. Creighton denied Attorney Royall's
petition and ruled that the trial must be held in Springfield.
Creighton, sixty-two years old, and with over twenty years' experience on the bench, had a splendid reputation as a dispassionate
judge with a kind and considerate disposition.[12] During the course
of James's trial, he treated Attorney Royall and his black assistant
courteously. Judge Creighton, however, simply did not agree with
Royall's assessment of the situation in the community. It was appropriate to hold the trial in Springfield, he ruled, because "there was
no feeling at present existing against the negro in this county." To
support his claim that the area was free of racism, Creighton mentioned that "negroes sit with whites on juries" and that black attorneys were "treated with every courtesy and respect" in court.
Creighton declared: "The disturbances occurring in the recent past
were not race riots at all. It was simply a case of a lawless mob taking
charge and using the [George] Richardson case as an excuse for
their violence. A hundred lawless ruffians do not affect public sentiment at all. In no county in the state does so little prejudice exist
against the colored race as in the county of Sangamon. In the opinion of the court there is no ground in fact to support a change of
venue."[13]

Judge Creighton's ruling reflected the opinion of many middle-
and upper-class Springfielders, both black and white, that the riot
was solely the work of hoodlums and riffraff. To Royall, Creighton's
refusal of a change of venue was a clear signal that Joe James's defense before a local all-white jury would be fraught with difficulty.
Having failed to get James's trial moved out of Springfield, he attempted to argue that, at the most, James could only be found
guilty of manslaughter. Joe James was a stranger in Springfield. He
did not know the Ballard family and was unfamiliar with their
neighborhood. Even if the prosecution could prove that James had
entered the Ballard house that Fourth of July evening, no evidence
indicated that he ever intended to commit a crime. To convict a man
of first-degree murder, one had to establish his intention to kill.
Royall pointed out that James was fleeing when Clergy Ballard
caught up with him, thus raising the possibility that he had acted in
self-defense. The defense also reminded the jury that James was in-
toxicated at the time of the murder and produced a number of wit-

nesses who had seen him drinking in the Levee just before the incident. "The killing of Clergy Ballard was not murder," the black attorney concluded, "for murder must be premeditated and done with malice aforethought."[14]

The prosecution, conducted by State's Attorney Frank Hatch and his assistant William St. Johns Wines, never established a motive for Ballard's murder but successfully wove "a web of circumstantial evidence" that fatally ensnared Joe James. Since no one except Clergy Ballard ever got a good look at the assailant the night of the murder, the prosecution's identification of the killer was flawed. Although when the prosecution asked members of the Ballard family if they saw the guilty man in the courtroom, all pointed to Joe James without hesitation, their identification was suspect. Not only had James's picture appeared in the newspapers several times, but Ballard's sons had been part of the search party that had beaten James the morning after the attack. Thus they had had plenty of opportunity to get a good look at the defendant before the trial. The prosecution further insisted that Clergy Ballard had been defending his family and home. James, "in entering it, whatever his purpose may have been, deserved to be hanged. The man who entered the Ballard home on the night of the crime, was himself responsible for the subsequent events and should hang." In vain the defense established, in cross-examining the Ballards, that no one had ever seen who had entered or left the house in the first place. Blanche Ballard, the victim's daughter, even admitted that it had been too dark in her bedroom to tell whether the intruder was black or white. The first look the Ballard family had gotten at the assailant had been either when he was fighting with Ballard in the front yard or when he fled from the scene.[15]

Several pieces of evidence ultimately swayed the jury. One was that James had been discovered near the Ballard home only hours after the attack. The second was the assailant's clothing. Witnesses claimed that Ballard's attacker had worn light pants and a dark coat, and their description tallied with James's clothing. Furthermore, when Clergy Ballard had grappled with the intruder in his yard, he had ripped a piece of cloth from the front of his shirt and had knocked his cap off. Homer Ballard, the eldest son, found both the cap and piece of shirt in the yard and turned them over to the police. An inmate at the jail and several police officers identified the cap as James's. When they arrested him and examined his clothing, the officers claimed, the piece of cloth Ballard had ripped away in the fight fit the hole in the shirt Joe James was wearing. James was not armed when arrested, but later in the day a detective found a short-bladed, bloodstained knife not far from where he had been sleeping off his liquor. Though no one could identify who had entered the Ballard home, and though no one had gotten a good look at the man Ballard fought with, the accumulated circumstantial evidence—especially the torn shirt—was enough for the jury to find James guilty.[16]

On 16 September James took the stand to testify in his own defense. Many hoped he would show signs of remorse or shed new light on the case, but they were disappointed. During the entire proceedings James had remained reserved, "silent, motionless and seemingly disinterested." On the stand he continued to be calm and restrained. The jury heard the same story James had told the police and press from the beginning: he was a stranger in Springfield; he had gotten drunk in a number of Levee saloons and at some point had passed out. He never knew the Ballards and remembered nothing of that evening after he left the last saloon.

James did give the prosecution an unpleasant surprise, however, when he told the court that he was only nineteen years old—too young, under state law, for the death penalty. Under rigorous cross-examination, James finally admitted that he did not know how old he was, and police officers testified that he had told them he was in his early twenties. The defense apparently made no attempt to get further information on James's age, and the issue was dropped even though it might have spared him from the gallows. Perhaps his lawyers simply did not know whom to contact. None of James's family wrote him or appeared in Springfield until shortly before his execution. Several days before the hanging, but too late to help, his mother offered to provide certification of his birthdate. Her son, she said, was not yet eighteen.[17]

As the trial ended, the defense hoped for a conviction for manslaughter, since, as Attorney Royall reminded the jury in his closing remarks, no evidence of premeditation existed. The jury decided on the first ballot that James was guilty of murder, but divided evenly over the appropriate penalty: half for life imprisonment, half for hanging. After ten ballots and several hours of quarreling, they finally settled on the death sentence and returned to the courtroom to announce their verdict. Extra armed deputies were stationed around the crowded room to prevent any outbursts, but the spectators remained silent as they listened to the decision. To the disappointment of news reporters, James heard the verdict with the same quiet impassivity he had shown throughout the trial. When

Judge Creighton asked him if he wished to say anything, James replied, "I have told all I know. I have nothing further to say," and was returned to his cell.[18]

Many in Springfield must have breathed a sigh of relief when, two days later, Joe James appeared before Judge Creighton to hear his death sentence pronounced. Royall and his assistant, who had conducted James's defense free of charge, announced they had no plans for an appeal, despite the "many loopholes through which we can carry the case to the supreme court." Unless James could come up with some money, Royall said, he would be unwilling to take this controversial and time-consuming step. He did mention that a few black residents were trying to raise funds for an appeal, but with little success. A white editor reported that "citizens of all classes, both white and colored, are satisfied with the verdict." Springfield's new black Law and Order League, for example, was pleased with the outcome of James's trial. The league had formed in response to the race riot to monitor and police black behavior downtown. Composed mostly of middle-class blacks, the league was determined to suppress black "immorality" and disorder, thus eliminating, as they saw it, a major cause of anti-black violence. League members viewed Joe James as precisely the kind of character likely to precipitate white attacks against the larger black community. When the league heard of the effort to raise money for James's appeal, it announced flatly that its "members will have nothing to do with the matter."[19] The rest of the black community must have been relieved, too. On the last day of James's trial, while the jury was deliberating over its verdict, many blacks prepared to evacuate, afraid that whites would riot again if James escaped the death penalty. The press reported that Springfield's blacks anxiously hoped that James's conviction might "allay to some extent the bitter feeling that has existed between the two races."[20]

Joe James's execution was scheduled for 23 October, and the press watched him carefully over the weeks for signs of weakening or emotional breakdown, hoping that he might talk about the Ballard murder and make some kind of confession. Meanwhile, the authorities planned carefully for the event. Only a limited number of citizens would be allowed to view the hanging, and the police would cordon off a large area near the jail. The city's old gallows, unused since 1898, was dragged out of the jail's basement and refurbished, and its trapdoor tested—within earshot of James and other inmates. Sheriff Charles Werner told frustrated reporters that James continued to be an ideal prisoner who was "unusually quiet and obedient" and who "says but little."[21]

During his last days in jail James underwent a conversion experience, and the press noted with approval that he spent much of his time reading the Bible and religious tracts. Encouraging James were a black minister and a white volunteer worker, Mrs. Mary Nickey, who dispensed religion and sympathy to the city's jail inmates. Both repeatedly urged James to confess to the murder as part of his repentance of past sins. In a long and intense discussion with Mrs. Nickey the day before the execution, James voiced what the press wanted badly to interpret as a confession. "When Sheriff Werner hangs me," he told Nickey, "he will not be hanging an innocent man." But since this statement was part of a conversation about how "love of liquor and women [had] made him a mark for the hangman's noose," James's statement that he was not innocent remained ambiguous. One writer remarked that perhaps Joe James felt that he was "meeting just punishment for some other crime he [had] committed in the past" or that he was expressing regrets about loose living.[22]

James prepared a written statement on the eve of his execution, which the press took as a more concrete admission of guilt, though it had the same fundamental ambiguity as his first "confession." It began: "I am sorry for the crime I committed. Drunkenness was the cause of it. In that I have sinned against Mr. Ballard, his family and each and every citizen. When the deed was committed I was a sinner." In a separate piece, James made a rambling impassioned plea for temperance, titled "Warning to all Evil Doers," in which he urged all young men to turn from drink and debauchery before it was too late. His final confession, however, again made it clear that he remembered nothing about the murder. "I did not remember the greatness of my crime," he wrote, "until I was brought to the city prison the next morning after I committed it." Did James, in the face of imminent death and in the painful throes of guilt over his past sins, simply decide to claim responsibility for a crime he knew nothing about? Was he convinced by his circumstances and spiritual advisors that it was prudent, for the safety of his soul, to do so? He did not—possibly could not—provide any details of the crime, of his whereabouts that July evening, or of his motives. Given the weight of circumstantial evidence against James, his confession understandably convinced the city's press that justice had been done. Even so, the confession was ambiguous enough that even today there is room for lively but fruitless debate over his guilt or innocence. After his death, newspapers revealed that, just before his execution, James told his mother that he was innocent of the crime, but guilty of having lived a sinful life.[23]

At 6:00 in the morning on 23 October, James was roused to prepare for his execution. After his last meal, he was again visited by his two spiritual advisors and spent the remainder of his time praying and singing hymns with them. Thus fortified, James, dressed in a new black suit, began the short march down the corridor to the gallows. Outside the jail, a crowd gathered at the edge of the police cordon, hoping to catch some glimpse of the proceedings inside. There were 147 witnesses present to watch the execution, among them Clergy Ballard's sons. Arms securely strapped to his sides, James passed through the crowd, mounted the gallows, and heard one final prayer from the black minister. Sheriff Werner then asked him if he had any final statements to make, but James shook his head and said, "Nothing." When the black hood was securely in place, Werner released the trapdoor, and a doctor pronounced James dead ten minutes later. The body was placed in a casket and carried out of the jail, under guard, to a nearby funeral home. That afternoon, when the funeral home opened its doors to the public, over seven thousand citizens filed silently past the casket for a last look at the convict. The crowd, mostly white, reportedly was well behaved, and the press claimed that many who viewed the body showed signs of sympathy for James. The next day, James's mother, who had not attended the execution, claimed her son's body. His coffin was loaded onto an Illinois Central car, and the black drifter made his final journey—home to a grave in Birmingham.[24]

White Rioters, White Justice

Immediately after Joe James's rapid trial and conviction in mid-September, State's Attorney Frank Hatch turned his energies to the prosecution of whites indicted for riot-related offenses. Hatch had worked tirelessly to gather evidence against rioters and declared that "no one who is guilty will be spared." As he scoured the city for witnesses and evidence, he received a number of anonymous death threats, which he dismissed with contempt.[25] He soon found, however, that few of his fellow white Springfielders were willing to serve as witnesses. Even those who clamored the loudest for law and order—Springfield's more affluent and influential citizens—proved reluctant to get involved in the trials.

Hatch attended the protest meeting of business and professional men just after the riot, hoping to recruit witnesses. When the meeting closed, he stood and announced that "this is the time to test the temper of the business men assembled here," and proceeded to distribute forms for members to fill out and provide the names of persons they had recognized in the mob. "There is not in this room today hardly a man who has not witnessed acts of violence," Hatch said as he handed out the forms, "and if you are anxious for speedy justice, bring the information which is now locked up within your breasts to my office." He challenged the crowd: "How many of you will have the nerve to sign your name to these cards and send them in?"[26] The state's attorney did not have to wait long for an answer. Few businessmen or professionals ultimately served as witnesses. The prosecution had to rely primarily on the police, detectives, the militia, and a few black citizens for evidence and testimony.

Despite the difficulty in gathering evidence, State's Attorney Hatch must have had high hopes of obtaining convictions for indicted rioters. After all, the belief that the riot was not due to racism, but to a crazy outburst of hooliganism was widespread, and the indictees were largely the poorer and less reputable members of the mob. Given that many held hoodlums and deviants responsible for the violence, it would have seemed logical that respectable white jurors would be eager to convict the "undesirables" tried before them as an object lesson to other potential troublemakers.

The first rioter tried was Abraham Raymer, the Russian Jewish peddler. Raymer allegedly was a ringleader during both nights of rioting, and he faced a charge of murder for the death of the elderly William Donnegan. The jury selection process was lengthy, for nearly one hundred men had to be dismissed, either because they admitted they were prejudiced against blacks, or because they had already formed opinions about Raymer from reading newspaper accounts of the riot.[27] Raymer's trial began 19 September, with Circuit Court Judge Creighton presiding.

In his opening statement, Assistant State's Attorney William St. Johns Wines explained that it was not necessary to prove that Raymer was the man who had assaulted Donnegan to convict him of murder. If he had been "in the crowd, aiding and abetting in the crime," he was guilty. Although a number of the prosecution's witnesses had difficulty identifying Raymer, in the end, accumulated evidence indicated that he had been involved in the attack on the Donnegan home. Especially damning was the testimony of Walter A. Townsend, the outspoken editor of the *Springfield Record*. The mob passed the *Record* offices on its way to Donnegan's. As Townsend and a friend stood outside the office to watch the crowd march by, the editor recognized Raymer among the leaders. Moreover, Raymer had earlier admitted to military investigators that he was in the crowd at Donnegan's lynching.[28]

The prosecution made a critical error, however, when Assistant State's Attorney Wines produced the bloodstained shirt Raymer wore the night of Donnegan's murder. Intending to work a dramatic effect upon the jurors, he declared that the shirt was spattered with Donnegan's blood, spilled when Raymer cut the old man's throat. The bloody shirt tactic backfired, for the defense attorneys knew that the blood on the shirt might well be Raymer's own. Had the prosecution not introduced the shirt, the defense probably could not have revealed that the police put the peddler through the so-called "sweating" process at the jail. The police had beaten and bloodied Raymer to extract information. The defense used this dramatic revelation of police brutality to portray Raymer as a helpless scapegoat, singled out by unprofessional city authorities desperate to pin blame for the riot on someone.[29]

On 23 September, Judge Creighton asked both sides to present their concluding remarks. The authorities, worried that disorder might result if Raymer were found guilty, posted extra deputies about the courtroom. At 9:00, eager citizens packed both the floor and gallery, as Assistant State's Attorney Wines began his two-hour summation for the prosecution. Wines compared Raymer's trial with Joe James's (which he had just helped to prosecute). In Raymer's case, he insisted, the evidence that the defendant had committed first degree murder was far more compelling. Reminding the jury of James's recent conviction, Wines asked, "Does not this man merit equal punishment[?]" "James admittedly did not go to the Ballard home seeking to satiate any lust for blood," he said. Raymer, on the other hand, "walked for many blocks leading a gang whom he knew full well was bent on murder and destruction."

Wines went on to point out that while Joe James "had no intent to murder," Raymer had clearly acted with premeditation: "Here is a young man who started out with no other object in view than murder. He knew that the gang which he joined . . . was out on a hunt for 'niggers.' Haven't we produced any amount of witnesses who swear that many members of the mob were shouting 'Let's get the niggers!' Does not Raymer himself admit shouting to people to come on? Will any reasonable man say that this defendant did not know what he was about? He went out to the residence of the old man Donnegan that night bent on murder. There was blood in his eye and murder in his heart." Wines finished his long speech, "one of the most forcible ever delivered in a Sangamon county court," one editor wrote, concluding that "if ever a man deserved hanging, that man is Abraham Raymer!"[30]

Shortly after 11:00, Raymer's attorney began the defense's closing arguments. Reminding the jury of the notorious bloody shirt, the lawyer denounced the city police as "brutes who had picked out this poor boy, who is as innocent as you or I." He also ridiculed many of the state's witnesses. Among those whose character he cast doubt on—appealing to racist sentiments—was Sarah Donnegan, the victim's widow: "what do you think of this woman—a white woman—marrying a negro forty years older than herself, when she herself was in the bloom of youth? I tell you she started out wrong and she has been erratic ever since."[31]

Creighton instructed the jury that it was not necessary to prove "that the defendant himself actually used the knife, or handled or adjusted the rope" used to hang Donnegan. Raymer's presence in the mob was enough to find him guilty. But when the jury returned to the hushed courtroom a little over three hours later, it declared Raymer not guilty. The verdict had taken only one balloting to decide. While the stunned prosecution attorneys looked on, spectators crowded to the courtroom exit to spread the news, and the pale and trembling defendant approached the jurors to thank them for their verdict.[32]

The not guilty verdict shocked the state's attorney, Judge Creighton, and the city's press and caused the city authorities to speculate that it might in fact be impossible to conduct fair and impartial riot trials in Springfield. It was clear to the prosecution that the jury had ignored the evidence presented and had disregarded the judge's instructions. The defense, however, read a happy omen in the not guilty verdict. They divined that this bold refusal to convict indicated Raymer likely would escape punishment on lesser charges. Assistant State's Attorney Wines noted grimly that "our jury lists as now composed seldom include that type of citizen who will do his full duty no matter what the outcome will be," but vowed that "convictions or no convictions, we will push these cases to the end." At the very least, he added, "we can and will teach criminals that they will have to face indictments and remain in jail until they are tried."[33]

The prosecution lost the next several cases, including one against Raymer for property damage. The state's attorneys used many of the same witnesses, again relying heavily on testimony from members of the state militia and city police force. In Raymer's second trial they felt they had persuasive new testimony: Harry Loper, the owner of the fancy restaurant sacked by the mob, confidently identified the peddler as one of those in the front ranks of the crowd. Loper had watched Raymer pitch bricks for over an hour. He was not likely to forget his face, he said, for three times he had had Raymer in his rifle sights, but dared not shoot lest he injure an innocent person in the milling crowd. Despite the prosecution's best efforts, the jury quickly acquitted Raymer a second time. About a week later, yet another jury acquitted a well-known thief and his two prostitute codefendants of charges of burglary and larceny. Police had found items stolen during the riot hidden in various parts of the brothel where the three defendants lived. In what the press termed a novel defense, the rioters' attorney offered the flimsy argument that some unidentified man must have sneaked into the house and secreted the stolen goods without the knowledge of its inhabitants. It took the jury less than three hours to vote for acquittal.[34]

After October's disappointing trials, State's Attorney Hatch decided to try to improve the quality of the jury lists. Accordingly, the old pool of jurors was purged to obtain "some of the most prominent business men in the city to act as jurors." Hatch wanted men of higher status on the list, hoping, no doubt, that they would be less sympathetic toward indictees of low standing and less vulnerable to intimidation. Among those singled out for possible jury duty, for example, were members of the Business Men's Association, the Chamber of Commerce, and "the select of the county," that is, merchants and larger landowners from more rural areas. The defense attorneys, on the other hand, made vigorous attempts to block this reform by trying to get better-off men excused from jury duty.[35] Apparently the final list was satisfactory to the prosecution. Armed with a reformed jury and what he felt was some of the best evidence of all the riot cases, Hatch began the prosecution of Abraham Raymer's third trial late in November. Raymer was tried on a charge of rioting, with the state's attorney attempting to prove only that he had been a member of the mob. When even the reform jury refused to convict Raymer, it became abundantly clear that all efforts to hold rioters accountable for their crimes would likely end in failure. Hatch considered the cases against Raymer the state's best. After three successive not guilty verdicts and the failure of higher-status jurors to convict, the prosecution of the rioters began to unravel.

The attorneys for the state now admitted gloomily that "it [would] be impossible to secure a conviction in Sangamon county."[36]

By the end of the year, Kate Howard's prophesy that her fellow citizens would never punish the rioters had been largely realized.[37] The riot's "Joan of Arc," however, did not live to see her predictions fulfilled. When a deputy sheriff came to her home to arrest her for murder in late August, she secretly took poison and collapsed later as she climbed the steps of the county jail.[38] Howard's co-rioters fared much better. The state's attorneys ultimately won only one minor victory out of over one hundred riot indictments: Abraham Raymer's conviction for petty larceny in his fourth trial in late December. He received a twenty-five dollar fine and thirty days in jail.[39] Some rioters avoided trial by pleading guilty to minor charges and were given light punishments by Judge Creighton. One rioter who pleaded guilty to petty larceny, for example, received a five-dollar fine and five days in jail. Another charged with the same crime was fined one dollar and locked up for a single day. A handful of indictments were dropped late in 1908 for a variety of reasons, but the bulk of the riot cases (including those involving police officers and a small number of blacks) were never tried and were eventually dismissed. The only rioter to receive a substantial penalty was teenager Roy Young, who had carelessly boasted in public about burning black residences. The boy made a complete confession to the police and was sent to the state reformatory before the riot trials began.[40]

Reading Race Out of Riot

Dismayed by repeated failures to bring rioters to justice, influential Springfield whites attempted to account for the meager results of months of work by able and determined prosecutors. The press and others claimed that racism had little to do with jurors' refusal to convict. Instead, the problem lay with their fear of reprisal. One editor concluded bluntly, "it is probably cowardice, and not sympathy with the mob spirit which is responsible for the farcical proceedings we are having in the circuit court."[41] He termed Abraham Raymer's second acquittal a "miscarriage of justice" and "contemptible," but argued that fear of mob retaliation had hampered the prosecution's efforts long before the trials began: "How many of those who are denouncing the jurors have gone to the state's attorney and told what they know of the rioting? How many of them are now willing to aid the cause of law and order by giving testimony against the men whom they saw and recognized among the rioters? It is all well enough to abuse the juries, but when we are doing this let us remember that some of the rest of us are cowards too."[42]

The press conceded that, since Joe James's trial, the city had been quiet. No threatening demonstrations occurred during the white rioters' trials. Even so, some insisted that August's "carnival of crime" had left its mark: "The danger is not now apparent, but the terror exists just the same. The [juror] is not faced with the excited and angry rioter, but he has before him the recollection of what occurred." The juror would also recall the city authorities' ineffectiveness in protecting persons and property from determined rioters and "knows that if he incur[s] the displeasure of the mob membership he is without assurance of protection." It was appropriate to condemn "jurors who haven't the nerve to do their duty," said the editor of the *Illinois State Journal*, but, he cautioned, it was difficult to criticize when "the yellow is in the neck of every mother's son of us."[43]

One highly publicized instance of attempted intimidation did take place. Walter A. Townsend, editor of the *Springfield Record*, served as a star prosecution witness in Abraham Raymer's murder trial. Unlike some of the lesser individuals who testified against Raymer, Townsend, because of his high standing in the community, was immune to the defense's tactic of undermining witnesses' credibility by character assassination. During and after the trial Townsend claimed he was the target of criticism and harassment. In an angry editorial published after Raymer's acquittal, he defended his role as a state's witness. For refusing to perjure himself on the stand, Townsend said, he had been denounced as a "nigger lover." He had also received threatening letters, and some of his readers cancelled their subscriptions, saying "they 'do not care to subscribe to a paper that stands for a nigger against a white man.'" Recounting in print what he had witnessed the night of Donnegan's murder, Townsend declared that he had "no apologies whatsoever to offer" to "those who would criticise [sic] a man for performing the plain duties of citizenship." He sarcastically invited other subscribers displeased with his testimony to be prompt in cancelling their subscriptions to the *Record*. "Such narrow-minded bigots," the editor fumed, "are not entitled to the privilege and pleasure of reading a newspaper that tells the truth and which is proud to stand for law and order."[44]

Factors other than the jurors' fear of retaliation likely contributed to the dearth of riot-related convictions in Springfield: for example, the jurors' own anti-black beliefs. Few in the white community ever expressed sympathy for the black victims of the violence, and many believed that blacks were to blame for the riot in the first place and that rioters had attacked only "bad Negroes." If a number of "undesirable" blacks had been driven out of town, then it was "a good riddance." Better-off whites concluded that the outbreak had ultimately worked some social and moral improvement in the capital. Moreover, the fear of persistent disorder and the perceived challenge to the authority of Springfield's white elite that together had helped create an initial resolve to pursue rioters dissipated after peace was effectively restored. Despite all their earlier angry rhetoric about "mob rule," better-off whites quickly lost interest in seeing anti-black violence punished. As influential whites grew more indifferent about the riot over time, the rift between whites of different classes that had been so evident during and immediately after the violence receded from view. And even though the press and prominent members of the white community complained about those who took the law into their own hands, the rioters and their sympathizers would not have missed their covert approval of violence against part of the community associated with sin and excess.

The most striking aspect of Springfielders' attempts to make sense of the riot was the persistent misinterpretation of the violence by both black and white spokesmen in the community. It was a view that might well have helped undermine white jurors' interest in convicting rioters. Most local observers denied that the outbreak was a race riot or a symptom of a determined "race war," as William English Walling called it. To be sure, Springfield's blacks did not go so far as to deny that they had been the rioters' major targets. They knew very well that the attacks were racially directed. Some black spokesmen did, however, tend to minimize the extent of white racism in the city by attributing the violence to a small, unrepresentative, and deviant segment of the white community. E. L. Rogers, the editor of the local black newspaper, the *Forum*, assured his readers that the rioters were "ignorant, ragged men, fool hoodlums" and "murderers, rogues and rapines [*sic*]." Echoing the white press, he singled out Raymer and Kate Howard as typical mob members: poor white trash, none of whom "own any property [or] who have any creditable standings [*sic*]."[45]

White spokesmen went a step further. They frankly denied that race was relevant at all to the violence. Whether such a view represented indifference or a sheer inability to analyze or confront the nature of their society, the result was the same: influential whites— the press, businessmen, clergymen, Judge Creighton, and others—

refused to acknowledge that the city had witnessed a race riot. From August on, white newspapers claimed that the violence had virtually nothing to do with interracial conflict. The rioters' intention "was not to avenge any public wrong or private grievance nor to purify the moral atmosphere of this community." It was purely "the spirit of loot" that motivated the mob—attacks on blacks were merely incidental.[46] Since better-off whites denied that racism existed in their city, they discounted the idea that anti-black prejudice played a role in the riot trials' not-guilty verdicts. They and a number of black spokesmen chose to avoid "the whole awful and menacing truth" that Walling wrote of: that systematic intimidation and discrimination had become a regular feature of northern life.[47] The sources and extent of Springfield's anti-black hostility thus went largely unremarked and unexamined in the wake of the riot. It was this combination of white complacency and widespread misinterpretation of the riot that prompted Walling to remark, "Springfield had no shame."

Springfielders were not alone or exceptional in reading race out of the riot. White denial that a *race* riot had occurred was evident in most northern commentary on the violence in Lincoln's hometown and was a reflection of a wider defensiveness about, or reluctance to admit, the extent and character of anti-black hostility in the North. Northerners were occasionally willing to concede that they had a "race problem"; anti-black collective violence, however, they preferred to view as an exclusively southern phenomenon. As northern whites defined it, the race problem did not stem from white shortcomings or unreasonable anti-black hostility. Rather, the problem was the simple presence of blacks—long unwelcome in the North— whom whites judged as naturally below American standards of civilization. Blacks' innate inferiority, according to popular racial stereotypes, placed them forever and immutably beyond inclusion in the political and social traditions, institutions, and ideologies whites used to define their culture. One contemporary observer succinctly summed up whites' prevailing ideas of blacks' place and destiny:

Ask the average man what the race problem is . . . and in all probability you will get some such answer as this: "The Negroes, as a rule, are very ignorant, are very lazy, are very brutal, are very criminal. But a little removed from savagery, they are incapable of adopting the white man's moral ideals. They are, in brief, an uncivilized, semi-savage people, living in a civilization to which they are unequal. Because they are spatially in a civilization to which they are morally and intellectually repugnant, they cannot but be as a foreign irritant. The problem is, How shall the body social adjust itself, daily, hourly, to this irritant?"[48]

Thus blacks, and not whites, were the "problem." If the civilized body social responded to the alien black irritant with attempts, such as that at Springfield, to punish or even expel blacks, then the logic of their view led many white northerners to blame blacks, and not to reassess the justice of excluding them from American "civilization."

In the North, then, whites generally either attributed Springfield's riot to black misbehavior or explained it away as an exceptional outbreak of hooliganism fostered by an unusually corrupt government in a city with a surfeit of saloons and brothels. According to an Aurora, Illinois, newspaper—and its position was typical of the northern press—Springfield had no race problem, but had simply reaped the wages of sin.[49] Only a handful of northern editorial voices, including William English Walling's, protested such facile dismissals of Springfield's riot. One such editor, for example, wrote with disgust that "the Northern papers talk wisely about the rigid and impartial enforcement of the law, and then fold their hands with an attitude of duty fully performed." The sources of Springfield's riot lay, he added, not with the capital's municipal or moral shortcomings, but with whites' "national indulgence in the perilous luxury of race prejudice, a Moloch, which ever demands to be fed with blood."[50]

The southern press also launched a spirited critique of northern race relations. Since mass anti-black violence occurred in the city proud of its association with the "Great Emancipator," the Springfield riot provided the South with a rare opportunity for self-righteous finger-pointing. Indeed, the riot presented Americans with "bitter irony in the fact that the largest force of state troops ever assembled in Illinois were summoned by the governor of Lincoln's state to protect the Negroes whom Lincoln emancipated from citizens in Lincoln's city."[51] Southern commentators repeatedly emphasized that Springfield proved that interracial conflict and anti-black violence were national, and not solely sectional, phenomena. Former Mississippi Governor James K. Vardaman, who had earned notoriety as a stridently anti-black politician, discussed the riot in an interview, touching upon most of the major themes seen in the southern press's response to the Illinois capital's troubles:

> No man reared north of the Mason and Dixon line understood the negro better than Lincoln. He said repeatedly that the two races could not live together in the same country on terms of social and political equality. These conflicts are liable to occur in any part of this republic where the negroes live in as large numbers as they do in Springfield, Ill.; and where the white man concedes to him the rights of citizenship

which he enjoys there. Such sad experiences as Springfield is undergoing will doubtless cause the people of the north to look with more toleration upon the methods employed by the southern people.[52]

Black Law and Order Leagues

America's blacks reacted to Springfield's violence with universal condemnation. Some, however—in particular, those influenced by Booker T. Washington's advocacy of black accomodation, self-help, and avoidance of conflict over political and social equality—placed a large share of the blame for race riots on blacks. Accommodationist blacks generally believed that only hard work, discipline, and success would win white recognition and respect. The nation's troubled race relations were not just due to white prejudice, they claimed, but were also caused by poor blacks, whose lack of education or deviant public behavior reinforced whites' view of the race as hopelessly inferior.[53] The appearance of new black law and order leagues in the wake of Springfield's violence reflected the accomodationists' tendency to blame fellow blacks for interracial conflict. These leagues were largely the work of more affluent citizens and were designed to monitor and regulate behavior in black urban neighborhoods. Black crime and publicly offensive conduct, they reasoned, increased white prejudice, led to increased discrimination, and, in the worst case, could precipitate anti-black violence like Springfield's.

Moreover, once provoked, white mobs attacked both respectable and offending blacks. Springfield's riot painfully demonstrated that one individual's crime could bring disaster to all blacks, regardless of their station. A black Chicago minister observed just after the Springfield outbreak: "The bad and lawless element of the negro race always has and will continue to affect the better element vastly more than the lawless element of the white will affect that race. Our people are judged by the worst element of our race, and unless we rise and condemn and fight against this lawless element we will be rightly judged."[54] To avoid a situation like Springfield's, where rioters held all blacks collectively liable for the misdeeds of a few, the minister advised better-off blacks to take a strong and vocal stand for law and order. He concluded that black Chicagoans "should form a law and order league, or a good citizens' league, to rid our community of negro lawbreakers" and to dispel whites' impression that more affluent blacks would tolerate or "harbor the criminals of our race."

Black self-help in the form of law and order leagues was not new, but Springfield's riot did temporarily inspire the creation of additional organizations committed to imposing social control over black communities.[55] In Chicago, Pittsburgh, Lafayette, Indiana, Washington, D.C., Atlanta, and elsewhere, prominent black citizens, alarmed by the news of the riot in the Illinois capital, and uneasy over the state of race relations in their own cities, gathered to pass resolutions and to establish organizations to supervise poor black neighborhoods. The new law and order leagues offered to help local authorities solve black crimes and pledged to help eliminate vice districts. Like Springfield's league, these groups also desired to purge their communities of "objectionable negro characters."[56] Most black law and order efforts remained symbolic only and were limited to speechmaking and the passing of resolutions. Moreover, not all concerned blacks accepted the narrow view that black misbehavior caused race riots or, as a black Chicago minister asserted, that "lynchings are caused by the prevalence of vice" among blacks.[57]

Springfield's own black law and order league survived little more than a year after the riot and had no tangible or lasting impact on black behavior there. The city administration probably posed one of the greatest obstacles to the goals of the black league, since it had little interest in eradicating vice in the capital. And the fate of Springfield's league was typical. As historian David Gerber points out, urban black law and order leagues generally achieved very little because of city governments' reluctance to clean up "neighborhoods which had long been officially accepted as centers of vice—and the fact that vice operators often had political influence also worked against reform." Given some whites' resentment of black success, it is doubtful that elimination of black "objectionable characters" would have prevented anti-black outbreaks anyway, which in this period were "as common as railroad wrecks."[58]

Local Impact of the Riot

By the winter of 1908–9, riot-related news had virtually disappeared from Springfield's newspapers. Minus a handful of black establishments, the Levee and vice district resumed business as usual. Crime, some of it interracial in nature, remained a problem there. Miscegenation, which the press had so severely condemned during and immediately after the riot, still occurred in the netherworld of the vice district, but, once more, newspapers reacted to it indifferently except insofar as it might occasionally provide humorous copy. For example, with a distinct lack of surprise or indignation, the press in December reported briefly that city police had discovered a house where "whites, negroes and Chinese were found living together" in a ménage that included "a French woman" and a Jew.[59] By winter the same newspapers that had singled out interracial crime and coupling as major factors behind August's outbreak were mentioning instances of such behavior in the same prosaic way as they reported changes in the weather.

Previous students of Springfield's riot have claimed that one of its major consequences was that "thousands of [blacks] left the city and never returned." The capital allegedly experienced "a mass exodus of the Black population from the city. Educated and prosperous Blacks were best able to make a move, and their loss severely weakened the remaining Black community."[60] Despite the rioters' efforts to drive them from the city, however, it appears that most black residents returned to the capital after a few weeks, determined to stay. For Springfield's blacks, the riot was a major, but short-term, disruption of life and work.

Many had fled the city: the more fortunate by carriage and train, others on foot. Some took refuge with friends and relatives in nearby towns and cities, while others drifted through rural areas, hungry and frightened, until the worst was over. Many riot refugees were sheltered at the State Arsenal under the protection of the militia. When the city seemed reasonably secure, most blacks simply went home. The riot did not affect Springfield's black population growth, for it increased by one-third between 1900 and 1910—at a faster rate than it had the previous decade (see Chapter 2, Table 2.2). Census and city directory records reveal that, four years later, most black riot victims still lived in Springfield. A comparison of residences of white rioters and black victims underscores blacks' desire to remain in the capital—the rioters seem to have left the city at a slightly higher rate than those whom they had hoped to drive out. Four years after the riot, 20 percent of the black victims seemingly had moved away, while one-quarter of the rioters had left Springfield.[61]

Better-off black citizens whose homes and businesses were damaged by the mob also generally chose to remain in Springfield. The black barbers, grocers, and other small shopkeepers cleaned up the debris, repaired broken windows and doors, and resumed business. All of the more than half dozen barbers whose businesses were sacked, for example, stayed in Springfield and were still working at their trade in the same places in 1910. The riot did affect black saloons, however. In 1907 the city had eleven of them, six of them on East Washington Street. Unlike other black businessmen, most downtown saloonkeepers did not reopen their places. By late 1908 the total number of black saloons had dropped to five, and only two were in the old Washington Street Levee. With few exceptions, former black saloonkeepers stayed on in Springfield, but they worked in different occupations. William Johnson, one of the two major black political ward captains, for example, sustained major losses when the mob sacked his saloon. He remained on the Levee but ran a pool hall instead of a drinking establishment after the riot. His rival, C. C. Lee, reopened his saloon a block away from Johnson's place on Washington Street.[62]

The city council and mayor probably made it more difficult for blacks to obtain liquor licenses for places in the Levee. Mayor Reece publicly pointed out that to deny blacks liquor licenses was against the law, but he may have done it anyway. Lee Osborne, a barber whose shop on East Washington Street was wrecked by the mob, re-opened his old place, but also had plans to set up a saloon in the Levee. Osborne felt it necessary to take unusual measures in apply-ing to the mayor for his permit. To his application he attached a number of written pledges in which he promised to prohibit gam-bling and to bar women from his saloon. He also pledged "that loaf-ers of [the] criminal element will not be tolerated and that there will be no misconduct of any kind." Osborne also won the support of the newly formed black law and order league and obtained the signa-tures of several businessmen and ministers of that organization for his application. The barber ultimately received his liquor license, but despite all of the elaborate assurances he had provided, the white press noted that "the issuance of the license was a surprise" because of "the sentiment of the [city] council." The council, it seems, was against issuing blacks saloon licenses after the riot, re-gardless of how respectable or upright the applicants were. Osborne reportedly gave his pledges to allay "any popular feeling which might exist against granting saloon licenses to negroes." His ability to run an orderly business was irrelevant, though, for "popular feel-ing" was against any black saloons because of "prejudice against the race, [which] will not be stilled or abated by assurance of any char-acter." After the riot, except for black saloons, black business in Springfield recovered rapidly, however.[63]

The city government was legally obligated to compensate riot vic-tims for their losses. It faced a flood of claims for injury and prop-erty compensation, with damage estimates eventually reaching at least $120,000. Black residents who had lost personal property (clothing, furniture, and the like) to fire and theft filed most of the riot claims. A special committee appointed by Mayor Reece to review the claims soon began to complain that black victims had "grossly padded" their estimates of losses. Whether such claim inflation actually took place is unclear, but the committee and the white press certainly wanted to keep the city's liability to a minimum. White newspapers, which had proved unsympathetic to the riot victims during the violence, subsequently ridiculed blacks' attempts to obtain compensation. For example, after reviewing the host of small claims under $100 that blacks had submitted for lost personal property, one editor complained that they were trying to cheat the government out of money. "Five-dollar patent leather shoes seem to have been a common thing in the 'levee' and the 'bad lands' district," he noted sarcastically. The victims "appear to have been well dressed men and women and nothing but the best was in their wardrobes." An unnamed city official reportedly quipped that if Levee and Badlands riot victims could afford such fancy attire, then the city ought to revise its tax code. How equitable the final compensations were is uncertain, but many had to wait for some time before their claims were settled. The city adopted a gradual system of payment that set aside a portion of its revenues each year to pay off riot claims. Eventually the city had to raise money by issuing and selling special bonds. The burden on the city budget, however, was such that nearly six years after the riot it had not yet retired its indebtedness on this bond issue.[64]

The 1908 riot embittered Springfield's black citizens, but it is unlikely that, as some claimed in later years, the violence marked a major turn for the worse in the city's race relations. Both the black and white press mentioned that race relations had been poor before the riot. The *Forum*, for instance, reported with alarm an increase in the number of white businesses refusing to serve blacks in the years before the riot. Springfield blacks who later wrote of the riot or who were interviewed about it disagreed as to whether it increased discrimination in the city or significantly worsened race relations. W. T. Casey, who in the 1920s published a short history of blacks in Sangamon County, insisted that "the riot left its indelible impress on the life of the body politic, and as the mind controls the body, so the moral effects of a lynching are far more far reaching than the material ones. Riots debase character; inflame passions; intensify race hatred—it has been so in Sangamon County. The writer has observed that the relations between the races [have] not been so cordial as [they were] before the 1908 riot. Incalculable injury has been done to the public weal. Time only will heal the wounds."[65]

The riot may have tempted more white businessmen to discriminate against blacks. At any rate, the practice of excluding blacks from restaurants, theaters, and hotels continued until nearly the middle of the twentieth century, in Springfield and elsewhere in the nation. Even in the late 1940s blacks were barred from many white establishments in the Illinois capital. Rev. Henry Mann, a local black minister who served a term as president of the local chapter of the National Association for the Advancement of Colored People, recalled that in the 1930s many white businesses downtown turned blacks away. "It wasn't anything to walk in any drugstore or anyplace like that and they'd refuse you," Mann said. "Eating in restaurants and things—you just didn't get anything. They'd just tell you no." Blacks encountered humiliating treatment in downtown theaters as well. "The Negroes had to go up in what we called 'peanut heaven,'" he remarked. "You didn't get to sit on the main floor. They'd give you that kind of consideration." In a speech before the Springfield Council of Churches in 1947, Alice Taborn, a black citizen, said she still detected "a decided effort to keep the negro in his 'place,' whatever that may be." She cited the city's transportation system to illustrate the tone of local race relations, mentioning "the bus driver who proclaims to the passenger in the corner next to him how he hates 'Negroes' and resents so much that he has to accommodate them, and you may understand my resentment when he passes me up when I have paid for my weekly [bus] pass."[66]

Rev. Mann and several other black residents who remembered life in Springfield early in the century claimed that such discrimination did not exist before the 1908 riot. It is clear from the angry articles in the *Forum*, however, that it was quite prevalent before the outbreak. The editor himself was refused service in downtown restaurants and campaigned to persuade Springfielders to boycott the discriminating white businesses whose names he published in the *Forum*. The recollections of Rev. Mann and other black residents suggest that, even though discrimination was not new to the city, blacks after the riot became more aware of, and sensitive to, its presence.[67] Certainly blacks' bitterness and anger over the violence and the court's failure to punish white rioters endured. Some blacks pointedly shunned businesses owned by whites whom they believed to be riot participants. Even as late as the 1970s, one black woman said she avoided shopping in a nearby grocery store because it was owned by the descendants of one of the alleged riot ringleaders.[68]

One area where Springfield blacks' interests were affected after
the riot was city politics. In 1911 the city government underwent a
major restructuring when the old ward-based, aldermanic system
was replaced by the city commission form then popular with many
urban Progressive reformers. Reform-minded Springfield citizens
had long been distressed by the corruption and inefficiency of the
old ward-based city council system and by the poor quality of city
water, which they claimed "was quite as unfit as the political machine then in power."[69] A flagrant attempt at ballot stuffing, plus
revelations that thousands of dollars were missing from the city's
coffers, generated widespread public outrage and made reform possible. The new system provided for five city commissioners to be
chosen in nonpartisan, at-large elections. The city's water supply
was upgraded, but in the long run, the new governmental structure
fell short of reformers' high hopes for increased probity and
efficiency.[70]

It is possible that reformers partly had the riot in mind when they
sought to clean up Springfield's government by changing to the
commission system. They had, after all, blamed the old ward-based
government for the violence because it gave blacks and lower-class
whites extensive political influence, which both allegedly abused. In
any event, the 1911 restructuring did significantly reduce blacks'
and working-class whites' roles in city politics. The black vote previously had had the potential to decide the outcome of elections for
aldermen who, to play it safe, courted the black vote and rewarded
black political workers with jobs and favors. Citywide at-large elections diluted Springfield's black vote, however, and removed the in-
centive for candidates for commissioner to solicit or reward support
from active black citizens. The composition of the city commission
over time illustrates the decline of blacks' and working-class whites'
influence. From 1911 to the late 1970s "only one city council member has resided on the east side where most of the city's blacks and
many of its working-class whites live. Most hail from the affluent,
largely middle-class west and south sides."[71] Also striking was the
decline in blacks' patronage rewards, especially the loss of positions
for blacks on the city police force. From 1911 to 1914 not a single
black patrolman or detective worked on the city force; from 1915 to
1918 between two and three black detectives were employed, but it
was not until 1919 that Springfield again had a black patrolman. By
1920 four black policemen worked for the city—two detectives and
two patrolmen—but still fewer than had been on the force in
1907.[72] No comparable decline took place in the city's fire depart-

ment, which continued to have one all-black unit, but the loss of police department jobs underscored blacks' diminished political role in the community following the 1911 reform of the government.

During the winter of 1908–9 Springfield's citizens made extensive plans for the centennial celebration of Abraham Lincoln's birthday on the twelfth of February. The prestigious Abraham Lincoln Centennial Association was formed to arrange a banquet and to invite well-known speakers, like William Jennings Bryan, to observe the holiday. The $25-per-plate dinner, a formal black-tie affair at the State Arsenal, was a great success. Present at the event were several foreign ambassadors, various government officials, and presidents and executives from large corporations, including Robert T. Lincoln, president of the Pullman Car Company. The gala celebration at the Arsenal, however, was for whites only. In the days before the banquet, the white press reported that Springfield's "negro residents are aggrieved because they have not been asked to participate in the coming celebration." Hence, a second, more modest gathering took place, as the city's black citizens met in St. Paul's A.M.E. Church to mark the Emancipator's birthday.

The segregation of the Arsenal celebration was not a product of the recent violence in the Illinois capital. Rather, it was a more symbolic instance of the anti-black feeling then widespread in the North. In praising Lincoln, northern whites that year generally ignored his historic connection to black Americans. The speeches at the Arsenal instead lauded him as an inspiring example of a self-made man and as a martyr to the glorious cause of union. It fell to those at St. Paul's to note and to honor Lincoln's "connection with his freeing of the colored race." Despite the segregation of the Arsenal banquet and the protests of local blacks, Springfield's white press concluded that the city had "acquitted itself with honor" by hosting the elaborate celebration. Springfield, said one editor, "did the handsome thing on the centennial of Lincoln's birth."[73]

NOTES

1. *SR*, 1 September 1908, 3 September 1908; *ISJ*, 2–3 September 1908, 5 September 1908; E. L. Rogers, "A Review of the Springfield Riot: The Alleged Cause and the Effect," *The Colored American Magazine* 15 (February 1909): 77; The Chicago Commission on Race Relations, *The Negro in Chicago: A Study of Race Relations and a Race Riot* (Chicago: University of Chicago Press, 1922), 68.

186The Sociogenesis of a Race Riot

2. Rogers, "A Review of the Springfield Riot," 77–78.

3. Manuscript schedules of the population census for Chicago, Illinois, 1910; CD, 1909.

4. *SR*, 3 September 1908; *ISJ*, 5 September 1908; *Directory of Sangamon County's Colored Citizens* (Springfield, Ill.: Springfield Directory Co., 1926).

5. *ISJ*, 4 September 1908; *SR*, 4 September 1908, 6 September 1908; "The So-called Race Riot at Springfield, Illinois," *Charities and the Commons* 50 (19 September 1908): 709–11; "Grand Jury Indictment of Springfield Police," *Charities and the Commons* 50 (12 September 1908): 683–84.

6. *SR*, 22 August 1908, 27–30 August 1908; *ISJ*, 22–23 August 1908, 28 August 1908, 25 September 1908.

7. *ISJ*, 7 July 1908, 15 September 1908, 18 September 1908; *SR*, 15 September 1908.

8. *ISR*, 1 September 1908; *ISJ*, 20 August 1908, 1 September 1908, 6 September 1908, 18–19 September 1908, 24 September 1908.

9. *ISJ*, 16 September 1908.

10. Ibid., 18 September 1908. Springfield's white newspapers were the major source of information on Joe James's trial and the rioters' trials. The circuit court records contain very little of the testimony given and consist mostly of lists of witnesses, judges' instructions to juries, and brief descriptions of the charges involved in specific cases.

11. *SR*, 8 September 1908.

12. Joseph Wallace, *Past and Present of the City of Springfield and Sangamon County, Illinois*, vol. 1 (Chicago: S. J. Clarke Publishing Co., 1904), 320–23.

13. *SR*, 8 September 1908.

14. *SR*, 15–16 September 1908; *ISJ*, 15–16 September 1908.

15. *SR*, 15 September 1908; *ISJ*, 6–7 July 1908, 15–16 September 1908.

16. *ISJ*, 6 July 1908, 16 September 1908, 18 September 1908; *SR*, 15 September 1908; *ISR*, 7 July 1908.

17. *SR*, 18 September 1908; *ISJ*, 24 August 1908, 17 September 1908, 15 October 1908.

18. *SR*, 18 September 1908; *ISJ*, 18 September 1908.

19. *SR*, 20 September 1908; *ISJ*, 19 September 1908, 21 September 1908, 15 October 1908.

20. *ISJ*, 19 September 1908.

21. Ibid., 21 September 1908, 8 October 1908, 21 October 1908.

22. Ibid., 23 October 1908.

23. Ibid., 24 October 1908.

24. Ibid.

25. *ISR*, 17 August 1908.

26. Ibid., 19 August 1908.

27. *SR*, 18 September 1908. For a detailed narrative of Abraham Raymer's first trial, see James Krohe, Jr., "Not Guilty! The Trial of Abraham Raymer after the Springfield Race Riots of 1908," *Illinois Times*, 11 August 1978.

28. *ISJ*, 20 September 1908; *SR*, 21–22 September 1908.

29. Krohe, "Not Guilty!"; *ISJ*, 4 September 1908, 22–23 September 1908; "Grand Jury Indictment," *Charities and the Commons* 50 (12 September 1908): 684.

30. *SR*, 23 September 1908.

31. Krohe, "Not Guilty!"

32. *ISJ*, 24 September 1908.

33. *SR*, 24 September 1908; *ISJ*, 25 September 1908.

34. *ISJ*, 7 October 1908, 9 October 1908, 18 October 1908; *SR*, 9–11 October 1908.

35. *ISJ*, 1 November 1908, 7 November 1908, 10 November 1908, 17 November 1908, 19 November 1908, 22 November 1908.

36. Ibid., 20–22 November 1908, 30 November 1908.

37. William English Walling, "The Race War in the North," *The Independent* 65 (3 September 1908): 532.

38. Howard's was not the last death connected with the riots. In December one of the whites who was shot during the first night of rioting in the Levee died in a Chicago hospital, having never recovered from his wound. He had been a worker in a railroad shop in Springfield. Like all of the other rioters who were identified as steam railroad employees, he worked for the C.P. & St. L. line. *ISJ*, 13 December 1908.

39. *ISJ*, 19–20 December 1908, 29 December 1908.

40. *ISJ*, 5 September 1908, 23 November 1908, 29 November 1908, 16 December 1908; *SR*, 4 September 1908. The indicted blacks had been charged with the assault on William Bowe, the city official who had been shot just outside the Badlands during the first night of the riots.

41. *ISJ*, 9 October 1908, 7 December 1908.

42. Ibid., 10 October 1908.

43. Ibid.

44. *SR*, 24 September 1908.

45. Rogers, "A Review of the Springfield Riot," 75–78; Margaret Ferguson Memoir, SSUO.

46. *SN*, 18 August 1908.

47. Walling, "The Race War in the North," 529–34.

48. Quincy Ewing, "The Heart of the Race Problem," *The Atlantic Monthly* 103 (March 1909): 389.

49. *ISJ*, 17 August 1908.

50. "The Lesson of Springfield," *The Public* 11 (4 September 1908): 534.

51. Graham Taylor, "The Race Riot in Lincoln's City," *Charities and the Commons* 50 (29 August 1908): 627–28; *Chicago Record-Herald*, 17 August 1908; W. A. Woodbridge, "Why the Difference?" *The Independent* 65 (10 September 1908): 605–6; "The Lesson of Springfield," 534–35.

52. *ISJ*, 18 August 1908. Springfield's newspapers published extensive excerpts of national press reaction to the riot.

53. August Meier, *Negro Thought in America, 1880–1915: Racial Ideologies in the Age of Booker T. Washington* (Ann Arbor: University of Michigan Press,

1963), 103, 105–6, 116–18, 161–255; August Meier and Elliott Rudwick, *From Plantation to Ghetto*, rev. ed. (New York: Hill and Wang, 1970), 193–212.

54. *Chicago Tribune*, 17 August 1908.

55. David A. Gerber, *Black Ohio and the Color Line, 1860–1915* (Urbana: University of Illinois Press, 1976), 417–33; Meier, *Negro Thought in America*, 135–36.

56. *Chicago Record-Herald*, 18 August 1908, 29 August 1908; *ISJ*, 24 August 1908; *Chicago Tribune*, 24 August 1908, 8 September 1908.

57. *Chicago Tribune*, 17–18 August 1908, 8 September 1908.

58. Gerber, *Black Ohio*, 426.

59. *ISJ*, 4 December 1908.

60. James Crouthemal, "The Springfield Race Riot of 1908," *Journal of Negro History* 45 (July 1960): 174; Rebecca Monroe Veach, *Growing up with Springfield: A History of the Capital of Illinois* (Springfield, Ill.: Boardman-Smith Funeral Chapel, 1973), 41.

61. CD, 1907–12; manuscript schedules of the population census for Springfield, Illinois, 1910. All of the rioters and victims identified from the newspaper lists and court records were traced in the census and city directory records through 1912. Since a number of rioters and victims "disappeared" from the city—not by moving, but because they died—these figures are not exact. It was, however, often possible to find out if a rioter or victim had died between 1908 and 1912, for the city directories often mentioned the deceased's name and date of death. Also the directories mentioned if wives of males previously listed were widows, thus providing a second way to determine if a male rioter or victim passed away in the four years after the riots. The handful of rioters and victims who died in these years were excluded from the calculation of the proportion of each group who had moved away from Springfield permanently.

62. CD, 1907–8, 1910–11.

63. *SN*, 17 August 1908, 20 August 1908, 22 August 1908; *ISJ*, 29 November 1908, 2 December 1908.

64. *ISJ*, 16 August 1908, 24 August 1908, 28–30 August 1908, 3 September 1908, 5 September 1908, 15 September 1908; *SN*, 20 August 1908; *SR*, 2 September 1908; D. O. Decker and Shelby M. Harrison, *City and County Administration in Springfield, Illinois* (New York: Russell Sage Foundation, 1917), 26, 123–26.

65. W. T. Casey, "History of the Colored People in Sangamon County," in *Directory of Sangamon County's Colored Citizens* (Springfield, Ill.: Springfield Directory Co., 1926).

66. Rev. Henry Mann Memoir, SSUO; Alice Taborn, "A History of Race Relations in Springfield, Illinois," typescript of a speech delivered 29 September 1947, Vertical File, "Springfield, Illinois Riot," SVC. For a detailed and extensive survey of patterns of discrimination in Springfield from 1911 to the 1980s, see Lawrence C. Golden, "Report on Racial Discrimination in

Springfield, Illinois," (unpublished manuscript submitted for the case of *McNeil, et. al. v. The City of Springfield, et. al.,* 1986).

67. Rev. Henry Mann Memoir; Margaret Ferguson Memoir; Taborn, "A History of Race Relations in Springfield, Illinois."

68. Margaret Ferguson Memoir.

69. Quote from Helen Van Cleave Blankmeyer, "The Story of the City Records," typescript, 1935, Illinois State Historical Library; James Krohe, Jr., ed., *A Springfield Reader: Historical Views of the Illinois Capital, 1818–1976* (Springfield, Ill.: Sangamon County Historical Society, 1976), 14; *SR,* 22 August 1908; Franz Schneider, Jr., *Public Health in Springfield, Illinois* (New York: Russell Sage Foundation, 1915), 58–64, 72–81, 86–95.

70. Blankmeyer, "The Story of the City Records." For a concise but thorough discussion of Springfield's city commission system of government, see Cullom Davis and James Krohe, Jr., "Springfield: An Evolving Capital," in Daniel Milo Johnson and Rebecca Monroe Veach, eds., *The Middle-Size Cities of Illinois: Their People, Politics, and Quality of Life* (Springfield: Ill., Sangamon State University, 1980), 195, 201–9, and Decker and Harrison, *City and County Administration in Springfield, Illinois.* On urban reform and the city commission system in Illinois in the Progressive era, see Daniel J. Elazar, *Cities of the Prairie: The Metropolitan Frontier and American Politics* (New York: Basic Books, Inc., 1970), 294–305.

71. Davis and Krohe, "Springfield: An Evolving Capital," 206–7.

72. CD, 1907–8, 1911–20.

73. Veach, *Growing up with Springfield,* 42; Bruce Alexander Campbell, *200 Years: An Illustrated Bicentennial History of Sangamon County* (Springfield, Ill.: Phillips Brothers, Inc., 1976), 202. *ISJ,* 31 January 1909, 5 February 1909, 12–13 February 1909.

Conclusion

When ambition, prompted by real education, causes the Negro to grow restless and he bestir himself to get out of that servile condition, then there is, or at least there will be, trouble, sure enough trouble.

Quoted in Ray Stannard Baker,
Following the Color Line

SPRINGFIELD's riot occurred in the context of the steady and marked deterioration of blacks' security in the United States that began in the late nineteenth century and continued after 1908. Race riots and lynchings represented the most extreme attempts by whites to subordinate black Americans, and riots like Springfield's were but the most visible and dramatic instances of anti-black violence. Although northern white newspapers gave frequent and conspicuous coverage to black crime and to lynchings in the South, they usually paid far less attention to small-scale attacks on blacks in the North. One suspects, though it would be difficult to prove, that there were many minor disturbances and potential riots that never reached the point of mass violence in northern cities. Although many communities probably had "close calls," the northern press may not have found such incidents newsworthy, and they went largely unrecorded. Such was not the case immediately after the Springfield riot. The press temporarily revealed the high level of general hostility and sporadic violence aimed at blacks that it usually passed over in silence.

While portraying the Springfield riot as an exceptional event attributable to the capital's alleged bad government and lax morality, carried out solely by deviant or drunken men, many observers at the same time betrayed considerable anxiety over the imminence of "race war" elsewhere in the North. It was a curious position, one in which the press, on the one hand, denied or minimized the implications of the Springfield riot and, on the other, looked anxiously about for signs of the next mob. As one northern writer warned, "the conditions in Springfield are not peculiar to that city. Almost every community in the country is face to face with the same possibilities. A mob may form in an hour."[1] For a brief time there was speculation that Springfield's riot had sparked a "contagion" of violent anti-black incidents. Newspapers reported numerous smaller, but potentially volatile, outbreaks of interracial violence in a number of northern communities late in the summer of 1908.

The first examples of "riot contagion" mentioned were those incidents in the cities and towns near Springfield precipitated by the appearance of black refugees from the riot. But soon city authorities in places like St. Louis and Chicago called up police reserves to prevent "sympathetic race riots," as they termed them. At the same time, newspapers claimed that a sharp increase in anti-black outbreaks occurred in both cities. In St. Louis, for instance, a routine arrest of a black newsboy on suspicion of robbery led to a nasty confrontation between city police and a mob that shouted, "Lynch the niggers!" and "Give 'em Springfield!"[2] Chicago's police were kept busy for several weeks as they were called on to keep a number of hostile white crowds from reaching riot proportions. Three days after the Springfield riot, Chicago blacks reportedly were the object of insults and, in some cases, unprovoked attacks by angry groups of whites. On 31 August, a pitched battle broke out between black and white Chicago dock workers, which police ended only after arriving in force and by "using their clubs freely." Finally, the press mentioned several instances of white lynch mobs forming in and near Chicago to hunt for blacks they thought guilty of various crimes.[3]

Smaller cities were not immune to the alleged "Springfield contagion." In Alton, Illinois, which had been troubled by a protracted battle over the integration of its public schools, it was noted that "considerable race feeling has arisen since the Springfield riots." Springfield's newspapers reported that "there have been many instances recently [in Alton] of negroes assaulted and severely beaten on the streets. A mob got after a negro in the downtown section and pursued him for blocks." Their rallying cry was said to be "Give him Springfield!"[4] Just after the Springfield riot, as many as four anti-black incidents appeared on a single page of the *Chicago Tribune;* three of them occurred in small northern communities and one in Oklahoma. During a minor fray in Evansville, Indiana (which had witnessed a serious race riot in 1903), two white men stabbed a black passerby, evidently without provocation. The whites "were discussing the Springfield riots" when a black man walked by, and "they lost their tempers and assailed the negro."[5] It is impossible to tell to what extent the smaller outbreaks of anti-black violence in August and September of 1908 were inspired by news of events in Springfield. The northern press insisted on the connection, but it is likely that northern newspapers were simply temporarily sensitized to attacks on blacks and thus devoted more than their usual coverage to the interracial violence that was in fact a frequent occurrence in the North.

Black Americans and others noted with dismay the decline of even liberal white interest in blacks' worsening plight in the North and whites' general lack of concern over the violence aimed against them. The editor of Boston's black *Alexander's Magazine* observed in 1906 that "the ranks of those who once stood for human rights are rapidly breaking and approaching the vanishing point, so that today, it is almost impossible to find a white man in the North or West who thinks about this problem so seriously as to be led to take a decided stand in behalf of justice." Surveying the widespread discrimination and anti-black violence of the decade, he concluded that, with respect to the "race problem," the only "thinking today is being done by the southern white people; the[ir] plea is for injustice."[6] The reaction of many northern whites—that Springfield's riot had nothing to do with racism—simply underscored the extent to which they could misinterpret or ignore the plight of blacks.

In his extensive travels and research on America's race problem, Ray Stannard Baker, a white reporter for *McClure's Magazine*, was struck by northern whites' lack of interest in, or knowledge of, blacks. "The people one ordinarily meets," Baker observed, "don't know anything about the Negro, don't discuss him, and don't care about him." The only whites he found who seemed at all interested in blacks were "a few politicians, mostly the lower sort, the charity workers and the police." In Boston, where he expected to detect some surviving trace of older abolitionist sentiments about blacks, Baker found "hesitation and withdrawal" among the whites he interviewed. The position of the "better class" in Boston and elsewhere in the North, he said, was this: " 'We have helped the Negro to liberty; we have helped to educate him; we have encouraged him to stand on his own feet. Now let's see what he can do for himself. After all, he must survive or perish by his own efforts.' "[7]

Reinforcing northern whites' general lack of concern over discrimination and anti-black violence was their persistent claim that only the South had serious interracial conflict. Edwin Todd noted in a scholarly exchange on the race problem in America in 1908, "We of the North are too fond of thinking that race prejudice exists only in the South."[8] In his monumental survey of American race relations in the 1940s, Gunnar Myrdal termed the process "passing the buck": northern whites complacently assumed that "Negroes are much worse off in the South," while southern whites pointed to the North's interracial sins, saying in effect, "the Negro problem is finally becoming national in scope." In the face of "an astonishing ignorance about the Negro on the part of the white public in the North," Myrdal concluded that "to get publicity is of the highest strategic importance to the Negro people."[9]

Little noticed by white Americans on Lincoln's birthday in 1909 were the beginnings of what would ultimately be a significant organizational challenge to their unawareness of and complacency about the state of the nation's race relations. In his indignant article on the Springfield riot, William English Walling urged a revival of "the spirit of the abolitionists" to combat anti-black violence. His challenge was quickly answered. Early in 1909 a call for a conference on race problems—composed by Oswald Garrison Villard and signed by several dozen educators, writers, and reformers—was published. After two conferences the National Association for the Advancement of Colored People was formally incorporated the following year. The leadership of the fledgling civil rights organization realized the importance of publicity in exposing the state of the nation's race relations. During its first forty years it gave high priority to combating anti-black aggression through publications and by fighting for anti-lynching legislation. Conferences, books, articles, investigations, and exposés were used to increase whites' awareness of the causes and nature of mob violence and to undermine the old stereotype of the criminal black by highlighting the widespread lawlessness of whites. Thus the baleful symbolism of the race riot in Lincoln's home town helped set in motion a program of organized dissent to America's dismal interracial status quo. In part born of "race war," the NAACP undertook its long battle against white indifference to violence against blacks.[10]

At first glance one is struck by how little it seemed to take to set off violent, organized, and sustained white aggression against blacks in the first decade of this century. Springfield's riot, for instance, cannot adequately be accounted for by referring to social strains such as sudden or dramatic changes in the black population, job or housing competition, or acrimonious labor disputes involving black strikebreaking. No war or severe economic depression inflicted generalized anxieties or frustrations upon Springfield's whites. Nor can responsibility for the violence be laid at the door of southern-born whites (or their descendants) who carried the "virus" of race hatred north with them as a peculiarly southern heritage. Finally, there was no discernible pattern of escalating pre-riot incidents involving blacks that might have raised white anger and fear to a fever pitch; the two incidents involving Joe James and George Richardson alone were enough to call forth a mob. What began as an attempt to punish the two jailed black suspects quickly turned into a massive and determined race war.

As the violence progressed, divisions and conflicts among whites over the riot became increasingly visible. What historian Barbara Fields has suggested for the South appears to apply to the urban North as well in this period: whites' social location helped shape the character and the content of their racial beliefs. Because different classes of whites had different experiences with blacks, "each class of whites had its particular variety of racialist ideology," despite the superficial consensus over white supremacy. Although anti-black prejudice could at times provide a unifying or rallying element for whites, Fields notes the "latent possibilities for discord" inherent in this diversity of white views.[11] The pattern of Springfield's violence indicates further that white behavior, as well as ideology, was influenced, not just by class, but also by ethnicity and geographical proximity to blacks. White racism and the propensity to riot varied with social location.

Class was the major dividing line. Better-off whites had the "luxury" of both social and geographical distance from blacks. Those blacks who settled in the urban North, for example, by and large did not settle in the neighborhoods of middle-class whites. With their tiny number of professionals and businessmen, neither did they pose threats to more affluent whites' job security. For the most part, better-off whites met blacks in the context of relations where blacks' status was clearly defined as subordinate. Whatever concerns they had about the "race problem" centered on issues of law and order, black crime, and disorderly behavior in downtown Springfield. This largely class-specific anti-black orientation was reflected in the attempts of influential whites to interpret the race riot as a "reform" that affected only "bad Negroes." The overwhelming impression one gets, however, is that better-off whites could and did ignore blacks in their community. They could afford to.

Not so for Springfield's working-class whites. Their behavior toward blacks was shaped by social conditions not shared by whites of higher standing in the city. Though no clear threat to their material interests was present, the possibility of black encroachment into working-class jobs and neighborhoods did exist. Their social and geographical distance from blacks could not be taken for granted. Moreover, some Springfield blacks had violated their subordinate place in society by openly expressing higher aspirations and by actually achieving a modest measure of power and material success. Blacks had won recognition in city politics, and their votes were both courted and rewarded. A significant number had managed to buy homes, and some had recently established successful businesses downtown. During the riot, the deviant character of this black progress was demonstrated by the selection of black achievers as prime targets for attack.

The danger of black success and aspirations was not peculiar to Springfield. As historian Michael Cassity points out, whites have often feared that "greater freedom for others necessarily implies a loss for themselves."[12] Neither was it purely a northern phenomenon. The Atlanta race riot of 1906, for example, was not the first nor the last time white rioters would be heard to shout, "Burn the place! It's too good for a nigger!" As one black editor remarked after Atlanta's violence, "There is evidence that the mob was not after the worst Negroes so much as they were after the best." He noted less affluent whites' hostility toward black success: "It need not surprise our friends that this element should become envious, and at times revolt because the intelligent and thrifty Negro nails the lie on their vulgar lip. . . . The shiftless, irresponsible and ignorant whites who make up the mob and spread the mob spirit are constantly picking quarrels with enterprising Negroes in order that they may have some excuse for carrying out the dictates of depraved and lawless ambition."[13] When Ray Stannard Baker investigated Atlanta's riot, he found many instances of "the extremes to which race feeling reaches among a certain class of Southerners." As evidence, Baker published excerpts from a letter written by a southern white worker: "I am, I believe, a typical Southern white workingman of the skilled variety, and I'll tell the whole world that I don't want any educated property-owning Negro around me." His only use for blacks, he added, was to do "labour that I don't want to have to perform myself." Should a skilled black threaten his job security, the worker said, "I will kill him."[14]

Opposition to black achievement was not new to the twentieth century. During the first half of the nineteenth century even small communities experienced riots inspired in part by white anger over

conspicuous black progress. There was sustained violence in Columbia, Pennsylvania, in 1834, for example, where whites complained of
"the success and aggressiveness of black artisans and working men."
Clearly targeted in Columbia's riot was Stephen Smith, a prosperous
coal and lumber dealer who violated whites' sense of "a fitting status
for a black man."[15] Whenever race riots broke out, of course, all
blacks were in danger. But Springfield's riot underscored the peril
of successful blacks that Ray Stannard Baker noted in 1906: "In several places in this country Negroes have been driven out by mobs—
not because they were criminal, or because they were bad citizens,
but because they were going into the grocery and drug business,
they were becoming doctors, dentists, and the like, and taking away
the trade of their white competitors."[16] By and large, however, those
who participated in urban race riots were not worried white doctors
and anxious grocers. Springfield's violence suggests that interracial
economic competition was not always directly relevant to anti-black
collective violence. And, if those Springfield rioters identified are
representative, then riot-prone whites in the early twentieth century
were generally from the ranks of the working class, and not proprietors and professionals.

For Springfield's white working class, collective violence represented the extreme end of a wide spectrum of strategies to keep
blacks in their place. Their seeming conviction that the only available remedy was to drive all blacks from the city indicated the extent
to which they felt blacks had violated the boundaries of their expected position in society. The desire for vengeance aside, the refusal of some blacks to accept their subordination ("the negro is too
fresh") and the success of others in achieving status, property, and
influence may have been perceived by some whites as an intolerable
affront. It was precisely over the issue of subordination of blacks
that the brief crisis of disagreement among whites of different
classes emerged. Working-class whites obviously wanted more of it.
Their social betters, however, saw little point in it, except insofar as
they wished to see more law and order downtown in general. Rioters
probably perceived that black subordination was not so important to
wealthier and more influential whites, who enjoyed social and phys-
ical distance from blacks. Better-off whites had little interest in keeping black Springfielders in their place, and other whites were quick
to resent this.

Rioters also perceived that middle- and upper-class whites were
partly responsible for the state of local race relations. First, they

made a black presence in Springfield possible by hiring blacks and by accepting blacks as customers. Some wealthier whites also "fronted" for blacks who wished to buy homes outside of recognized black neighborhoods. Worse, Springfield's political and business community had allowed blacks a small share of the power and rewards of local and state government. Thus rioters partly blamed their social betters for the "intolerable" state of affairs—and acted accordingly. They quickly and forcibly communicated their anger to better-off whites. Sacking Loper's elegant restaurant was but one expression of what rioters thought of whites who valued law and order over the enforcement of black subordination. Some whites, then, suddenly found that they, too, were singled out as enemies in the race war. To rid the city of blacks, rioters attempted to force businessmen, the press, and government officials to cooperate in their purge by severing ties to the despised race. As better-off whites panicked in the face of anonymous threats and occasional attacks, class differences over the meaning of the riot and blacks' place in the city were exposed. Springfield's race riot was not simply a conflict between blacks and whites—for a time, whites were pitted against whites as well.

Although middle- and upper-class whites were virtually absent from Springfield's active rioting, they were far more involved in its genesis and aftermath than they cared to admit. In the first place, they encouraged the rioters in the early stages of the violence by swelling the crowds and by initially praising the riot as "reform." With peace restored and Joe James sentenced to hang, and with the white rioters acquitted, the disagreement between whites of different classes on the position of blacks in the community was smoothed over. Peace, however, came partly at the expense of Springfield's blacks. Law and order prevailed, but not what all would regard as justice. Better-off whites largely refused to cooperate in identifying and prosecuting mob members; as jurors they repeatedly acquitted rioters. The striking lack of sympathy and concern for the riot victims manifested in the press, in white pulpits, and by white businessmen further illustrated just how little the "better sort" of white cared about blacks' welfare. Influential whites—not just in Springfield, but in the nation as a whole—tended to place most of the blame for the outbreak on blacks and dismissed white rioters as mere hoodlums. Once it became clear that there would be no further challenges to white authority in Springfield, better-off whites again spoke of the good that had come out of the violence. In effect, they ultimately gave their sanction—in word and deed—to working-class whites' violent reassertion of white supremacy, in turn helping to perpetuate a climate that fostered yet more anti-black violence.

Blacks who lived in a society where success might imperil them as much as the worst criminal behavior indeed faced a world of danger. No amount of accommodating rhetoric, deferential behavior, or respectability could ensure their security as long as such a large class of whites demanded and tried to enforce black subordination. Over the course of the late nineteenth and early twentieth centuries, it became increasingly difficult for black Americans to maintain the belief that hard work, achievement, and the adoption of middle-class values would win them the respect of whites or a secure place in American society. White collective violence against propertied, as well as poor, blacks in Atlanta, Springfield, and elsewhere made Booker T. Washington's cheerful predictions of racial progress sound ever more hollow and irrelevant. Riots like Springfield's also made it more difficult for blacks to view affluent whites as allies during racial conflicts. It was common in this period for many black spokesmen to portray wealthier whites and employers as their "friends" and to see working-class and poor whites as antagonistic to black progress. Wealthier whites were supposedly less racist than their working-class counterparts. The violence in Springfield, though, made painfully clear the limitations of the friendship of better-off whites. It is true that they were not among those who lynched, burned, and looted, but that did not mean that they were necessarily more free of anti-black attitudes, or that their views had no impact on events in Springfield. The response of influential whites—in the riot trials and elsewhere—left to Springfield's black community an enduring legacy of resentment and distrust.

Despite the fissure that appeared between whites of different status during the riot, Springfield's conflict involved no "class war" and saw no attack upon the prevailing economic structure within which both black and white workers struggled for survival and dignity. Race, and to a lesser extent, ethnicity, had long divided America's working class. As Gunnar Myrdal observed, racial diversity ensured that America's "lower class groups will, to a great extent, take care of keeping each other subdued."[17] Irish-Americans, for instance, themselves so long victims of prejudice and so heavily involved in labor organizing, were one of the ethnic groups with a strong and enduring hostility toward Afro-Americans. Organized labor did glean a reward from keeping blacks out of trades: the conservation of employment for whites in a competitive labor market. But exclusion could backfire, turning the black masses into a weapon for employers to use in breaking strikes and driving down wages. In such cases, though, it was often blacks, and not employers, who felt the brunt of white workers' anger.

Springfield's experience tells us that even before black economic competition and labor strife appeared on a large scale in northern cities after the Great Migration, unease and dissatisfaction already existed among many white workers over the presence of even small numbers of blacks in their communities. Before the social tensions of the World War I era, a firm foundation of white working-class hostility to black progress was well established. Springfield's riot was like the heat lightening that portends a gathering storm. When anxiety over black competition for jobs and housing later rose with the sudden increase in black migration, white workers' preexisting fears about racial boundaries and black subordination in American society were exacerbated. The result would be the worst series of northern race riots in the American experience.

NOTES

1. Henry B. Chamberlain, "Some Reflections on the Springfield Race Riot," *Chicago Record-Herald*, 30 August 1908; Allen H. Spear, *Black Chicago: The Making of a Negro Ghetto, 1890–1920*, (Chicago: University of Chicago Press, 1967), 47.

2. *SN*, 19 August 1908; *Chicago Tribune*, 16 August 1908.

3. *SR*, 18 August 1908; *SN*, 21 August 1908; *Chicago Tribune*, 2 September 1908, 7 September 1908; *Chicago Record-Herald*, 2 September 1908.

4. *SR*, 23 August 1908; August Meier and Elliot M. Rudwick, "Early Boycotts of Segregated Schools: The Alton, Illinois Case, 1897–1908," *Journal of Negro Education* 36 (Fall 1967): 394–402.

5. *Chicago Record-Herald*, 17 August 1908.

6. "What of the Future?" *Alexander's Magazine* 2 (15 October 1906): 10.

7. Ray Stannard Baker, *Following the Color Line: An Account of Negro Citizenship in the American Democracy* (New York: Doubleday, Page & Company, 1908), 117–18.

8. "Discussion of the Paper by Alfred H. Stone 'Is Race Friction between Blacks and Whites in the United States Growing and Inevitable?' " *American Journal of Sociology* 13 (May 1908): 832.

9. Gunner Myrdal, *An American Dilemma: The Negro Problem and Modern Democracy*, vol. 1 (New York: Harper & Row, 1944), 46–49, and vol. 2, 819–36.

10. Mary White Ovington, *The Walls Came Tumbling Down* (New York: Harcourt, Brace and Company, 1947); Charles Flint Kellogg, *NAACP: A History of the National Association for the Advancement of Colored People, 1909–*

200   The Sociogenesis of a Race Riot

1920 (Baltimore: Johns Hopkins Press, 1967); Robert L. Zangrando, *The NAACP Crusade against Lynching, 1909–1950* (Philadelphia: Temple University Press, 1980).

11. Barbara J. Fields, "Ideology and Race in American History," in J. Morgan Kousser and James M. McPherson, eds., *Region, Race and Reconstruction: Essays in Honor of C. Vann Woodward* (New York: Oxford University Press, 1982), 156–60.

12. Michael J. Cassity, *Chains of Fear: American Race Relations since Reconstruction* (Westport, Conn.: Greenwood Press, 1984), xiii–xvi.

13. Ovington, *The Walls Came Tumbling Down*, 63–66; "What of the Future?," *Alexander's Magazine* 2 (15 October 1906): 15; "Atlanta's Negro Mania," *Alexander's Magazine* 3 (15 November 1906): 40. For accounts of the 1906 Atlanta riot see Baker, *Following the Color Line*, 10–11, 84–86; Richard Hofstadter and Michael Wallace, eds., *American Violence: A Documentary History* (New York: Alfred A. Knopf, Inc., 1970), 237–40; W. E. B. Du Bois, "The Atlanta Massacre," *The Independent* 61 (4 October 1906): 779–80; Charles Crowe, "Racial Massacre in Atlanta, September 22, 1906," *Journal of Negro History* 54 (April 1969): 150–73; Joseph Boskin, ed., *Urban Racial Violence in the Twentieth Century*, 2d ed. (Beverly Hills, Calif.: Glencoe Press, 1976), 22–23.

14. Baker, *Following the Color Line*, 84–85, 298–99. Conspicuous black success was also one major contributing factor to the race riot in Wilmington, North Carolina, in 1898. See Richard Maxwell Brown, ed., *Strain of Violence: Historical Studies of American Violence and Vigilantism* (New York: Oxford University Press, 1975), 208–10. A more detailed description of the Wilmington outbreak may be found in H. Leon Prather, Sr., *We Have Taken a City: Wilmington Racial Massacre and Coup of 1898* (Cranbury, N.J.: Associated University Presses, 1984).

15. Brown, *Strain of Violence*, 207.

16. Baker, *Following the Color Line*, 288–89.

17. Myrdal, *An American Dilemma*, 68.

Appendix

Table 2.1 Major Springfield Industries and Their Workforces, 1912 and 1914

Company	Employees, 1912	Employees, 1914
Illinois Watch Co.	900	940
Racine-Sattley Co. (agricultural implements)	500	450
Desnoyer Shoe Co.	400	550
A. L. Ide & Son (metalwork)	—	100
United Zinc and Chemical Co.	350	175
Springfield Boiler & Manufacturing	—	100
F. R. Coats Co. (jewelers' tools, watch parts)	90	—
Lincoln Park Coal and Brick Co.	—	111

Compiled from Louise C. Odencrantz and Zenas L. Potter, *Industrial Conditions in Springfield, Illinois* (New York: The Russell Sage Foundation, 1916), 4; Newton Bateman and Paul Selby, eds., *Historical Encyclopedia of Illinois and History of Sangamon County*, vol. 2 (Chicago: Munsell Publishing Company, 1912), 783–86.

Table 2.2   Leading Occupational Categories, Springfield, Illinois, 1910

Occupation	Number
Extraction of minerals	
miners	2,489
Manufacturing and mechanical industries	
laborers, building and hand trades	631
carpenters	566
miscellaneous metal industries	396
machinists, millwrights, toolmakers	393
builders and building contractors	265
painters, glaziers, varnishers	253
iron and steel industries	165
blacksmiths, forgemen	164
laborers, iron and steel industries	159
engineers, stationary	154
compositors, linotypers, and typesetters	146
shoe factory operatives	142
electricians, electrical engineers	124
plumbers, gas and steam fitters	121
boilermakers	117
cigar and tobacco factory workers	113
Transportation	
draymen, teamsters, expressmen	398
laborers, railroad	261
railroad conductors and motormen, street railways	170
locomotive engineers	150
switchmen, flagmen, yardmen	142
Trade	
clerks	363
deliverymen	302
salespersons	506
Domestic and personal service	
servants (male)	261
servants (female)	973
bartenders	207
saloon keepers	179
barbers, hairdressers, manicurists	161
janitors and sextons	146
porters (except in stores)	123
waiters	94
Total[a]	15,250

Compiled from U. S. Bureau of the Census, *Thirteenth Census of the United States Taken in the Year 1910: Population*, 4:274–79.
[a]Total excludes professional category (733) and clerical workers (1,031).

Table 2.3 Sangamon County Coal-Mining Statistics, 1906–10

	1906	1907	1908	1909	1910
Number of mines	40	38	37	37	36
Average number of miners	4,310	4,294	4,507	4,993	4,435
Average number of other mine employees	1,984	2,053	2,046	1,996	2,581
Total mine workers	6,294	6,347	6,553	6,989	6,995
Average price paid per ton mined	$.53	$.56	$.56	$.56	$.56[a]
Average days in operation	169	191	188	166	173
Tons of coal mined	4,155,431	4,876,621	5,082,626	5,334,148	5,153,322

Compiled from the Illinois Bureau of Labor Statistics' *Annual Coal Report* for the years 1906–10.

[a]Figure is average for hand-mined coal in the Fourth District, which contained Sangamon County.

Table 2.4 Blacks in Illinois Cities, 1890–1910

	Number of Blacks	Percent of Population
1890		
Chicago	14,271	1.3
Springfield	1,798	7.2
Quincy	1,771	5.6
Peoria	864	2.1
East St. Louis	772	5.1
Danville	246	2.1
1900		
Chicago	30,150	1.8
Springfield	2,227	6.5
Quincy	2,029	5.6
East St. Louis	1,799	6.1
Peoria	1,402	2.5
Danville	638	3.9
1910		
Chicago	44,103	2.0
East St. Louis	5,882	10.1
Springfield	2,961	5.7
Quincy	1,596	4.4
Peoria	1,569	2.3
Danville	1,465	5.2

Compiled from *Thirteenth Census, 1910*, 2:504.

Table 2.5   Leading Occupations of Black Males, Springfield, Illinois, 1907

Occupation	Number	Percent of Total Black Male Workers
Laborer	299	28.1
Porter	163	15.3
Miner	158	14.9
Driver/teamster	67	6.3
Waiter	41	3.9
Janitor	39	3.7
Barber	25	2.4
Cook	24	2.3
Houseman	17	1.6
Hostler	13	1.2
Coachman	13	1.2
Bartender	12	1.1
Subtotal	871	81.9
Miscellaneous occupations	193	18.1
Total	1,064	100.0

Compiled from R. L. Polk & Co., *Springfield City Directory for the Year Commencing October 1st, 1907* (Springfield Ill.: R. L. Polk & Co., 1907).

Table 2.6   White Foreign-Born Residents in Three Wards, Springfield, Illinois, 1910

	Ward 1		Ward 6		Ward 7		Total in City
	Number	Percent	Number	Percent	Number	Percent	Number
Russians	575	54.7	183	17.4	108	10.3	1,051
Italians	62	22.5	20	7.3	102	37.0	276
Germans	439	20.6	496	23.3	169	8.0	2,217
Irish	193	19.1	209	20.7	50	4.9	1,012
Others	589	31.7	561	38.2	98	18.5	2,344
Total	1,858	48.2	1,469	38.1	527	13.6	6,900

Compiled from *Thirteenth Census, 1910*, 2:516.

Table 3.1 Comparison of the Age Characteristics of Three
Categories of Rioters

Rioters	Mean Age	Median Age	Number
Indictees	28.2 years	26 years	41
Arrestees	27.8 years	24 years	49
Injured	28.5 years	26 years	26
Combined	27.6 years	25 years	116

Table 3.2 Comparison of Age of Rioters and White Springfield
Males over Ten Years Old

Age	White Springfield Males, 1910		Rioters, 1908	
	Number	Percent	Number	Percent
10–14	1,985	10.2	3	2.6
15–19	2,019	10.4	28	24.1
20–24	2,217	11.4	24	20.7
25–34	4,520	23.2	32	27.6
35–44	3,683	18.9	18	15.5
45–64	3,867	19.9	7	6.0
65 and older	1,118	5.8	4	3.5
Total	19,451	100.0	116	100.0

Age data for white Springfield males for 1910 was compiled from *Thirteenth Census,
1910*, 2:480.

Table 3.3   Comparison of Ethnicity of Rioters and Springfield's White Population, 1910

Place of Birth	Springfield Whites, 1910		Rioters, 1908	
	Number	Percent of White Population	Number	Percent of Rioters
Germany	2,127	4.40	1	.9
Russia	1,051	2.20	2	1.7
Ireland	1,012	2.10	2	1.7
England	726	1.50	5	4.4
Austria	487	1.00	1	.9
Italy	276	.57	4	3.5
Scotland	246	.51	0	0.0
Canada	168	.35	2	1.7
Hungary	145	.30	0	0.0
Sweden	116	.24	0	0.0
Others	546	1.20		
Total	6,900	14.20	17	14.8

Compiled from *Thirteenth Census, 1910*, 2:504, 516.

Note: For the white population, $N = 48{,}699$. For the rioters, $N = 115$.

Table 3.4   Comparison of Ethnic Background of American-Born Rioters and Springfield's White Population, 1910

American-Born, Both Parents	Springfield, 1910		Rioters	
	Number	Percent of Total Whites	Number	Percent
German	3,548	7.3	3	2.6
Irish	2,224	4.6	11	9.6
English	586	1.2	2	1.7

Compiled from *Thirteenth Census, 1910*, 2:504, 516; manuscript schedules of the population census for Springfield, Illinois, 1910.

Note: For the white population, $N = 48{,}699$. For rioters, $N = 115$.

Table 3.5   Occupations of Springfield Rioters, 1908

Occupation	Number	Occupation	Number
High white-collar		*Skilled, (continued)*	
druggist/proprietor	1	meat cutter	1
real estate dealer	1	paperhanger	2
hotel proprietor	1	plumber	2
Low white-collar		printer	1
banker, watch factory	1	tailor	1
contractors (small)	2	*Semi-skilled*	
feed yard operator	1	bartender	8
clerks	2	brakeman, railroad	1
grocery clerk	1	cook, restaurant	1
saloon clerk	1	laundry worker	2
hotel clerk	1	lineman, telephone	1
saloon proprietor	2	car repairman,	
restaurant proprietor		railroad	2
(small)	1	miner	18
letter carrier	1	streetcar driver	2
boardinghouse		streetcar conductor	1
proprietor	1	tinner, apprentice	1
photographer	1	flagman, railroad	1
student	1	operative, watch	
traveling salesman	1	factory	2
Skilled		operator, telephone	1
barber	2	*Unskilled*	
baseball player	1	cement worker	3
blacksmith	6	caller, railroad	1
boilermaker	2	helper, railroad	1
bookbinder	1	saloon porter	3
bricklayer	2	domestic	1
carpenter	2	laborer	14
cigar maker	1	peddler	4
engineer, railroad	2	teamster	4
fireman, railroad	3	elevator operator	1
glazier	1	saloon waiter	1
house painter	3	yardman	1
machinist	2		

Table 3.6 Occupations of Indictees, Arrestees,
and Injured Rioters, 1908

	Indicted	Arrested	Injured	Subtotal
High white-collar	0	1	2	3
Low white-collar	7	6	4	17
Skilled	10	14	10	34
Semi-skilled	15	17	10	42
Unskilled	15	13	6	34
Criminal	3	0	0	3
Total	50	51	32	133

Table 3.7 Homeownership among Indictees, Arrestees,
and Injured Rioters, 1910

	Indictees	Arrestees	Injured	Total
Owns home	3	5	2	10
Rents home	7	9	3	19
Boards with parents who own home	2	6	7	15
Boards with parents who rent home	5	6	4	15
Boards with relatives who own home	0	1	1	2
Boards with relatives who rent home	1	0	1	2
Boards with non-kin who own home	0	2	0	2
Boards with non-kin who rent home	5	7	0	12
Live-in domestic	1	2	0	3
Prison inmate	1	1	0	2
Total	25	39	18	82

Homeownership data were located in the manuscript schedules of the population census for Springfield, Illinois, 1910.

Table 3.8   Residential Location of Rioters by Ward, 1908

Ward	Indictee	Arrestee	Injured	Combined Number	Combined Percent
1	10	8	12	30	24.0
2	6	6	2	14	11.2
3	3	8	6	17	13.6
4	0	3	3	6	4.8
5	2	10	2	14	11.2
6	4	8	6	18	14.4
7	12	8	6	26	20.8
Total	37	51	37	125	100.0

Addresses were obtained from R. L. Polk, *Springfield City Directory for the Year Commencing October 1st, 1908* (Springfield, Ill.: R. L. Polk & Co., 1908).

Table 3.9   Marital Status of Springfield Rioters

Status	Number	Percent
Married	27	26.2
Single	68	66.0
Widowed	4	3.9
Divorced	4	3.9
Total	103	100.0

Compiled from manuscript schedules of the population census of Springfield, Illinois, 1900 and 1910, from newspaper articles, and from county marriage records.

Table 4.1   Occupations of Black Riot Victims

Occupation	Number
High white collar/professional	
proprietor, theater and restaurant	1
undertaker	1
Low white collar, including small proprietors	
boardinghouse keeper	1
messenger, statehouse	1
proprietor, bicycle shop	1
proprietor, grocery	1
proprietor, restaurant	3
proprietor, saloon	4
proprietor, upholstery shop	1
Skilled	
barber	7
carpenter	1
shoemaker	2
Semi-skilled	
bartender	4
cook	2
miner	5
Unskilled	
domestic	3
janitor	2
laborer	8
laundress	2
porter	9
restaurant man	1
teamster	1
watchman	1
Total	62

Table 4.2 Block-Length Street Sections with One
Black Household, by Ward, 1907

Ward	Sections with One Black Home
1	25
2	6
3	22
4	12
5	5
6	37
7	15

Compiled from R. L. Polk, *Springfield City Directory for the Year Commencing October 1st, 1907* (Springfield, Ill.: R. L. Polk & Co., 1907).

Bibliography

A Note on Springfield Sources

Extensive histories of the Illinois capital were published in the late nineteenth and early twentieth centuries. In general these local histories are highly anecdotal and self-congratulatory, but they do contain an abundance of detail unavailable elsewhere. Several provide biographical sketches of middle- and upper-class citizens. The most useful of these early histories is Newton Batemen and Paul Selby, eds., *Historical Encyclopedia of Illinois and History of Sangamon County*, 2 vols., (Chicago: Munsell Publishing Company, 1912). Others include *History of Sangamon County, Illinois* (Chicago: Inter-State Publishing Company, 1881); Joseph Wallace, *Past and Present of the City of Springfield and Sangamon County, Illinois*, 2 vols., (Chicago: S. J. Clarke Publishing Co., 1904); *History of Springfield, Illinois: Its Attractions as a Home and Advantages for Business, Manufacturing, Etc.* (Springfield, Ill.: Illinois State Journal Print, 1871). Additional biographies of turn-of-the-century Springfielders may be found in the *Portrait and Biographical Album of Sangamon County, Illinois* (Chicago: Chapman Bros., 1891).

For the period before the Civil War, the most detailed book-length work remains Paul M. Angle's *"Here I Have Lived": A History of Lincoln's Springfield, 1821–1865* (Springfield, Ill.: The Abraham Lincoln Association, 1935). There are a small number of locally produced recent works on Springfield's history. See, for example, Rebecca Monroe Veach, *Growing up with Springfield: A History of the Capital of Illinois* (Springfield, Ill.: Boardman-Smith Funeral Chapel, 1973); Cullom Davis and James Krohe, Jr., "Springfield: An Evolving Capital," in Daniel Milo Johnson and Rebecca Monroe Veach, eds., *The Middle-Size Cities of Illinois: Their People, Politics, and Quality of Life* (Springfield, Ill.: Sangamon State University, 1980); James Krohe, Jr., *A Springfield Reader: Historical Views of the Illinois Capital, 1818–1976* (Springfield, Ill.: Sangamon County Historical Society, 1976); and Bruce Alexander Campbell, *200 Years: An Illustrated Bicentennial History of Sangamon County* (Springfield, Ill.: Phillips Brothers, Inc., 1976). Three state histories provided good supplementary material on the capital's history, economy, and politics: Ernest Ludlow Bogart and John Mabry Mathews, *The Modern Commonwealth, 1893–1918* (Chicago: A. C. McClurg & Co., 1922); John H. Keiser, *Building for the Centuries: Illinois, 1865 to 1898* (Urbana: University of Illinois Press, 1977), and Donald F. Tingley, *The Structuring of a State: The History of Illinois, 1899–1928* (Urbana: University of Illinois Press, 1980).

Springfield was one of several cities that the Russell Sage Foundation elected to study intensively in the early twentieth century. The result was an indispensable and rich source on the Springfield community. Shelby M. Harrison's *Social Conditions in an American City: A Summary of the Findings of the Springfield Survey* (New York: The Russell Sage Foundation, 1920) is a condensation of a number of independent investigations into the capital's economy, geography, government, educational and recreational facilities, public health, housing, and correctional system. Unfortunately, the Russell Sage investigators paid scant attention to the black community; when blacks were mentioned at all, it was usually in the context of discussions about crime or bad housing conditions. Though focusing on Springfield's changing land use, Clarence Woodrow Sorensen's "The Internal Structure of the Springfield, Illinois, Urbanized Area" (Ph.D. dissertation, University of Chicago, 1951) contains much useful information on the city's economic development and its impact on residential patterns from the 1850s to the 1950s. A more limited discussion of Springfield's land use may be found in Goeffrey Roger Gleave, "The Central Business District of Springfield, Illinois, 1884–1959" (Masters Thesis, University of Illinois, Urbana, 1959).

One of the best sources for exploring Springfield's political scene early in the century is its newspapers. Helen Van Cleave Blankmeyer's unpublished manuscript, "The Story of the City Records" (typescript, 1935, Illinois State Historical Library, Springfield), provides a brief history of Springfield's city administrations in the nineteenth and twentieth centuries. Blankmeyer also describes the scandals that prompted the reform of the city government in 1911. A short but incisive sketch of the character of Springfield's politics may be found in Elise Morrow, "Springfield, Illinois," *Saturday Evening Post,* 27 September 1947. On Springfield's vice district and its connection with local politics, see William L. Clark's *Hell at Midnight in Springfield; Or a Burning History of the Sin and Shame of the Capital City of Illinois,* 4th ed. (Milan, Ill.: 1914). Clark's account is lurid and sensationalistic, but it does provide a rare glimpse into life in the Levee. See also Illinois General Assembly, Senate, Vice Committee, *Report of the Senate Vice Committee* (Chicago: 1916).

Material on Springfield's black community is scarce. Only two short historical sketches exist; one is in the *History of Sangamon County, Illinois,* published in 1881. Another is W. T. Casey, "History of the Colored People in Sangamon County," in *Directory of Sangamon County's Colored Citizens* (Springfield, Ill.: Springfield Directory Co., 1926). Other than crime news, the city's four white newspapers reported very little pertaining to blacks. In 1908 there were two black papers in Springfield. One, the *Forum*, has been preserved. The *Forum* was published weekly with short issues that relied heavily upon reprinted material from larger, more successful black presses. It did, however, provide biographical information on successful black citizens not available elsewhere and gave short descriptions of their homes, businesses, and social activities. The *Forum*'s young editor, E. L. Rogers, repeatedly urged Springfield's blacks to protest against unequal treatment by white businesses, and his editorials constituted one of the major sources of information on local patterns of discrimination.

A second major source on the black community in Springfield was the interviews with black Springfielders conducted by the Oral History Office of Sangamon State University in Springfield. Beginning in the 1970s, interviews were conducted with many older Springfield residents, and the Oral History Office made a special effort to seek out blacks who had lived in the city early in the century. As was the case with the *Forum*, these interviews helped illuminate turn-of-the-century patterns of discrimination and the local black response to worsening race relations. The interviews also provided information on work, housing, the character of various neighborhoods, city government, immigrants, and local race relations in the years after the riots.

Manuscripts

G. Cullom Davis Papers. University Archives. Sangamon State University. Interviews. Oral History Office. Sangamon State University.

Sangamon County, Illinois. Circuit Court Clerk's Office. Circuit Court Files. 1908–9.

Sangamon County, Illinois. Circuit Court Clerk's Office. Defendant's Index. Vol. 11. May 1907–January 1909.

Sangamon County, Illinois. County Clerk's Office. Index to Birth Records. 1877–1916.

Sangamon County, Illinois. County Clerk's Office. Index to Marriage Records. 1864–1919.

Sangamon County, Illinois. County Clerk's Office. Record of Births. 1877–1916.

Sangamon County, Illinois. County Clerk's Office. Record of Marriages. 1864–1919.

Springfield, Illinois. Illinois Regional Archives Depository. Sangamon State University, Springfield, Illinois. Springfield Burial Record. 1908–16.

United States. National Archives. Manuscript Schedules of the 1900 Population Census for Springfield, Illinois.

United States. National Archives. Manuscript Schedules of the 1910 Population Census for Springfield, Illinois.

Vertical File. "Springfield Race Riot." Sangamon Valley Collection, Lincoln Library. Springfield, Illinois.

Published Government Documents

Illinois. Adjutant General. *Biennial Report of the Adjutant General of Illinois to the Governor and Commander-In-Chief, 1907–8.* Springfield: State Printers, 1909.

Illinois. Bureau of Labor Statistics. *Annual Coal Report.* Springfield: 1890–1915.

Illinois. General Assembly. Senate. Vice Committee. *Report of the Senate Vice Committee, Created under the Authority of the Forty-Ninth General Assembly.* Chicago: State Printers, 1916.

Springfield, Illinois. *Reports of the Officers of the City of Springfield, Illinois.* 1886–1906. Sangamon Valley Collection, Lincoln Library.

Springfield, Illinois. *The Springfield City Code, Comprising the Laws of the State of Illinois Relating to the Government of the City of Springfield, and the Ordinances of the City Council.* Springfield, Ill.: 1902. Sangamon Valley Collection, Lincoln Library.

U.S. Bureau of the Census. *Negro Population, 1790–1915.* Washington, D.C.: Government Printing Office, 1918.

———. *Special Reports: Occupations at the Twelfth Census.* Washington, D.C.: Government Printing Office, 1904.

———. *Thirteenth Census of the United States Taken in the Year 1910: Manufactures.* Washington, D.C.: Government Printing Office, 1912.

———. *Thirteenth Census of the United States Taken in the Year 1910: Mines and Quarries, 1909.* Washington, D.C.: Government Printing Office, 1913.

———. *Thirteenth Census of the United States Taken in the Year 1910: Population.* 4 vols. Washington, D.C.: Government Printing Office, 1913–14.

U.S. Census Office. *Twelfth Census of the United States Taken in the Year 1900: Population.* 2 vols. Washington, D.C.: Government Printing Office, 1901.

Newspapers

Chicago Record-Herald
Chicago Tribune
Forum
Illinois State Journal
Illinois State Register
Illinois Times
Springfield News
Springfield Record

Secondary Sources

Allport, Gordon W. *The Nature of Prejudice.* Reading, Mass.: Addison-Wesley Publishing Company, 1954.

Altgeld, John P. *Live Questions.* Chicago: George S. Bowen & Son, 1899.

Angle, Paul M. *Bloody Williamson: A Chapter in American Lawlessness*. New York: Alfred A. Knopf, 1952.

"The Atlanta Mob Spirit." *Alexander's Magazine* 3 (15 October 1906): 15.

"Atlanta's Negro Mania." *Alexander's Magazine* 3 (15 November 1906): 39–41.

"Atlanta Outdone." *The Independent* 65 (20 August 1908): 442–43.

Ayers, Edward L. *Vengeance and Justice: Crime and Punishment in the Nineteenth-Century American South*. New York: Oxford University Press, 1984.

Baker, Ray Stannard. *Following the Color Line: An Account of Negro Citizenship in the American Democracy*. New York: Doubleday, Page & Company, 1908.

Barnum, Darold T. *The Negro in the Bituminous Coal Mining Industry*. The Racial Policies of American Industry. Report No. 14. Philadelphia: University of Pennsylvania Press, 1970.

Bergesen, Albert. "Official Violence during the Watts, Newark, and Detroit Race Riots of the 1960s." In *A Political Analysis of Deviance*, edited by Pat Lauderdale. Minneapolis: University of Minnesota Press, 1980.

Black, Donald. *The Behavior of Law*. Orlando, Fla.: Academic Press, 1976.

———. "Crime as Social Control." *American Sociological Review* 48 (February 1983): 34–45.

———. "The Elementary Forms of Conflict Management." In *New Directions in the Study of Justice, Law, and Social Control*, edited by Melvin J. Lerner. New York: Plenum Press, 1990.

———. "Social Control as a Dependent Variable." In *Toward a General Theory of Social Control*. 2 vols., edited by Donald Black. Orlando, Fla.: Academic Press, 1984.

Bloombaum, Milton. "The Conditions Underlying Race Riots as Portrayed by Multidimensional Scalogram Analysis: A Reanalysis of Lieberson and Silverman's Data." *American Sociological Review* 33 (February 1968): 76–91.

Borchert, James. *Alley Life in Washington: Family, Community, Religion, and Folklife in the City, 1850–1970*. Urbana: University of Illinois Press, 1980.

Boskin, Joseph, ed. *Urban Racial Violence in the Twentieth Century*, 2d ed. Beverly Hills, Calif.: Glencoe Press, 1976.

Brier, Stephen. "The Career of Richard L. Davis Reconsidered: Unpublished Correspondence from the *National Labor Tribune*." *Labor History* 21 (Summer 1980): 420–29.

Brophy, Ira N. "The Luxury of Anti-Negro Prejudice." *Public Opinion Quarterly* 9 (Winter 1945–46): 456–66.

Brown, Richard Maxwell, ed. *American Violence*. Englewood Cliffs, N.J.: Prentice-Hall, Inc., 1970.

———. *Strain of Violence: Historical Studies of American Violence and Vigilantism*. New York: Oxford University Press, 1975.

Capeci, Dominic J., Jr. *The Harlem Riot of 1943*. Philadelphia: Temple University Press, 1977.

Caplan, Nathan S., and Paige, Jeffery M. "A Study of Ghetto Rioters." *Scientific American* 219 (August 1968): 15–21.

Cassity, Michael J. *Chains of Fear: American Race Relations since Reconstruction.* Westport, Conn.: Greenwood Press, 1984.

Chamberlain, Henry B. "Some Reflections on the Springfield Riot." *Chicago Record-Herald,* 30 August 1908.

The Chicago Commission on Race Relations. *The Negro in Chicago: A Study of Race Relations and a Race Riot.* Chicago: University of Chicago Press, 1922.

Chudacoff, Howard P. *Mobile Americans: Residential and Social Mobility in Omaha, 1880–1920.* New York: Oxford University Press, 1972.

Clark, Dennis. *The Irish Relations: Trials of an Immigrant Tradition.* East Brunswick, N.J.: Associated University Presses, 1982.

Colson, Elizabeth. "Social Control and Vengeance in Plateau Tonga Society." *Africa* 23 (July 1953): 199–212.

Cook, Adrian. *The Armies of the Streets: The New York City Draft Riots of 1863.* Lexington: University Press of Kentucky, 1974.

Cook, Raymond Allen. *Fire From the Flint: The Amazing Careers of Thomas Dixon.* Winston-Salem, N.C.: John F. Blair, 1968.

Cooney, Mark. "The Social Control of Homicide: A Cross-Cultural Study." S.J.D. diss., Harvard University, 1988.

Crouthemal, James. "The Springfield Race Riot of 1908." *Journal of Negro History* 45 (July 1960): 164–81.

Crowe, Charles. "Racial Massacre in Atlanta, Sept. 22, 1906." *Journal of Negro History* 54 (April 1969): 150–68.

Davis, Natalie Zemon. *Society and Culture in Early Modern France.* Stanford, Calif.: Stanford University Press, 1975.

Decker, D. O., and Harrison, Shelby M. *City and County Administration in Springfield, Illinois.* New York: Russell Sage Foundation, 1917.

Deutsch, M., and Collins, Mary E. *Interracial Housing: A Psychological Evaluation of a Social Experiment.* Minneapolis: University of Minnesota Press, 1951.

DeVries, James E. *Race and Kinship in a Midwestern Town: The Black Experience in Monroe, Michigan, 1900–15.* Urbana: University of Illinois Press, 1984.

Dixon, Thomas, Jr. "Booker T. Washington and the Negro." *Saturday Evening Post* 178 (19 August 1905): 1–2.

———.*The Clansman: An Historical Romance of the Ku Klux Klan.* New York: Doubleday, Page & Co., 1905.

Dobkowski, Michael. *The Tarnished Dream: The Basis of American Anti-Semitism.* Westport, Conn.: Greenwood Press, 1979.

Dollard, John. *Caste and Class in a Southern Town.* New Haven, Conn.: Yale University Press, 1937.

DuBois, W. E. B. *The Philadelphia Negro: A Social Study.* Philadelphia: 1899.

Duis, Perry R. *The Saloon: Public Drinking in Chicago and Boston, 1880–1920.* Urbana: University of Illinois Press, 1983.

Elazar, Daniel J. *Cities of the Prairie: The Metropolitan Frontier and American Politics.* New York: Basic Books, Inc., 1970.

Ellsworth, Scott. *Death in a Promised Land: The Tulsa Race Riot of 1921.* Baton Rouge: Louisiana State University Press, 1982.

"E. L. Rogers." *The Colored American Magazine* 15 (February 1909): 74.

Ewing, Quincy. "The Heart of the Race Problem." *The Atlantic Monthly* 103 (March 1909): 389–97.

Feldberg, Michael. *The Philadelphia Riots of 1844: A Study of Ethnic Conflict.* Westport, Conn.: Greenwood Press, 1975.

———. *The Turbulent Era: Riot and Disorder in Jacksonian America.* New York: Oxford University Press, 1980.

Fields, Barbara J. "Ideology and Race in American History." In *Region, Race and Reconstruction: Essays in Honor of C. Vann Woodward,* edited by J. Morgan Kousser and James M. McPherson. New York: Oxford University Press, 1982.

Fine, Sidney. "Chance and History: Some Aspects of the Detroit Riot of 1967." *Michigan Quarterly Review* 25 (Spring 1986): 403–23.

Flynn, Charles L., Jr. "The Ancient Pedigree of Violent Repression: Georgia's Klan as a Folk Movement." In *The Southern Enigma: Essays on Race, Class, and Folk Culture,* edited by Walter J. Fraser, Jr., and Winfred B. Moore, Jr. Westport, Conn.: Greenwood Press, 1983.

Frazier, E. Franklin. *The Negro Family in the United States.* Chicago: University of Chicago Press, 1939.

Fredrickson, George M. *The Black Image in the White Mind: The Debate on Afro-American Character and Destiny, 1817–1914.* New York: Harper & Row, 1971.

Friedman, Lawrence M., and Percival, Robert V. *The Roots of Justice: Crime and Punishment in Alameda County, California, 1870–1910.* Chapel Hill: University of North Carolina Press, 1981.

Gerber, David A. *Black Ohio and the Color Line, 1860–1915.* Urbana: University of Illinois Press, 1976.

———. "Lynching and Law and Order: Origin and Passage of the Ohio Anti-Lynching Law of 1896." *Ohio History* 83 (Winter 1974): 33–50.

———. "A Politics of Limited Options: Northern Black Politics and the Problem of Change and Continuity in Race Relations Historiography." *Journal of Social History* 14 (Winter 1980): 235–55.

Gilje, Paul A. "The Baltimore Riots of 1812 and the Breakdown of the Anglo-American Mob Tradition." *Journal of Social History* 13 (Summer 1980): 547–64.

———. *The Road to Mobocracy: Popular Disorder in New York City, 1763–1834.* Chapel Hill: University of North Carolina Press, 1987.

Gluckman, Max. *Custom and Conflict in Africa.* Oxford: Basil Blackwell, Ltd., 1956.

Granovetter, Mark S. "The Strength of Weak Ties." *American Journal of Sociology* 78 (May 1973): 1360–80.

Grant, Robert B. *The Black Man Comes to the City: A Documentary Account from the Great Migration to the Great Depression, 1915 to 1930.* Chicago: Nelson-Hall Company, 1972.

Grimshaw, Allen D. "Actions of the Police and the Military in American Race Riots." *Phylon* 24 (Fall 1963): 271–89.

————. "Changing Patterns of Racial Violence in the United States." *Notre Dame Lawyer* 60 (Symposium, 1965): 534–48.

————. "Factors Contributing to Colour Violence in the United States and Britain." *Race* 3 (May 1962): 3–19.

————. "Lawlessness and Violence in America and Their Special Manifestations in Changing Negro-White Relationships." *Journal of Negro History* 44 (January 1959): 52–72.

————. "Negro-White Relations in the Urban North: Two Areas of High Conflict Potential." *Journal of Intergroup Relations* 3 (Spring 1962): 145–58.

————, ed. *Racial Violence in the United States.* Chicago: Aldine Publishing Company, 1969.

————. "A Study in Social Violence: Urban Race Riots in the United States." Ph.D. diss., University of Pennsylvania, 1959.

————. "Three Views of Urban Violence: Civil Disturbance, Racial Revolt, Class Assault." *American Behavioral Scientist* 11 (March-April 1968): 2–7.

————. "Urban Racial Violence in the United States: Changing Ecological Considerations." *American Journal of Sociology* 64 (September 1960): 109–19.

Grimsted, David. "Rioting in Its Jacksonian Setting." *American Historical Review* 77 (April 1972): 361–418.

Gutman, Herbert G. *The Black Family in Slavery and Freedom, 1750–1925.* New York: Pantheon Books, 1976.

————. "The Negro and the United Mine Workers of America." In *The Negro and the American Labor Movement,* edited by Julius Jacobson. Garden City, N.Y.: Doubleday & Company, 1968.

————. "Persistent Myths about the Afro-American Family." *Journal of Interdisciplinary History* 6 (Autumn 1975): 181–210.

————. *Work, Culture and Society in Industrializing America.* New York: Alfred A. Knopf, 1976.

Hair, William Ivy. *Carnival of Fury: Robert Charles and the New Orleans Race Riot of 1900.* Baton Rouge: Louisiana State University Press, 1976.

Hammett, Theodore M. "Two Mobs of Jacksonian Boston: Ideology and Interest." *Journal of American History* 62 (March 1976): 845–68.

Harlan, Louis R. *Booker T. Washington: The Wizard of Tuskegee, 1901–1915.* New York: Oxford University Press, 1983.

Harris, Robert L. "Coming of Age: The Transformation of Afro-American Historiography." *Journal of Negro History* 67 (Summer 1982): 107–21.

Harris, William H. *The Harder We Run: Black Workers since the Civil War.* New York: Oxford University Press, 1982.

Haynes, George Edmund. "Conditions Among Negroes in the Cities." *Annals of the American Academy of Political and Social Science* 49 (September 1913): 105–19.

Haynes, Robert V. *A Night of Violence: The Houston Riot of 1917.* Baton Rouge: Louisiana State University Press, 1976.

Hellwig, David J. "The Afro-American and the Immigrant, 1880–1930: A Study of Black Social Thought." Ph.D. diss., Syracuse University, 1973.

Hershberg, Theodore, ed. *Philadelphia: Work, Space, Family, and Group Experience in the Nineteenth Century.* New York: Oxford University Press, 1981.

Hicken, Victor. "The Virden and Pana Mine Wars of 1898." *Journal of the Illinois State Historical Society* 52 (Summer 1959): 263–78.

Hine, Darlene Clark, ed. *The State of Afro-American History: Past, Present, and Future.* Baton Rouge: Louisiana State University Press, 1986.

Hofstadter, Richard, and Wallace, Michael, eds. *American Violence: A Documentary History.* New York: Alfred A. Knopf, Inc., 1970.

Horton, James Oliver, and Horton, Lois E. *Black Bostonians: Family Life and Community Struggle in the Antebellum North.* New York: Holmes & Meier Publishers, 1979.

Ihlder, John. *Housing in Springfield, Illinois.* New York: Russell Sage Foundation, 1914.

Jackson, Kenneth T. *The Ku Klux Klan in the City, 1915–1930.* New York: Oxford University Press, 1967.

Janowitz, Morris. "Patterns of Collective Racial Violence." In *Violence in America: Historical and Comparative Perspectives,* edited by Hugh Graham Davis and Ted Robert Gurr. New York: Bantam Books, 1969.

———. *Social Control of Escalated Riots.* Chicago: University of Chicago Press, 1968.

Jeffress, Philip W. *The Negro in the Urban Transit Industry.* The Racial Policies of American Industry. Report No. 18. Philadelphia: University of Pennsylvania Press, 1970.

Jensen, Richard. *The Winning of the Midwest: Social and Political Conflict, 1888–1896.* Chicago: University of Chicago Press, 1971.

Jordon, Winthrop. *The White Man's Burden: Historical Origins of Racism in the United States.* New York: Oxford University Press, 1974.

———. *White over Black: American Attitudes toward the Negro, 1550–1812.* Chapel Hill: University of North Carolina Press, 1968.

Katzman, David M. *Before the Ghetto: Black Detroit in the Nineteenth Century.* Urbana: University of Illinois Press, 1973.

Keiser, John H. "Black Strikebreakers and Racism in Illinois, 1865–1900." *Journal of the Illinois State Historical Society* 65 (Autumn 1972): 313–26.

———. *Building for the Centuries: Illinois, 1865 to 1898.* Urbana: University of Illinois Press, 1977.

Kellogg, Charles Flint. *NAACP: A History of the National Association for the Advancement of Colored People.* Vol. 1, *1909–1920.* Baltimore: Johns Hopkins University Press, 1967.

Kephart, W. M. *Racial Factors and Urban Law Enforcement*. Philadelphia: University of Pennsylvania Press, 1957.

Kincaid, Larry. "Two Steps Forward, One Step Back: Racial Attitudes during the Civil War and Reconstruction." In *The Great Fear: Race in the Mind of America*, edited by Gary B. Nash and Richard Weiss. New York: Holt, Rinehart and Winston, Inc., 1970.

Kleppner, Paul. *The Cross of Culture: A Social Analysis of Midwestern Politics, 1850–1900*. New York: The Free Press, 1970.

Krohe, James, Jr. *Midnight at Noon: A History of Coal Mining in Sangamon County*. Springfield, Ill.: Sangamon County Historical Society, 1975.

―――. "Not Guilty! The Trial of Abraham Raymer after the Springfield Race Riots of 1908." *Illinois Times*, 11 August 1978.

―――. *Summer of Rage: The Springfield Race Riot of 1908*. Springfield, Ill.: Sangamon County Historical Society, 1973.

―――, ed. *A Springfield Reader: Historical Views of the Illinois Capital, 1818–1976*. Springfield, Ill.: Sangamon County Historical Society, 1976.

Kusmer, Kenneth L. *A Ghetto Takes Shape: Black Cleveland, 1870–1930*. Urbana: University of Illinois Press, 1976.

Lane, Roger. *The Roots of Violence in Black Philadelphia, 1860–1900*. Cambridge, Mass.: Harvard University Press, 1986.

―――. *Violent Death in the City: Suicide, Accident, and Murder in Nineteenth-Century Philadelphia*. Cambridge, Mass.: Harvard University Press, 1979.

Lee, Alfred McClung, and Humphrey, Norman D. *Race Riot*. New York: Dryden Press, 1943.

"The Lesson of Springfield." *The Public* 11 (4 September 1908): 534–35.

Lewis, Ronald L. *Black Coal Miners in America: Race, Class, and Community Conflict, 1780–1980*. Lexington: University Press of Kentucky, 1987.

Licht, Walter. *Working for the Railroad: The Organization of Work in the Nineteenth Century*. Princeton: Princeton University Press, 1983.

Lieberson, Stanley, and Silverman, Arnold R. "The Precipitants and Underlying Conditions of Race Riots." *American Sociological Review* 30 (December 1965): 887–98.

Litwack, Leon. *North of Slavery: The Negro in the Free States, 1790–1860*. Chicago: University of Chicago Press, 1961.

―――. "The Ordeal of Black Freedom." In *The Southern Enigma: Essays on Race, Class, and Folk Culture*, edited by Walter J. Fraser, Jr., and Winfred B. Moore, Jr. Westport, Conn.: Greenwood Press, 1983.

Logan, Rayford W. *The Betrayal of the Negro: From Rutherford B. Hayes to Woodrow Wilson*. New enl. ed. New York: Collier Books, 1965.

Luebke, Frederick. "The Germans." In *Ethnic Leadership in America*, edited by John Higham. Baltimore: Johns Hopkins University Press, 1978.

MacKenzie, Barbara K. "The Importance of Contact in Determining Attitudes toward Negroes." *Journal of Abnormal and Social Psychology* 43 (1948): 417–41.

Marsden, Peter V., and Campbell, Karen E. "Measuring Tie Strength." *Social Forces* 63 (December 1984): 482–501.

Martin, Waldo E. *The Mind of Frederick Douglass.* Chapel Hill: University of North Carolina Press, 1984.

Meier, August. *Negro Thought in America, 1880–1915: Racial Ideologies in the Age of Booker T. Washington.* Ann Arbor: University of Michigan Press, 1963.

Meier, August, and Rudwick, Elliott. *Along the Color Line: Explorations in the Black Experience.* Urbana: University of Illinois Press, 1976.

Meier, August, and Rudwick, Elliott. *Black History and the Historical Profession, 1915–1980.* Urbana: University of Illinois Press, 1986.

Meier, August, and Rudwick, Elliott. "Early Boycotts of Segregated Schools: The Alton, Illinois Case, 1897–1908." *Journal of Negro Education* 36 (Fall 1967): 394–402.

Meier, August, and Rudwick, Elliott. *From Plantation to Ghetto.* Rev. ed. New York: Hill and Wang, 1970.

Miller, Kelly. "The Negro as a Workingman." *American Mercury* 6 (November 1925): 310–13.

Morrow, Elise. "The Cities of America: Springfield, Illinois." *Saturday Evening Post* 220 (27 September 1947).

Moss, Frank. *The Story of the Riot.* New York: The Citizens' Protective League, 1900. Reprint. New York: Arno Press, 1969.

Myrdal, Gunnar. *An American Dilemma: The Negro Problem and Modern Democracy.* 2 vols. New York: Harper & Row, 1944.

Nash, Gary B., and Weiss, Richard, eds. *The Great Fear: Race in the Mind of America.* New York: Holt, Rinehart and Winston, Inc., 1970.

National Association for the Advancement of Colored People. *Thirty Years of Lynching in the United States, 1889–1918.* New York: 1919.

Newby, I. A. *Jim Crow's Defense: Anti-Negro Thought in America, 1900–1930.* Baton Rouge: Louisiana State University Press, 1965.

Odencrantz, Louise C., and Potter, Zenas L. *Industrial Conditions in Springfield, Illinois.* New York: Russell Sage Foundation, 1916.

Osofsky, Gilbert. *Harlem: The Making of a Ghetto, Negro New York, 1890–1930.* New York: Harper & Row, 1966.

Ovington, Mary White. *Half a Man: The Status of the Negro in New York.* London: Longmans, Green & Co., 1911.

———. *The Walls Came Tumbling Down.* New York: Harcourt, Brace and Company, 1947.

Pettigrew, Thomas F. "Attitudes on Race and Housing: A Social-Psychological View." In *Segregation in Residential Areas: Papers on Racial and Socioeconomic Factors in Choice of Housing,* edited by Amos H. Hawley and Vincent P. Rock. Washington, D.C.: National Academy of Sciences, 1973.

Philpott, Thomas L. *The Slum and the Ghetto: Neighborhood Deterioration and Middle-Class Reform, Chicago, 1880–1930.* New York: Oxford University Press, 1978.

Pleck, Elizabeth Hafkin. *Black Migration and Poverty: Boston, 1865–1900.* New York: Academic Press, 1979.

Potter, Zenas L. *The Correctional System of Springfield, Illinois.* New York: Russell Sage Foundation, 1915.

Prather, H. Leon, Sr. *We Have Taken a City: Wilmington Racial Massacre and Coup of 1898.* Cranbury, N.J.: Associated University Presses, 1984.

"Race War in Springfield." *The Public* 11 (21 August 1908): 492–93.

Raper, Arthur F. *The Tragedy of Lynching.* Chapel Hill: University of North Carolina Press, 1933.

Redding, Jay Saunders. "The Negro in American History: As Scholar, as Subject." In *The Past Before Us: Contemporary Historical Writing in the United States,* edited by Michael Kammen. Ithaca, N.Y.: Cornell University Press, 1980.

Report of the National Advisory Commission on Civil Disorders. Washington, D.C.: Government Printing Office, 1968.

Rice, Roger L. "Residential Segregation by Law, 1910–1917." *Journal of Social History* 34 (May 1968): 179–99.

Richards, Leonard L. *"Gentlemen of Property and Standing": Anti-Abolition Mobs in Jacksonian America.* New York: Oxford University Press, 1970.

Rieder, Jonathan. "The Social Organization of Vengeance." In *Toward a General Theory of Social Control,* 2 vols., edited by Donald Black. Orlando, Fla.: Academic Press, 1984.

Rogers, E. L. "A Review of the Springfield Riot: The Alleged Cause and the Effect." *The Colored American Magazine* 15 (February 1909): 75–78.

"The Riot at Springfield." *The Outlook* 89 (22 August 1908): 869–70.

Rose, Arnold M., Atelsek, Frank J., and McDonald, Lawrence R. "Neighborhood Reactions to Isolated Negro Residents: An Alternative to Invasion and Succession." *American Sociological Review* 18 (October 1953): 497–507.

Rose, John C. "Movements of the Negro Population as Shown by the Census of 1910." *American Economic Review* 4 (June 1914): 281–92.

Rosen, Ruth. *The Lost Sisterhood: Prostitution in America, 1900–1918.* Baltimore: John Hopkins University Press, 1982.

Rudé, George. *The Crowd in History: A Study of Popular Disturbances in France and England, 1730–1848.* New York: Wiley, 1964.

Rudwick, Elliott M. *Race Riot at East St. Louis, July 2, 1917.* Carbondale: Southern Illinois University Press, 1964.

Saxton, Alexander. "Race and the House of Labor." In *The Great Fear: Race in the Mind of America,* edited by Gary B. Nash and Richard Weiss. New York: Holt, Rinehart and Winston, Inc., 1970.

Sitkoff, Harvard. "Racial Militancy and Interracial Violence in the Second World War." *Journal of American History* 58 (December 1971): 661–81.

"The So-called Race Riot at Springfield, Illinois." *Charities and the Commons* 50 (19 September 1908): 709–11.

Spear, Allen H. *Black Chicago: The Making of a Negro Ghetto, 1890–1920.* Chicago: University of Chicago Press, 1967.

Spero, Sterling D., and Harris, Abram L. *The Black Worker: The Negro and the Labor Movement.* New York: Columbia University Press, 1931.

Stone, Alfred Holt. "Is Race Friction between Blacks and Whites in the United States Growing and Inevitable?" *American Journal of Sociology* 13 (March 1908): 676–97.

Swan, Alex L. "The Harlem and Detroit Riots of 1943: A Comparative Analysis." *Berkeley Journal of Sociology* 16 (1971–1972): 75–93.

Taylor, D. Garth. "Housing, Neighborhoods, and Race Relations: Recent Survey Evidence." *Annals of the American Academy of Political and Social Science* 441 (January 1979): 26–40.

Taylor, Graham. "The Race Riot in Lincoln's City." *Charities and the Commons* 50 (29 August 1908): 627–28.

Thernstrom, Stephan. *The Other Bostonians: Poverty and Progress in the American Metropolis, 1880–1970.* Cambridge, Mass.: Harvard University Press, 1973.

Thernstrom, Stephan, ed. *Harvard Encyclopedia of American Ethnic Groups.* Cambridge, Mass.: Harvard University Press, 1980.

Thoden van Velzen, H. U. E., and van Wetering, W. "Residence, Power Groups and Intra-Societal Aggression: An Enquiry into the Conditions Leading to Peacefulness within Non-Stratified Societies." Part 2. *International Archives of Ethnography* 49 (1960): 169–200.

Thornbrough, Emma Lou. *The Negro in Indiana: A Study of a Minority.* Indianapolis: Indiana Historical Bureau, 1957.

Tingley, Donald F. *The Structuring of a State: The History of Illinois, 1899–1928.* Urbana: University of Illinois Press, 1980.

Tuttle, William M., Jr. *Race Riot: Chicago in the Red Summer of 1919.* New York: Atheneum, 1970.

Voegeli, Jacque V. *Free but Not Equal: The Midwest and the Negro during the Civil War.* Chicago: University of Chicago Press, 1967.

Waller, Altina L. "Community, Class and Race in the Memphis Riot of 1866." *Journal of Social History* 18 (Winter 1984): 233–46.

Walling, William English. "The Race War in the North." *The Independent* 65 (3 September 1908): 529–34.

Waskow, Arthur I. *From Race Riot to Sit-In, 1919 and the 1960s: A Study in the Connections between Conflict and Violence.* Garden City, N.Y.: Doubleday and Company, 1966.

Watts, Eugene J. "Police Priorities in Twentieth-Century St. Louis." *Journal of Social History* 14 (Summer 1981): 649–73.

"We Would Not Dramatize Our Ills." *Alexander's Magazine* 3 (15 December 1906): 62–63.

"What of the Future?" *Alexander's Magazine* 2 (15 October 1906): 9–15.

Williamson, Joel. *The Crucible of Race: Black-White Relations in the American South since Emancipation.* New York: Oxford University Press, 1984.

———. *New People: Miscegenation and Mulattoes in the United States.* New York: The Free Press, 1980.

Wilner, Daniel M., Walkley, Rosabelle P., and Cook, Stuart W. *Human Relations in Interracial Housing: A Study of the Contact Hypothesis.* Minneapolis: University of Minnesota Press, 1955.

Wittke, Carl. *The Irish in America.* Baton Rouge: Louisiana State University Press, 1956.

Zangrando, Robert L. *The NAACP Crusade against Lynching, 1909–1950.* Philadelphia: Temple University Press, 1980.

Zunz, Olivier. *The Changing Face of Inequality: Urbanization, Industrial Development, and Immigrants in Detroit, 1880–1920.* Chicago: University of Chicago Press, 1982.

——, ed. *Reliving the Past: The Worlds of Social History.* Chapel Hill: University of North Carolina Press, 1985.

Index

Alabama, 15, 59
Alexander's Magazine, 192
Allport, Gordon W., 3, 144–45, 147
Alton, Illinois, 15, 77, 191
Arson, 46, 127–28, 139–40, 161
Atlanta, 179; race riot, 195–96, 198
Auburn, Illinois, 129

Badlands, 16, 66–67, 69–70, 72, 73,
    80–81, 126, 136, 182; attack on, 35–
    43, 94–96, 99, 101, 104, 107, 116, 117,
    128, 130–31, 133, 135, 137–39, 145–
    47
Baker, Ray Stannard, 190, 192, 195–96
Ballard, Blanche, 19, 164
Ballard, Clergy, 19, 23, 26, 111, 118,
    134, 142–43, 160–68
The Birth of a Nation, 24
Black, Donald, 143–44
Black law and order leagues, 178–79; in
    Springfield, 166, 178–79, 181
Black self–defense: in Springfield riot,
    34–35, 39–40, 42, 94, 101–2, 104,
    136–37
Bloomington, Illinois, 28, 130, 159, 163
Boston, 64, 192
Brittin, Arthur, 129
Brown, Richard Maxwell, 6
Bryan, William Jennings, 185
Buffalo, Illinois, 129–30

Burton, Scott, 35, 37–39, 41, 99, 102,
    131
Businesses, black: 16, 61–62, 64–65, 72,
    82, 84, 115, 136–37, 139–40, 194–
    95; destroyed in riot, 32–35, 53n, 94,
    104, 128, 130–35, 148, 179–81,
    195; saloons, 18, 34, 62, 72, 80–82,
    94, 104, 115, 132–35, 180–81
Businessmen, white: opinions on riot,
    47–49, 84–86, 126–29, 148, 152, 159–
    60, 168–69, 172, 174–76, 197; sued
    for discrimination, 83–84; threatened
    by rioters, 126–29, 197
Butler, Edith A., 127–28
Butler, William J., 124, 127–29

Canadians, 107
Carpenter, Edith, 65, 136–37
Casey, W. T., 182–83
Cassity, Michael, 195
Chafin, E. W., 31–32
Chatham, Illinois, 114
Chicago, 55, 79, 159, 178–79, 191; race
    riot of 1919, 4, 60, 108
Chicago, Peoria, and St. Louis Railroad,
    93; employees as rioters, 93, 111,
    142–43, 161–62, 187n
Chicago Tribune, 99, 130, 191–92
Churches, black, 64, 185
The Clansman, 24–25

Class position: of black riot victims, 8–9, 195–96, 198; of white rioters, 8–9, 194–96, 198. *See also* Rioters, white

Coal miners, 56, 58–59, 61, 63, 110, 129; black, 7, 58–59, 61–62, 67–68, 71, 107, 109–10; immigrant, 7, 59, 63, 68, 71, 107; in riot, 95, 102–3, 109–11, 145

Coal mining: in Illinois, 55–56, 61, 63, 109–10, 129; in Springfield and Sangamon County, 16, 55–59, 107, 109, 111, 145

Cohn, Nathan, 35

Columbia, Pennsylvania: race riot of 1834, 196

Contact hypothesis, 144–46

Courts: *See* Sangamon County Circuit Court

Creighton, James A., Judge, 163, 166, 169–71, 173, 175–76

Crime, 73; and blacks, 21–23, 50–51n, 73, 134–35, 178–80, 194; in Springfield, 20, 23–24, 73–74, 76–78

Criminals: in Springfield riot, 8, 47–48, 73–74, 78, 85–86, 95, 97, 101, 110–11, 113–14, 118, 159–61, 163, 172, 175

Danville, Illinois, 60

Debose, Albert, 140

Democratic party, 74, 81; and blacks, 79, 81–82, 108–9, 132–34; press, 47, 74, 78, 81

Deneen, Charles, Governor, 27, 29, 32, 40, 99

Depression, economic, 61, 193–94; of 1907, 57–59

Detroit: race riot of 1943, 4, 145, 147

Discrimination, 58–59, 62–63, 65, 115, 144, 150–51, 178, 182–83, 192–93; black resistance to, 83–84. *See also* Segregation

Dixon, Thomas, 24–25

Donnegan, William, 43–46, 96, 99, 131, 136, 138–39, 169–71, 174

Douglass, Frederick, 151

Drugs, 24, 73, 81, 113, 134–35, 160

Duncan, Clarke, 137, 139

Duncan, Otis, 137–38

East St. Louis: race riot of 1917, 4, 60

Elections: black vote in, 79–82, 131–33; and local option, 75–76; vote fraud in, 74–75, 80–82, 132–33, 184

English immigrants, 107–8, 110, 137

Evansville, Indiana: race riot of 1903, 2, 191–92

Ferguson, Margaret, 62, 64–65, 136–39, 146–47, 149

Fields, Barbara, 194

Fire department, 27, 31, 35–36; blacks in, 81–82, 127, 184–85

Florville, William, 61–62

Florville, William, Jr., 64, 149–50

Following the Color Line, 190

Forum, 21–22, 25–26, 42–43, 72–73, 80–81, 83–84, 150, 158–59, 175, 182–83

Gerber, David A., 21, 81, 179

Germans, 55, 68, 107–9, 124

Gluckman, Max, 144

Grand jury: investigation of Springfield riot, 100–101, 112, 158–59

Griffith, D. W., 24

Grimshaw, Allen, 3–6

Hallam, Mabel, 25–26, 28, 41–42, 118, 142–43, 158–59, 161

Hallam, William, 25, 28, 111, 143, 159

Hanes, Murray, 29, 96, 100

Hankins, Blanche, 44–45

Harvey, Clarence, 140–43, 146–47

Hatch, Frank, State's Attorney, 164, 168–69, 171–72

Hopkins, Alice, 65–66, 71

Housing: black residential, patterns in Springfield, 7, 43, 66–67, 71, 79, 84, 89n, 109, 116–17, 136, 140–42, 195; condition of, for Springfield's blacks, 66–68, 72; interracial conflict over, 3, 6, 71, 84, 109, 136, 140–42, 144–50, 193, 195–97, 199. *See also* Badlands; Levee; Rioters, white

Hubbard, William, 149, 153n

Humphrey, Ernest, 97, 138–39

Humphrey, Norman, D., 145, 147

Illinois Bureau of Labor Statistics, 58

Illinois Senate Vice Committee, 76–77

Illinois State Arsenal, 27–29, 40–41, 44,
    131, 138, 180, 185
Illinois State Journal, 42, 57–58, 124–25,
    174
Illinois state militia, 1, 27–29, 32, 34,
    37, 39–41, 43–46, 96, 98, 100–102,
    135–37, 139–40, 151–52, 159, 169–
    70, 172
Illinois State Register, 47, 129
Illinois Watch Company, 20, 57, 63, 142
Immigrants, 7, 62–64, 106–10, 152; ra-
    cial attitudes of, 23, 59, 71, 109, 137,
    147; residential location of, 68, 71.
    See also individual ethnic groups
The Independent, 2, 104
Irish, 55, 68, 106–10, 116; and anti-
    black hostility, 108–9, 118, 133–34,
    198
Italians, 68, 107, 109

Jackson, Madge, 71
James, Joe, 15–20, 26–28, 31, 49n, 159,
    194; opinion of Springfield blacks of,
    160–61, 166; trial of, 160–68, 170,
    174, 197
Jensen, Richard J., 110.
Jews, 68, 71, 97, 107; businesses
    attacked, 33–34, 107, 128; in riot, 35,
    97, 106, 138–39, 147. *See also* Raymer,
    Abraham
Johnson, William, 132–33, 181

Kanner, Isadore, 128
Kentucky, 55, 104–5, 139

Labor conflict and racial violence, 3, 6,
    129, 145, 150–51, 191, 195–96, 198–
    99; in Springfield, 7, 58–59, 84, 108–
    10, 115, 118, 125, 132, 148, 193–96
Lee, Alfred M., 145, 147
Lee, C. C., 132–33, 181
Lee, William, 93–96, 111, 117–18
Levee, 16, 20, 22–24, 32–35, 37, 40–41,
    43–44, 67, 71–74, 76, 81–82, 94–97,
    101–2, 104, 107, 113, 117, 126, 128,
    131, 161, 179–80, 182; police cleanup
    of, after riot, 159–60; targeted in riot,
    131–35, 139, 146–47, 181
Lincoln, Abraham, 2, 29, 61–62, 74, 79,
    81, 96, 176–77, 185, 193

Lincoln, Robert T., 185
Lithuanians, 68, 71, 107–9
Local Option League, 75, 77, 91n
Loper, Henry, 27–30, 32, 34, 38, 40, 48,
    62, 93–96, 98, 100, 103, 113–14, 126,
    131, 172, 197
Lynching, 179, 190–91, 193, 198; in
    South, 1, 104–5, 162, 176, 190, 195;
    in Springfield, 38–39, 41, 43–46, 95–
    97, 99–100, 130, 138–39, 148, 162,
    182. *See also* Burton, Scott; Donnegan,
    William

Mann, Rev. Henry, 71, 183
Memphis: race riot of 1866, 133
Middle class, black, 43–44, 63–64, 140,
    175, 180–82; cultural values of, 22,
    72–73, 161, 166, 178–79, 198; occu-
    pations of, 63–65; resentment of, by
    black working class, 65–66; life-style
    of, 65–66, 136, 140; neighborhoods,
    66–67, 135–40; targeted by rioters,
    135–48, 151, 195, 198
Middle class, white: neighborhoods, 67–
    68, 148–50, 184, 194; opinions on
    riot, 46–49, 73–79, 82, 84–86, 100–
    101, 106, 118, 125–29, 131–32, 134–
    35, 147–48, 152, 159–61, 163, 168–
    69, 172, 175–76, 184, 194, 196–98;
    rioters, 114, 197–98; at riot scene,
    28–29, 85, 95–98, 197
Migration, black: during World War I
    era, 4, 6–7, 199; to Springfield, 7
Migration, white, 55, 104–6
Miller, Kelly, 150–51
Miscegenation, 23–25, 37, 135, 139,
    171, 179–80
Morris, Wilbur, City Police Chief, 27–28
Murray, George W., 96
Myrdal, Gunnar, 193, 198

National Association for the Advance-
    ment of Colored People, 2, 183, 193
Newspapers: black press, 21–22, 64, 72–
    73, 80–81, 83–84, 150, 175, 182–83,
    192; inflammatory coverage of inter-
    racial conflict, 20, 26, 40–43, 104,
    134–35, 159, 179; southern, 1, 104,
    177–78; in Springfield, 19, 21, 23–24,
    41, 47–49, 57–58, 73–74, 78, 80–83,

85, 95–98, 102–3, 106, 113–14, 134,
139, 152, 160, 171, 173–76, 179–80,
182, 197; on Springfield riot, 48, 106,
176–78, 190–92, 197. *See also Forum*
Nickey, Mary, 167–68

Occupations, in Springfield, 57; of
blacks, 7, 58–59; of rioters, 62–66,
80–82, 107, 115, 130, 148–49, 151,
180–81, 184–85. *See also* Rioters,
white
O'Toole, Fergus, 106, 113

Pana, Illinois, 129
Pawnee, Illinois, 97, 129–30
Peoria, Illinois, 28, 60, 77
Philadelphia, 79
Pleasant Plains, Illinois, 129–30
Police: activity after riot, 159–60, 162,
166; black, 81–82, 127, 184–85; performance in riot, 26–30, 32, 34, 37,
40–41, 43–44, 97, 104, 106, 112–14,
116, 131, 142, 159–60, 170–74; and
riot prevention and control, 3–5, 191;
in Springfield, 5, 19, 75, 112; testimony in riot trials, 100–102, 159,
164–65, 169
Polish immigrants, 68, 71, 107–9
Politics: corruption in, 74–82, 84–85,
132–34, 177, 179, 184, 190; and
interracial competition, Springfield,
7, 79–82, 84, 108–9, 131–34, 184,
195, 197
Prohibitionists, 16, 31–32, 75–79
Prostitution, 16, 21, 23–24, 47, 74, 76,
95, 103, 113, 134–35, 160, 172

Quincy, Illinois, 60

Race riots, 179, 190–93, 195–96; in Atlanta, 195–96; in Civil War era, 4,
133; in Evansville, Indiana, 2, 191; in
Greensburg, Indiana, 2; in Jacksonian
era, 4, 98, 196; in New York, 2, 98;
sociological and psychological explanations of, 2–10, 57–58, 60–61, 84,
109–15, 118, 141–51, 192–94; in
Springfield, Ohio, 2; in World War I
era, 3–8, 84, 108, 145, 199; in World
War II era, 3–5, 145, 147

Racial attitudes, 41–43, 63, 72–73, 80,
104–5, 108–9, 125, 140–41, 144–51,
182–83, 185, 190–93, 198; and white
disunity over, 9–10, 47–49, 82, 84–
86, 95–97, 100, 118, 126–29, 134–35,
147–51, 159–61, 169, 173–78, 194–
98. *See also stereotypes,* racial; discrimination; segregation
Railroads, in Springfield, 55–57, 63, 93,
111; rioters as employees of, 93–94,
111, 117–18, 142–43, 161–63, 187n
Raymer, Abraham, 97, 101, 106, 113,
138–39, 169–75
Reece, Roy, Mayor, 31, 40, 80, 127, 134,
181–82
Reform: 84–85, 179; of city government, 74–80, 132, 184–85
Relational distance: and anti-black violence, 141–51
Republican party, 74; and blacks, 79–
82, 108–9, 118, 132–34
Residential proximity: and anti-black
violence, 144–47, 150, 194. *See also*
Relational distance
Restrictive covenants, 149–50
Richards, Leonard, 98
Richardson, George, 26–28, 31, 111,
158–59, 163, 194
Riot contagion, 190–92. *See also* Rumors
Rioters, white: 6–8, 178–79, 195–96,
198–99
Rioters, white, in Springfield, 84–86,
94–95; age of, 98, 103–4, 115–16,
142; and anonymous threats, 100,
126–29, 143, 161–62, 168, 197; arrested, 40, 95, 98–99, 103–4, 106–7,
109, 111, 115–16; ethnicity and birthplace of, 98, 104–10, 142, 194; hit-
and-run attacks by, 43–46, 96–97,
135–47, 151–52, 161; identification
of, 8–9, 94–103, 105–6, 119n, 142,
188n; indicted, 97–100, 102–4, 106–
7, 109, 111–16, 159, 169, 173; injured
or killed, 30, 34–35, 38–40, 45, 101–
4, 109, 111–12, 115–16, 128, 187n;
marital status, 117; motivation, 126,
132–34, 140–51, 160–62, 194–99;
occupations of, 58–59, 84, 98, 110–
15, 142, 145, 148, 150–51, 161–62;
politics and, 82, 108–9, 195; residence

and homeownership of, 40, 98, 115–
18, 142, 145–50, 180, 194; selectivity
of criminal justice system and, 98–
103, 107, 112–14; sex of, 98, 103–4;
social networks of, 101, 111, 133–34,
142–43, 160–62; southern element
among, 7–8, 104–6, 194; trials of (see
Sangamon County Circuit Court)
Riot refugees, black, 37, 40–41, 44,
129–31, 135–36, 138, 140, 180
Riot souvenirs, 41, 100, 113–14
Riot trials. See Sangamon County Circuit
Court
Riot victims, black: 8, 178, 195–96, 198
Riot victims, black, in Springfield, 37–
39, 100, 118, 129–53, 180–81; com-
pensation for injury and property
loss, 46, 181–82; identification of, 9,
130–31, 153–54n, 188n; injured or
killed, 32, 37–39, 45, 45–46, 95, 99,
129–31, 151–52; residential location
of, 130–31, 137–42
Riot victims, white, 33–34, 37, 127–28
Riverton, Illinois, 129
Rock Island, Illinois, 77
Rogers, Rev. E. B., 131–32
Rogers, E. L., 42–43, 73, 80–81, 83–84,
158–59, 175, 183
Royall, O. V., 162–63, 165–66
Rudé, George, 8
Rudwick, Elliott, 4
Rumors: during Springfield riot, 42–
44, 139
Russell Sage Foundation: investigation
of, of conditions in Springfield, 56,
63, 67–68, 72, 76
Russian immigrants, 68, 71, 107–9

St. Johns Hospital, 35, 45, 102–3
St. Louis, 97, 140, 191
saloons, 16–17, 20, 23, 40, 62, 72, 74–
78, 81–82, 160, 177, 180–81; and saloonkeepers, 74–75, 106, 115, 126,
132–35, 181
Sambo and His Funny Noises, 124–25, 151
Sangamon County, 56, 58–59, 60, 63–
64, 97, 106, 109, 129–30, 182–83, 191
Sangamon County Circuit Court:
records on rioters, 98–99; trial of Joe
James, 160–68, 170, 174, 183, 197;

trials of rioters, 100, 138–39, 152,
168–74, 197–98
Schools: and interracial conflict, 3, 191
Segregation: black challenges to, in
North, 3; exclusion of blacks from
towns, 129–30, 153n; in South, 104;
in Springfield, 68–71, 83–84, 133,
148–51, 182–83, 185
Shand, Richard J., Colonel, 27–28, 34,
37, 39–40
Springfield Business Men's Club: opinions of, on riot, 47–49, 127–29, 152,
169
Springfield City Council, 76, 79, 81,
181, 194
Springfield, Illinois: black population,
16, 60–62, 64, 66–67, 180, 193; early
history, 55–57, 61–64; economy, 55–
58, 63; housing, 66–68, 72; manufacturing, 55, 57–58, 63, 68, 115;
population, 16, 55–56, 103, 105–8,
121n; residential patterns, 66–73,
117–18, 140–42, 148–50; transportation, 55–57, 63, 115, 183
Springfield, Illinois, race riot: compensation of riot victims, 46, 128–29,
181–82; death and injury toll of, 45–
46, 128, 130–31; events precipitating,
18–20, 25–28, 158–59, 193–94; local
impact of, 179–85, 198; local persistence of violence after, 151–52, 161–
62; property damage and losses in,
45–46, 127–30, 181–82
Springfield News, 41–42, 114, 152
Springfield Record, 42, 47, 78, 169–70,
174
Stereotypes: ethnic, 106, 124, 126; racial, 21–25, 42, 72–73, 104–5, 124–
25, 160, 176–79, 178, 193. See also
Racial attitudes
Streetcars, 63; employees as rioters, 111,
143
Strikebreaking, 3, 59; blacks and, 6, 61,
148; in Springfield, 7, 59, 193, 198–
99
Sullivan, Richard M., 80
Sunday, Billy, 77

Taborn, Alice, 183
Tennessee, 55, 105

Texas, 104–5
Thayer, Illinois, 129
Todd, Edwin, 192–93
Townsend, Walter A., 169–70, 174
Tuttle, William M., 4, 108

Unions, 61, 63, 115, 162–63, 198–99
United Mine Workers, 59–61, 88n, 145

Vardaman, James K., 105, 177–78
Vengeance, 142–44, 160–61, 196
Vice districts, 20, 76–77, 179; in Spring-
   field, 73–77, 81, 95, 159–60, 179–80.
   See also Levee
Villard, Oswald Garrison, 193
Virden: strikes in coal mines and inter-
   racial conflict in, 7, 59, 61, 88n, 129

Walling, William English, 2, 46–48, 85,
   96, 102, 104–6, 125–26, 148, 175–77,
   193

Washington, Booker T., 178, 198
Washington, D.C., 179
Werner, Charles, Sheriff, 26–28, 34, 37,
   39–40, 43, 166–68
Williamson County, Illinois, 56
Willis, Samuel, 46, 139–40
Wines, William St. Johns, Assistant
   State's Attorney, 164, 169–73
Witnesses: black, 169; intimidation of,
   100, 161–62, 174; of riot, 78, 102,
   112; at trial of Joe James, 164; unwill-
   ingness of, to testify, 99–102, 142,
   168–69, 173–75, 197
Women, 116; as riot participants, 30,
   95, 103, 172; as riot spectators, 28.
   See also Kate Howard

Young, Edward C., Major General, 43,
   45

Roberta Senechal de la Roche is a professor of history at Washington and Lee University.